Stealing Time

"Time is more than the passing of minutes or hours. It is the space for love, arts, politics, passions, safety, connections, humanity. This compelling book illuminates time and its violent theft by state and corporate border bureaucracies. It is an analytical, provocative and necessary read."
—Prof. Elizabeth Stanley, *Victoria University of Wellington, Australia*

"This outstanding volume takes our understanding of state crime and the undocumented migration process in an important new direction. By employing the concept of temporality, Monish Bhatia and Vicky Canning have brought together an innovative group of scholars who, collectively, weaponise what they call 'migrant time'. Through this lens of temporality each of the chapters offers powerful new insights into the state's repertoire of violence against asylum seekers and refugees while simultaneously bringing to the fore the resistance that this 'hidden' form of repression engenders in those subject to its harms."
—Prof. Penny Green, *Queen Mary University, UK*

"In this remarkable volume, we see vividly how time itself is an object and target of power, and rather than a natural fact, is produced through governance. By taking migration as their central framework of analysis, the contributors to this book provide a profound and memorable critical investigation of state power and the subtle violence of bureaucracy. This book is a landmark event in consolidating the incipient field of critical studies of temporality, and in situating human mobility and borders at the heart of understanding the place of time in social domination."
—Prof. Nicholas De Genova, *University of Houston, USA*

"Time, and the loss of time, is not just incidental in the treatment of migrants who are subject to state power. It is structural and directed as well as emphatic in its effects. This powerful book driven by two renowned scholars, Monish Bhatia and Victoria Canning, delivers this message in a clear and creative manner through chapters from the frontlines of migration scholarship. A must read."
—Dr. Devyani Prabhat, *University of Bristol, UK*

"Monish Bhatia and Victoria Canning bring together a stellar group of scholars from around the world to discuss how punitive migration laws steal time – which is literally our most valuable resource. This study of temporality is chock full of useful theoretical insights. Migrants are at the mercy of the host state and often have no choice but to wait for decisions, appointments, interviews, and legal and policy changes. Migrants spend countless hours building families, friendship networks, and communities – only to have that stolen away when they are detained and deported. While in immigration detention, detainees count time up – instead of down as they do in prison – as their release dates are nearly always uncertain. These are just some of the ways the authors and editors theorize temporality in the migration context. This beautifully put together collection is a must-read for any student of migration."

—Professor Tanya Golash Boza, *Associate Professor of Sociology at the University of California, USA*

Monish Bhatia · Victoria Canning
Editors

Stealing Time

Migration, Temporalities and State Violence

Editors
Monish Bhatia
School of Law
Birkbeck, University of London
London, UK

Victoria Canning
School for Policy Studies
University of Bristol
Bristol, UK

ISBN 978-3-030-69896-6   ISBN 978-3-030-69897-3 (eBook)
https://doi.org/10.1007/978-3-030-69897-3

© The Editor(s) (if applicable) and The Author(s) 2021
This work is subject to copyright. All rights are solely and exclusively licensed by the Publisher, whether the whole or part of the material is concerned, specifically the rights of translation, reprinting, reuse of illustrations, recitation, broadcasting, reproduction on microfilms or in any other physical way, and transmission or information storage and retrieval, electronic adaptation, computer software, or by similar or dissimilar methodology now known or hereafter developed.
The use of general descriptive names, registered names, trademarks, service marks, etc. in this publication does not imply, even in the absence of a specific statement, that such names are exempt from the relevant protective laws and regulations and therefore free for general use.
The publisher, the authors and the editors are safe to assume that the advice and information in this book are believed to be true and accurate at the date of publication. Neither the publisher nor the authors or the editors give a warranty, expressed or implied, with respect to the material contained herein or for any errors or omissions that may have been made. The publisher remains neutral with regard to jurisdictional claims in published maps and institutional affiliations.

Cover illustration: Biwa Studio

This Palgrave Macmillan imprint is published by the registered company Springer Nature Switzerland AG
The registered company address is: Gewerbestrasse 11, 6330 Cham, Switzerland

Dedicated to those whose time is stolen by borders.

Foreword: Adrift in the Global Migration Regime

A dense web of technologies of control exercised by states, supranational institutions and increasingly international corporations shapes and patterns timings, timelines and tempo of migrant lives, from the fragmented, protracted and dangerous journeys to reach safety and hope for a better life, to the choreographed rituals of citizenship ceremonies and the sudden accelerations of forced removals.

Through an examination of everyday ruptures, transits, beginnings and endings in the lives of those increasingly disenfranchised by omnipresent borders, particularly people seeking asylum and 'unwanted' migrants, this edited book offers a captivating conceptual and empirical journey into the unexpected contingencies and detours, the necessarily fluid aspirations and desires, the frustrated hopes and helplessness of lost time, that feature prominently in the lives of migrants and refugees.

In uncovering the everyday impact of migration governance on migrants and the many ways in which human existence is shaped, defined and confined within the narrowing spaces of immigration laws and the violence of borders and immigration enforcement practice, the book invites the readers to see the *stealing* of time not as a side-effects rather a structural component of migration governance—an active, deliberate and inherently harmful one, the editors explain in the Introduction. The stealing of time, in its many forms, contributes to produce docile and exploitable subjects and, in doing so, it is central to the process of illegalisation of migration, observed by several critical migration scholars. The illegalisation of migration is a global phenomenon, affecting a growing number of migrants and forms of mobility; a process that co-opts into a permanent state of uncertainty and precariousness groups of immigrants who, until not long ago, were granted secure and permanent legal status and rights.

Drawing on contributions from established and up-and-coming scholars, migrant rights activists and border crossers, this collection is an important addition to an emerging body of scholarship in migration studies on temporal dimensions in the analysis of migration governance and migrant experiences. Importantly, it builds on a range of analytical perspectives and positionalities, and from a wide range of case studies, which capture different stages in migration trajectories and a variety of contexts and spaces where the lives of 'unwanted' migrants unfold, from camps to detention centres, from asylum reception centres to border crossings. The list of countries covered in the collection is noticeable, from Afghanistan to Manus Island, from Mexico to the USA, from Syria to Jordan, Turkey and the EU, all contributing to shed light on how multiple regimes and logics of time both produce, and are produced by and in migration processes. This brings to the fore questions currently at the margin of migration scholarship, including concerns with the role of time in the governance of migrant bodies on the move as well as in the process of settlement; the impact of multiple regimes and logics of time on migrant biographies and everyday lived experiences, and the salience of policy timelines and timings to the structuring of migrants' social relations and everyday lives and aspirations.

Birmingham, UK
November 2020

Nando Sigona

Nando Sigona is a Professor and the Director of the Institute for Research into Superdiversity (IRiS) and a Research Associate at the University of Oxford's Refugee Studies Centre. His work investigates the migration and citizenship nexus. This is achieved through in-depth examination of a range of experiences of societal membership including, but not limited to, those of: EU families; refugees; Roma, undocumented migrants, racialized minorities, unaccompanied minors, dual citizens, 'failed' asylum seekers and stateless people. Nando is one of the founding editors of *Migration Studies, an International Academic Journal* published by Oxford University Press and the editor of the book series *Global Migration and Social Change* by Bristol University Press.

His recent work includes *Unravelling Europe's 'Migration Crisis'* (Policy Press, 2017), *Within and Beyond Citizenship* (Routledge, 2017), The *Oxford Handbook on Refugee and Forced Migration Studies* (Oxford University Press, 2014) and *Sans Papiers: The Social and Economic Lives of Undocumented Migrants* (Pluto Press, 2014).

Acknowledgments

This book has been a long project in the making. When it began, we did not foresee the implications of a global pandemic, nor the exacerbated impacts this would have for people living within and between borders. As such, we are particularly thankful to all contributors who have worked to finalise *Stealing Time* under remarkable and—for us at least—unprecedented conditions.

We owe gratitude to many more, and so in alphabetic order we would like to thank: Dalia Abdelhady, Birkbeck Criminology Department, Border Criminologies, Mary Bosworth, Jon Burnett, DIGNITY—the Danish Institute Against Torture, Andrew Douglas, Liz Douglas, European Group for the Study of Deviance and Social Control, Igor Fink, Harm and Evidence Research Collaborative, Andrew Jefferson, Martin Joormann, Shahram Khosravi, Lisa Matthews, Migrant Artists Mutual Aid, Migration Mobilities Bristol, Ida Nafstad, Scott Poynting, Amina Rafique, Safety 4 Sisters, Ann Singleton, Statewatch, Trampoline House Copenhagen, Aaron Winter.

And of course—thanks, as always, to our families and friends.

About This Book

This book draws together empirical contributions which focus on conceptualising the lived realities of time and temporality in migrant lives and journeys. *Stealing Time* uncovers the ways in which human existence is often overshadowed by legislative interpretations of legal and illegalised. It unearths the consequences of uncertainty and unknowing for people whose futures often lay in the hands of states, smugglers, traffickers and employers that pay little attention to the significance of individuals' time and thus, by default, their very human existence.

Overall, the collection draws perspectives from several disciplines and locations to advance knowledge on how *temporal* exclusion relates to social and personal processes of exclusion. It begins by conceptualising what we understand by 'time', and looks at how temporality and lived realities of time combine for people during and after processes of migration. As the book develops, focus is trained on temporality and survival during encampment, border transgression, everyday borders and hostility, detention, deportation, and the temporal impacts of border deaths.

Stealing Time both conceptualises and realises the lived experiences of time with regard to those who are afforded minimal autonomy over their own time: people living in and between borders.

Introduction: Contested Temporalities, Time and State Violence

Time is an enigma. At once, time is something we can understand and agree on, and yet often have little conceptualisation of: it is our collective human existence, our daily lives and the years that go by. Time is history and it is the future, something we have watched over or wait to unfold. By all accounts, time in the every day is a simplistic notion that perhaps few of us stop to focus on. That is, until time becomes our ally or our enemy, something that we can control or lose all autonomy over.

The multifarious nature of time and temporalities have been explored and theorised by many social scientists, physical scientists and theorists as a social category (Durkheim, 1912, 2016) as experiential and culturally specific (Mead, 1932, 2002; Turner, 1967) and as a physical attribute inherent to evolution (Hawking, 1989). These have laid foundations for understanding what is meant by time, and if or how such a concept can ever be universal. However, as decolonial scholars have addressed, such constructions may not draw us to understanding how certain forms of time are perforated by globalised inequalities, exclusion and racialised forms of injustice (De Genova, 2002; El-Enany, 2020).

It is this aspect of time and temporality that this collection seeks to address, specifically in the context of migration. The idea for this book came about in early 2018 at a symposium at Birkbeck, University of London (Criminology Department).[1] The foundations were laid in discussions grappling with state power and control over migrant time, and how this is exercised in ways which seem unconnected to what might normatively be recognised as 'time'. Rather than a universal or even culturally specific experience that is inherent to human existence, migrant time is regularly governed by policy, law and legislation, by militarised interference and patrols at national and international borders. It is bureaucratised in the every day through surveillant forms of governance which require migrants to 'prove' their right to move across borders or stay within borders (Abdelhady et al., 2020; Stumpf, 2011). It is visa applications, welfare applications, hours of asylum interviews. It is waiting for decisions and appointments, avoiding state actors and officials or facing them in banal and repetitive interviews.

As Melanie Griffiths has shown in depth, migrant time can be slow and monotonous, with days, weeks and even years passing in a sense of stuckness, waiting for papers or family reunifications. It might be in indefinite immigration detention, where (unlike prison) people count time up, rather than counting time down. It may then be frenzied—a quick dispersal or relocation to another house or part of the country, or a newly announced deportation with little time to gather ones thoughts or things, to say goodbye to loved ones or plan for what may come next (Griffiths, 2013, 2014; see also Canning et al., 2017; Stumpf, 2011; and Gomberg-Muñoz, and Silver et al., in this volume).

In short, migrant time is governed and human autonomy thus reduced. This power is exercised by states and their representatives, supranational states (such as the European Union) and—increasingly in the context of neoliberal governance—by corporations. It is therefore part of a micro, meso and macro web of actors and affiliates who collectively and individually seeks to determine the path that many people can go down, or not.

---

[1] Organised by Monish Bhatia, Gemma Lousley and Sarah Turnbull, entitled *Borders, Racisms and Harms: A Symposium*. More information is available here: http://www.bbk.ac.uk/events/rem ote_event_view%3Fid%3D466.

Our focus here is not on those with national identities that sit at the top of the Passport Index—dominated by European countries—the relatively rich traveller who is able to move quite freely and without significant risk. Rather we focus on those who are increasingly disenfranchised by intensified borders, including people who travel without papers/are undocumented; people who are forced to migrate due to persecution or conflict and may be seeking asylum; and those who fall under the broad umbrella of migrating for economic reasons. These are not monolithic or completely separate demographics, as is often presented. Instead, as McMahon and Sigona evidence (2018), individuals may have complex and multifaceted reasons for crossing borders, or indeed staying behind (see Schuster et al., this volume). In any case, we consider this juxtaposition of rights to be a toxic and (for many) lethal one: those who *least need* to cross borders—holiday travellers, financial elites and sun-seekers—are those with most ability and scope to do so, whilst those who may *most need* to for personal security or poverty alleviation are instead caught in nefarious bordered webs.

It is for this reason that we have titled this book *Stealing Time*. In the discussions at Birkbeck and since, we considered multiple angles from which we wish to conceptualise migration and temporality in the context of this collection. We drew first from Khosravi's earlier reflections on stolen time and the way in which temporalities are experienced in immigration detention, deportation and the fear of both (2016; 2018). As Khosravi noted, time is, for all of us, a form of capital that is unequally distributed in relation to rights and autonomy. This echoed well with how we perceive this particular liminal period. However, since *stolen* denotes something of the past, we moved to present this bureaucratically violent process in the active tense, and the here and now. That is, stealing time is a way to emphasise that such endeavours are not a thing of the past either in the global bordering sense or for people affected by bordering. It is active, deliberate and inherently harmful. Cohen and Taylor (1976) show us that time can be given as a punishment—time that belongs to someone else. For instance, those given custodial sentences have their time abstracted by courts and through the sanctioning of prison time. For people in such situations, time is not a resource but rather a controller. It is here also that the meaning of time becomes linked to ongoing harm and criminality, since representations of illegal activity lay with migrants (Yahya, Chapter 2). And yet, as Bhatia (Chapter 9), Canning (Chapter 6) and Iliadou (Chapter 10) evidence, it is the lethal or harmful exercising of state power that aligns more accurately to mass atrocities such as deaths at borders, state inflicted death and temporal harm.

As such, this book invites the contributors and the reader to consider the actions—and inactions and omissions—of processes which reduce people's autonomy or sense of self, but whose control over temporality often remains in the hands of something much bigger than themselves. This structured reduction in autonomy should not be conflated with migrant agency. We do not contest that this exists through individual's lives and personal decisions, which is well evidenced in migrant solidarity platforms and acts of resistance (see for example Edward and Lindberg, this volume). Furthermore, we do not wish to force a unified collection within which all authors offer the same or even similar perspectives. Instead, we aim to *complicate* our collective understanding of time, temporalities, migration and state violence. It is for this reason that we have attempted to build a globalised perspective of the various ways in which time and temporalities relate to migration. As we will outline below when setting out the structure of this book, contributions focus on country contexts that take us through Afghanistan, Australia, Britain, Denmark, France, Germany, Greece, India, Iran, Jordan, Manus Island, Mexico, Sweden, Syria, Turkey and the USA. The chapters include contributions from people who have been held at or within borders, as well as who have researched the lived realities of border controls. It is a collection by activists, scholars, researchers and border crossers, and as such aims to provide a meaningful platform for which discussions regarding temporalities and the stealing of time can develop across these perceived boundaries.

Migratory Journeying and the Value of Migrant Lives

As we have hinted thus far, the complex nexus of time and space is felt differently across migratory journeys; from the first point of mobilisation, to the barriers and borders between reaching host or 'safe' countries. Even then, as sovereign states push further *towards* criminalising mobility and push *against* migrant rights and movement, 'safe' countries are increasingly safe in name only. The illegalisation of everyday rights such as accessible housing and work (Boochani, 2018; El-Enany, 2020; Mayblin, 2019), as well as the criminalisation of care and humanitarianism (Fekete et al., 2017), has increasingly made the lives of migrant populations more difficult, and in some places the facilitation of detention and deportations easier. Meanwhile, reductions in family reunification can leave loved ones stranded across countries and continents, where all concerned are unsure of how they can move forward, or if they ever will do so as a unit.

In capitalist societies, time is associated with money and success. Therefore, time is a form of capital, similar to money, which can be invested, saved or wasted (Cohen and Taylor, 1976). In this collection we ask what happens to the time people have spent in the countries, where they live deportable and liminal lives, or where they are deported from. For instance, long-term residents or even citizens (such as those belonging to the Windrush generation in Britain), who have worked, built networks, learned languages, paid taxes, fallen in love or had children, are routinely illegalised and sent to countries they may have little link with. The time people have *invested* to achieve these goals is lost by deportation. The time people have *spent* to accumulate social and cultural capital is thwarted by deportation. This is the stealing of time.

Migration can be perceived and studied as a spatial process, and the temporal aspects of migration have received much less attention. The everyday life of illegalised migrants and people seeking asylum is essentially characterised by waiting, either for papers, for people or for deportation. As Bourdieu highlighted, and from which Yahya draws in Chapter 2, 'the all-powerful is he who does not wait but makes others wait… waiting implies submission' (2000: 228). To keep people waiting is an exercise of power over other people's time. We therefore suggest that the temporal frame of migration and waiting is crucial to understanding what promotes social, political and economic ex/inclusion. The exclusion by current border regimes is not only spatial but also temporal; keeping people in prolonged waiting, depriving people of possibilities and embedding the loss of life chances.

Structure of This Book

This book draws together empirical contributions which focus on conceptualising the lived realities of time and temporality in migrant lives and journeys. *Stealing Time* uncovers the ways in which human existence is often overshadowed by legislative interpretations of 'the legal' and 'the illegalised'. It unearths the consequences of uncertainty and unknowing for people whose futures often lay in the hands of states, smugglers, traffickers and employers that pay little attention to the significance of individuals' time and thus, by default, their very existence.

This book aims to both realise the lived experiences of time with regard to those who are afforded minimal autonomy over their own time: people living in and between borders. Overall, this collection draws perspectives from several disciplines and locations to advance knowledge on how *temporal* exclusion relates to social and personal processes of exclusion. It begins by conceptualising what we understand by 'time', and looks at how temporality and lived realities of time combine for people during and after processes of migration. As the book develops, focus is trained on temporality and survival during encampment, border transgression, everyday borders and hostility, detention, deportation and ultimately border deaths.

Indeed, some focus more explicitly on how time is experienced by people affected by migration rather than people who are themselves mobilising. This is how the journey through this text begins. In Chapter 1, Liza Schuster, Reza Hussaini, Mona Hossaini, Razia Rezaie and Muhammad Riaz Khan Shinwari begin in Afghanistan, documenting the lives of people who are 'left behind' in the aftermath of family members and loved ones migrating. We are introduced to the gendered realities of Afghan migration, which sees predominately men mobilise, and charts how time is stolen for women who are less likely to 'move around'. As they show in both empirical and poetic depth, this waiting is sustained by hope: for reunification, to move themselves, or see their loved ones return.

In Chapter 2 we move from Afghanistan to Syria, where Karam Yahya journeys us through the decisions people make when crossing borders, and the endless boundaries one must overcome in going forward and whilst 'stuck' at camps. Drawing on his experience of first arriving in Jordan as an aid worker, and later when fleeing Syria, we see first-hand the relentless barriers that must be negotiated. But more than physical borders, Yahya exposes bordering as a *process*: not only during a journey, but a temporal engagement bound in social contracts that requires constant negotiation through bureaucratic complexities, lost time and Othering in host countries.

From here, Isabel Meier and Giorgia Donà take us through France, Germany and the UK where they document the implications of asylum regimes. Through their research across the three countries, they outline life narratives which focus on timescapes as a specific liminal experience for people seeking asylum: a process which draws out multiple temporalities—rather than fixed—documenting how these unfold through administrative, economic and affective practices and experiences. Importantly, Chapter 3 highlights ways in which certain aspects of human experience are intensified by these state-controlled temporalities, emphasising the harms of stress, loneliness and financial precarity.

Shifting to the Southern Hemisphere, Behrouz Boochani and Omid Tofighian train our gaze on what they term 'the weaponization of time' in Australian territories. Focussing on Boochani's experience of six years held on Manus Island and in Manus Prison, and the endemic harms embedded in deterrence policies, Chapter 4 offers us a meticulous insight into the stealing of time as torture. Moreover, the dynamic between Boochani and Tofighian solidly introduces us to the value of organised resistance and solidarity across borders and bordering.

Chapter 5 moves our focus back into Northern Europe, where Stanley Edward and Annika Lindberg draw attention to the state implemented violence inherent to both immigration detention (in Sweden) and deportation centres (in Denmark). Highlighting these mechanisms as a form of racialised global apartheid, Lindberg first highlights how hopes and dreams are manipulated in immigration detention as a means to motivate people who are detained to leave, whilst simultaneously stealing their time. In the second section, Edward outlines his own hopes against the deportation regime which held him in partial confinement in Denmark. As with Boochani and Tofighian, Edward's insight exemplifies the agency held by people to organise, and use hope against the very regimes which steal time. Whilst the Danish authorities aim to motivate people to leave through deportation centres, Edward uses hope as a motivation to persevere.

The focus on Northern Europe continues in Chapter 6 with Victoria Canning, who outlines the ways in which violent bureaucracies have intersectional impacts for survivors of violence. Drawing specifically on research in Britain, Denmark and Sweden, she outlines the lived experience of women who are trapped in temporal limbo, and the human cost of such existential confinement. Whilst asylum regimes may be harmful for all or most who pass through them, for survivors of sexualised or domestic violence the emotional impacts of previous traumas can be compounded by fears or threats of deportation or detention, lack of access to psychological support, and feelings of loss from the past or for the future. This infliction of autonomy harm, she argues, is the bureaucratised stealing of time.

From here, Chapters 7 and 8 complement each other in addressing the experiences of people who are returned from the United States to Mexico. In Chapter 7, Alexis Silver, Melissa Manzanares and Liron Goldring focus on young Mexican migrants who are returned or deported, and who face irrecoverable loss of time, social investment and—for some—money to enable the rebuilding of life elsewhere. They highlight how such significant changes to their social environment can result in culture shock, particularly for those who have spent many years (or even a majority of their life) in the USA. In Chapter 8, Ruth Gomberg-Moñoz draws us further into grasping the complexity of rebuilding one's life after deportation. She highlights that time is systematically wasted and efforts to rebuild life are stalled. Moreover, Gomberg-Moñoz invites us to consider whether state negligence towards people who are deported is a consequence of bureaucratic failure, or a form of failed remitters in their nations of citizenship.

In Chapter 9, Monish Bhatia shifts our focus to the toxic residues of colonialism and Hindu nationalism in India. The chapter uncovers ongoing state-sanctioned killings across the Indo–Bangladesh borders— which he terms the violent stopping of migrant time. Bhatia further explores the contemporary internal bordering regime, citizenship practices and mass disenfranchisement and time theft of undocumented Muslims. Those who are illegalised increasingly find themselves in limbo, marginalised and even subject to confinement in detention centres. The chapter is dense and complex, and uncovers the historic past and the present anti-Muslim and xenophobic politics and practices in India.

The closing chapter of this collection takes us to Greece, and specifically the Greek Island of Lesvos. In a devastating indictment of the violence of the European Union's strategy towards militarised borders and deterrence of migrants, Evgenia Iliadou outlines the reality of death at Europe's borders. Reflecting on activist work and empirical research, she conceptualises thanatopolitical harms of governance when control is exercised in place of humanitarianism. In considering how pushbacks facilitate deaths at sea, Iliadou addresses death as the politicised stealing of time, and of life. Moreover, such theft does not end there, but continues when bodies are not recovered, and dignity in death is often even withheld through burial for those whose bodies are recovered from the sea.

Final Note from the Editors

In all, this collection aims to encourage a complicated and critical sense of temporality that can place migrant lives as active agents, but which also facilitates a recognition that states and (increasingly) their corporate allies hold significant power over individual decisions, exclusions and life trajectories. Lives lost to borders are not only stolen, but violently stopped. This is the loss of friendships, family, love, birthdays, celebrations and everything else that forms much of human life. Above all we ask you to consider this: as we stated earlier, what we do with our time is a form of capital, linked with our own perceptions of success or failure— it is unlike any other capital we possess. We may lose money or friends, and work to claim them back. We might lose a sentimental object that, in essence, cannot seem replaceable, but with which another can replace its function. But no matter how rich we are or what cultural capital we accumulate, we can never, ever re-accumulate time that is lost. That is a commodity that is out of human reach, and which for those most affected by bordering, is often stolen.

Monish Bhatia
Victoria Canning

References

Abdelhady, D., Gren, N. & Joormann, M., 2020. Introduction. In: D. Abdelhady, N. Gren & M. Joormann, eds., *Refugees and the Violence of Welfare Bureaucracies in Northern Europe*. Manchester: Manchester University Press.

Boochani, B., 2018. *No Friend but the Mountains: Writing from Manus Island*. London: Picador.

Bourdieu, P., 2000. *Pascalian Meditations*. Stanford: Stanford University Press.

Canning, V., Caur, J., Gilley, A., Kebemba, E., Rafique, A. & Verson, J., 2017.*Migrant Artists Mutual Aid: Strategies for Survival, Recipes for Resistance*. London: Calverts Publishing.

Cohen, S. & Taylor, L. 1976. *Escape Attempts: The Theory and Practice of Resistance to Everyday Life*. London: Allen Lane.

De Genova, N., 2002. Migrant 'Illegality' and Deportability in Everyday Life. *Annual Review of Anthropology*, 31, pp. 419–447.

Durkheim, E., 1912, 2016. *The Elementary Forms of Religious Life*. Oxford: Oxford University Press.

El-Enany, N., 2020. *Bordering Britain: Law, Race and Empire*. Manchester: Manchester University Press.

Fekete, L., Webber, F. & Edmond-Pettitt, A., 2017.*Humanitarianism: The Unacceptable Face of Solidarity*. London: Institute of Race Relations.

Griffiths, M., 2013. Frenzied, Decelerating and Suspended: The Temporal Uncertainties of Failed Asylum Seekers and Immigration Detainees. *Centre on Migration, Policy and Society*, Working Paper No. 105.

Griffiths, M., 2014. Out of Time: The Temporal Uncertainties of Refused Asylum Seekers and Immigration Detainees. *Journal of Ethnic and Migration Studies*, 40, pp. 1991–2009.

Hawking. S., 1989. *A Brief History of Time*. New York: Bantam Press.

Khosravi, S., 2016. Deportation as a Way of Life for Young Afghan Men. In: R. Furman, D. Epps & G. Lamphear, eds., *Detaining the Immigrant Other*. Oxford: Oxford University Press.

Khosravi, S., June/July 2018. Stolen Time. *New Statesman*. pp. 33–34.

Mayblin, L., 2019. Imagining Asylum, Governing Asylum Seekers: Complexity Reduction and Policy Making in the UK Home Office. *Migration Studies*, 7(1), pp. 1–20.

McMahon, S. & Sigona, N., 2018. Navigating the Central Mediterranean in a Time of 'Crisis': Disentangling Migration Governance and Migrant Journeys. *Sociology*, 52(3), pp. 497–515.

Mead, G. H., 1932, 2002. *The Philosophy of the Present*. New York: Prometheus Books.

Stumpf, Juliet P., July 23, 2011. Doing Time: Crimmigration Law and the Perils of Haste. *UCLA Law Review*, 58, No. 1705, 2011, *Lewis & Clark Law School Legal Studies*, Research Paper No. 2011-25.

Turner, V. W., 1967. *The Forest of Symbols: Aspects of Ndembu Ritua*. Ithaca: Cornell University Press.

Contents

1 'My Beloved Will Come Today or Tomorrow': Time and the 'Left Behind' 1
   Liza Schuster, Reza Hussaini, Mona Hossaini, Razia Rezaie, and Muhammad Riaz Khan Shinwari

2 Journey and Encampment Observations: Liminality and the "Protracted Refugee Situation" 25
   Karam Yahya

3 Micropolitics of Time: Asylum Regimes, Temporalities and Everyday Forms of Power 39
   Isabel Meier and Giorgia Donà

4 The Weaponisation of Time: Indefinite Detention as Torture 65
   Omid Tofighian and Behrouz Boochani

5 Contested Dreams, Stolen Futures: Struggles Over Hope in the European Deportation Regime 83
   Annika Lindberg and Stanley Edward

6	Compounding Trauma Through Temporal Harm *Victoria Canning*	105
7	"Starting from Scratch?": Adaptation After Deportation and Return Migration Among Young Mexican Migrants *Alexis M. Silver, Melissa A. Manzanares, and Liron Goldring*	127
8	The Mexico City Runaround: Temporal Barriers to Rebuilding Life After Deportation *Ruth Gomberg-Muñoz*	151
9	State Violence in India: From Border Killings to the National Register of Citizens and the Citizenship Amendment Act *Monish Bhatia*	171
10	"Violence Continuum": Border Crossings, Deaths and Time in the Island of Lesvos *Evgenia Iliadou*	197
Epilogue		223
Index		229

Notes on Contributors

Monish Bhatia is a Lecturer in Criminology at the Birkbeck, University of London—School of Law. His research interests lie in the areas of asylum, state racism and violence, specifically the treatment of individuals by the criminal justice and immigration systems. He has published several articles and chapters, and is the co-editor of *Media, Crime and Racism* (2018), *Critical Engagements with Border, Racisms and State Violence* (Critical Criminology, 2020), and *Race, Mental Health and State Violence* (Race & Class, 2021).

Behrouz Boochani is Adjunct Associate Professor of Social Sciences at UNSW, author and journalist and was incarcerated as a political prisoner by the Australian government on Manus Island and then held in Port Moresby (Papua New Guinea). In November 2019 he escaped to New Zealand where he has been accepted as a refugee. His book *No Friend But the Mountains: Writing from Manus Prison* (Picador, 2018) has won numerous awards including the 2019 Victorian Prize for Literature.

Victoria Canning is a Senior Lecturer in Criminology at the University of Bristol. Her research and teaching interests lie in the areas of gendered harms, state power and violence, specifically in trajectories of violence in the lives of women seeking asylum. She has published several articles, chapters and books, including, *Gendered Harm and Structural Violence in the British Asylum System* (winner of the British Criminology Society book prize, 2018), *Sites of Confinement: Prisons, Punishment and Detention* (2014) and *From Social Harm to Zemiology* (2021, with Steve Tombs).

Giorgia Donà is a Professor co-director of the Centre for Migration, Refugees and Belonging at the University of East London. Her research focuses on conflict and displacement, child and youth migration, psychosocial perspectives and forced migration, refugee voices and representation, and multi-modal narratives. Recent publications include: *The Marginalised in Genocide Narratives* (2019), *Forced Migration: Current Issues and Debates* (2019, edited with Alice Bloch), and *Child and Youth Migration: Mobility-in-Migration in an Era of Globalisation* (2014, edited with Angela Veale).

Stanley Edward is a migrant activist, co-founder of Castaway Souls of Denmark/Europe, member of the Silent University, Freedom of Movements, and the Bridge Radio Denmark.

Liron Goldring was an undergraduate research assistant at Purchase College during the time of research. She will obtain a masters (MSW) from the Hunter College Silberman School of Social Work in May, 2020. Her current research focuses on conspiracy theories and anti-Semitism in the United States.

Ruth Gomberg-Muñoz is an Associate Professor of Anthropology at Loyola University Chicago. Her ethnographic work with undocumented people and their family members examines how members of mixed-status families navigate law and society in the United States and Mexico. Her most recent NSF-funded project is a collaboration with deportee rights activists in Mexico City and anti-deportation organizers in Chicago. She is the author of two books, *Labor and Legality: An Ethnography of a Mexican Immigrant Network* (2011, 2020) and *Becoming Legal: Immigration Law and Mixed Status Families* (2016), as well as numerous scholarly articles and other writings.

Mona Hossaini holds an M.A. in Kashmir and South Asian studies from UNESCO Madanjeet Singh Institute for the South Asia Foundation, India. Prior to her current role as a Gender Development Expert with the Afghanistan Justice Organization, she has conducted research for different NGOs and INGOs.

Reza Hussaini has 10 years experience working with Research and Higher Education institutions in Kabul, Afghanistan. His research areas include gender, peace processes, human right and migration. 2015–2018, he was Research Manager at the Afghanistan Center at Kabul University.

Evgenia Iliadou is a postdoctoral research fellow at the Department of Politics, University of Surrey. She has conducted extensive ethnographic research in Greece and Lesvos on refugee crisis, border harms, temporal violence, vulnerability and the lived experiences of border crossers. She has worked for fifteen years as an NGO practitioner in refugee camps and detention centres, in Lesvos and the Greek mainland, and she has been member of various activist networks supporting people on the move.

Annika Lindberg is a visiting postdoctoral researcher at AMIS, University of Copenhagen, and member of the Freedom of Movements Research Collective. She researches state violence and bureaucratic power in the field of migration control, detention and deportation.

Melissa A. Manzanares is a doctoral student at the University of North Carolina at Chapel Hill. Her research interests include international migration, the labor market experiences of migrants, legal status, and gender. Her current research focuses on the connection between human trafficking and migration.

Isabel Meier joined the Sociology Department at University of Northampton in December 2019, following a position as postdoctoral researcher in the Space and Political Agency Group at Tampere University. Her research interests are broadly centred around the politics of asylum, bordering, race and emotions. Isabel holds a Ph.D. from the University of East London where she was a recipient of the Excellence Scholarship. Drawing on her own experience as activist in the UK and

Germany, her thesis explored the emotional politics of bordering and emergent political possibilities.

Razia Rezaie has an M.A. from Graduate School of Society and Culture at Ritsumeikan Asia Pacific University, Japan. Her dissertation was on Afghan economic migrants in Japan and their transnational experience. Together with the other authors, she worked at ACKU on the Hopes, Fears and Plans of Afghan Families Project on which this paper is based.

Liza Schuster is based at City, University of London, spent six years working in Afghanistan, most recently with these co-authors based at the Afghanistan Centre at Kabul University (ACKU). Together they explored representations of migration in Afghan popular culture; the fears, hopes and plans of Afghan families; and the development of Afghan migration policy.

Muhammad Riaz Khan Shinwari is a young Afghan scholar, recently returned to Afghanistan after years in Pakistan as a student and exile. He was part of a research team at ACKU working on Pashtu Landays. Riaz is currently teaching English and looking for opportunities for further study.

Alexis M. Silver is an Associate Professor of Sociology and Latin American, Caribbean, and Latinx Studies at Purchase College—State University of New York. She researches migration, youth, and transnational families in the United States and Mexico. Her book, *Shifting Boundaries: Immigrant Youth Negotiating National, State and Small Town Politics*, was published in 2018 by Stanford University Press.

Omid Tofighian is an award-winning lecturer, researcher and community advocate, combining philosophy with interests in citizen media, popular culture, displacement and discrimination. He is Adjunct Lecturer in the School of the Arts and Media, UNSW and Honorary Research Associate for the Department of Philosophy, University of Sydney. His publications include the translation of Behouz Boochani's multi-award winning book *No Friend but the Mountains: Writing From Manus Prison* (Picador, 2018); and co-editor of 'Refugee Filmmaking', *Alphaville: Journal of Film and Screen Media* (2019).

Karam Yahya was born and raised in Damascus, Syria before moving with his family to Amman, Jordan. Karam graduated from Hashimite University in 2013 and started his work at Za'atari refugee camp before himself crossing borders from Jordan to Germany as the situation in Syria (followed by Jordan) deteriorated. He later returned to the Mediterranean on sea rescue missions serving as a cultural mediator and a contact person with "Action for Education" in Chios Island and Idomeni, as well as participating in several search and rescue missions through Jugend Rettet (Search and Rescue). Currently, Karam is a Master's student at Humboldt University Berlin where his primary focus is mental health and well-being for migrants arriving in host societies.

1

'My Beloved Will Come Today or Tomorrow': Time and the 'Left Behind'

Liza Schuster, Reza Hussaini, Mona Hossaini, Razia Rezaie, and Muhammad Riaz Khan Shinwari

The sound of the *bukhari*, a tin stove used for warmth and boiling water, being scraped clean in preparation for lighting, pulled me from a deep sleep. Sakina saw that I was awake and began to sing what sounded like a lullaby. She keened the names of her husband, her son and nephews, interwove them with place names—Istanbul, Germany, France and the song became a lament. She was calling for them to come home, to come back to the family, telling them she missed them, the children

---

L. Schuster (✉) · R. Hussaini
City, University of London, London, UK
e-mail: liza.schuster.1@city.ac.uk

M. Hossaini
South Asia Foundation, New Delhi, India

R. Rezaie
Ritsumeikan Asia Pacific University, Beppu, Japan

M. R. K. Shinwari
Afghanistan Centre at Kabul University, Kabul, Afghanistan

© The Author(s), under exclusive license to Springer Nature Switzerland AG 2021
M. Bhatia and V. Canning (eds.), *Stealing Time*,
https://doi.org/10.1007/978-3-030-69897-3_1

missed them and the house was empty without them. I pulled myself upright, huddled in the *kampal* and sat listening in the white light from the window as the snow fell softly outside. Her tears gathered on her eyelashes, then slid down her cheeks. Her voice broke on a sob. We sat in silence for a moment, and then she got up to empty the bucket of cinders. When she returned, she said 'no one wants their children to leave. We want them to go to work in the morning, and to come home every evening to eat the food we cook and play with their children. But here there is no work – only fear'. At that point, her husband had been gone seven years, her son five and her nephew three (Schuster Fieldnotes, Pule Khumri, December 2012; all names have been changed).

Introduction

For centuries, Afghan men have been driven from home by poverty, and more recently by various forms of persecution (Safri, 2011). Throughout this time, women in particular have waited for fiancés, husbands, fathers and sons to return, their lives sharply constrained by the absence of adult men (and boys) on whom they have traditionally had to depend for protection and provisions. The Soviet Invasion in 1979 caused whole families to flee, as they have continued to do from the successive conflicts afflicting Afghanistan, mostly to neighbouring Iran and Pakistan. As the men returned to fight, or moved on looking for work, women, children and the elderly were then left behind in camps or the towns where they had settled. Still more recently, Afghan families have waited to be sent for, to join male family members in Australia, North America and Europe, to begin a new life abroad. While it has been clear for some time that migrants are as likely to be women as men (Morokvasic, 1984; Phizacklea, 1983), and Afghan women do go abroad to study, or as part of family units, it still remains extremely rare for Afghan women to move alone,[1] especially without papers. At a time when it is more and more

---

[1] Afghan boys make up by far the largest proportion of unaccompanied minors arriving in Europe—in 2018, the latest date for which figures are available, 86% of unaccompanied minors were male, and the largest group (16%) were Afghan (Eurostat, 2019). Occasionally, a girl does travel alone, and since 2015 UNHCR have documented more women travelling with children

difficult to get visas, and when the journey has become more and more dangerous, many Afghan women are left behind, to wait to be sent for, or at least for a visit from loved ones who manage to get papers.

In recent decades, these periods of waiting have been dictated more and more by states determined to control who, how and for how long people enter their territories. The time spent by migrants stuck in transit or at the border extends the limbo of their families back home. While those recognised by states as refugees have the right to bring their families to join them 'immediately', with some honourable exceptions, bureaucrats do little to facilitate reunification, when not actively working against it. In particular, since 2016 European states have shifted towards grants of subsidiary protection that do not carry the right to family reunification. Those with 'lesser' status have to satisfy stricter income and housing conditions, which means that families remain separated for years.

As states keep people seeking asylum at a distance, trapping them in 'a powerful geography of exclusion' (Mountz, 2011) that ruptures their lives, it is important to remember the collaterally excluded, those left waiting 'at home'. Those that are left behind create 'new mental maps (and clocks)' through their connections to the time-space of family members abroad (Leutloff-Grandits, 2017, p. 124) and are sustained by 'the changing dynamics of hope created in the meeting point between their everyday lives and geopolitical realities' (Brun, 2015). Faced with these realities, families in Afghanistan try to minimise risk and maximise success, deciding who should leave and with whom. Families decide whether it would be better for one person to travel alone, sparing wives, children or elderly parents serious physical dangers, but risking prolonged separations, or to travel together risking serious harm, but perhaps increasing the chance of being able to stay. The borders make themselves felt in homes across Afghanistan, first as families negotiate who should cross which borders, sharing stories of others who have failed or succeeded in their attempts. As these decisions are negotiated, the border slips in between those who will leave and those who will stay,

---

but it is more common for women to travel in family groups, though they are sometimes separated en route, either by the smugglers or at borders as some family members may make it through but others are trapped behind the fences (Freedman, 2016, p. 19).

separating them and keeping them separated for months and years. As time passes, for many the abstract border that they cannot see from an Afghan home is almost palpable. Those who wait to hear news of the traveller are trapped within their homes, waiting to hear whether those who have left have reached safety and are yet in a position to return home for a visit or to send for them. But these left behind people are too often invisible because rendered immobile in their own homes, both because of social norms and because of the ongoing conflict in Afghanistan.

The Left Behind

Khosravi (2018) has described the time stolen from migrants deported from Europe, from those held in detention and forced to wait in limbo. But time is also stolen from those 'left behind'. The lives of the left behind are marked by waiting, a waiting that is heavily gendered. While boys and men also wait to be sent for by fathers, fiancées or wives, their situation is different to that of their mothers and sisters, as patriarchal norms send them into the streets to look for and take up employment, or to go to school or the bazaar in spite of the risks of becoming 'collateral damage' in the ongoing conflict (Mountz, 2011). However, women and girls are much less likely to be able to move around. In particular, the risk to life and limb outside means that women are increasingly obliged to 'lose their time' at home (Hussaini et al., 2020) in protracted waiting over which they have no control, trapped by the patriarchy of both sending and receiving states.

Increasingly scholars are focusing on the costs imposed on the 'left behind', including the 'not (yet) migrants' (Elliot, 2016, p. 102) who share many of the challenges facing forced migrants, in particular those in protracted displacement due to conflict. The concept of protracted displacement is understood as a particularly acute form of 'protracted uncertainty', framed by the concepts of 'waiting' and 'hope' (Brun, 2015, p. 20). As Elliot puts it 'the life of the migrants' spouse is characterised by a particular type of expectant and urgent waiting—a waiting that is often extended across years' (2016, p. 105).

1 'My Beloved Will Come Today or Tomorrow'

تاوی نن خم سبا به راشم
جانانه میاشتی دی شمیرم تیر شو کلونه

You said I am going and will return soon
I counted the months but now years have passed since your migration
(Shaheen, 1994)

Those 'left behind', but who expect or hope either to leave or to welcome a loved one home one day, have no idea when the waiting will end. They live in an uncertain, future-oriented present, in which time leaches away, and which is framed by conflict and fear, fear for themselves and fear for the migrant undertaking a dangerous journey.

'Left behind' is a term that has come to describe those wives (Aysa & Massey, 2004), parents (Fuller, 2017), children (Dreby, 2007) and, less often, husbands (Hoang & Yeoh, 2011) who remain while others leave. Some of that work has examined the impact of being left behind on family structures, on gender roles, on economic relations and on the temporal and spatial immobility imposed on these women by virtue of their gender and the absence of husbands and or fathers (Brun, 2015; Boccagni & Baldassar, 2015), though there is less written on those left behind in countries in conflict. The migration of husbands from some patriarchal societies can create a space for women to take on more responsibility within the family, and occasionally to move into the labour market, should economic conditions and social norms permit (Aysa & Massey, 2004), with this access to wages allowing them greater agency and participation in family decision-making. This has certainly occurred in Afghanistan, but to an extremely limited extent, as we discuss below.

This chapter draws on research conducted in Afghanistan since 2012, including a study by Schuster of what happens to those forcibly deported and to their families (2012–2013), and two related projects (2016–2018) in which she and a team of five Afghan researchers analysed the place of migration in Afghan oral culture, and conducted interviews with families over eighteen months to explore their fears, hopes and plans for the future.[2] While much of the fieldwork for the first study was ethnographic

---

[2] The authors would like to acknowledge the support of the ESRC who funded the research, and to thank the families who gave their time and trusted us with their fears, hopes and plans, our colleagues Osted Shakur and Belgheis Alavi Jafari, and the editors for their comments.

and conducted in the capital of Baghlan province, Pule Khumri, the security situation in 2016–2018 meant that this fieldwork was confined to Kabul. Although the focus of this work was not waiting or being left behind, these were sub-themes that emerged both from the interviews and from the poetry we collected.

One hundred and nine interviews were conducted by Hossaini and Razaie with members of eighteen families (six Pashtun, six Hazara, five Tajik and one Sikh) resident in Kabul in their homes. They focused on the hopes, plans and fears of families for their future, and were repeated at four to seven week intervals. Migration was a recurring theme in these interviews, as people discussed their plans for themselves or their children, family members abroad, or voiced disapproval of or fear for others who were leaving. As Hossaini and Razaie are women, most of the interviews were with the wives and daughters of the families, especially since they were conducted during the day, when the men were less likely to be home. The families were recruited by snowball sampling, and although not a criterion for inclusion in the study, all have some family members abroad. Hossaini and Razaie recorded and transcribed the interviews and wrote up their observations. They also conducted the preliminary analysis, which was then developed by them with Hussaini and Schuster. The interviews were translated into English collectively by Hussaini, Hossaini, Rezaie and Schuster.

The verses cited here are *Landay, the* anonymous two line poems in Pashtu, most often composed and shared among women (Grima, 1992; Majruh, 2003), and cited by Afghans of every social class and age (Schuster & Shinwari, 2020). Most of those cited came from collections by Benawa (1958), Laiq et al. (1982) and Majruh (2003) as indicated. Where there is no name, the Landay was collected by Shinwari from social media, social networks, overheard in public or seen on the back windows of taxis. Aside from the Majruh verses (where the original Pashtu version was not provided), all other translations of the Landays were a collaboration between Schuster and Shinwari.

We are also grateful to our Afghanistan Centre at Kabul University (ACKU) colleagues who welcomed us into their family.

Waiting and Watching

تکل به کله د راتلو کړې
زه دې د لارې څوکیداره کړم مینه

When will you decide to come back to me
You have made me a watcher of the way
(Shaheen, 1994)

For centuries, Afghan men have left home as *gharib* (itinerant workers), peddlers, traders and merchants, leaving families behind for months or years (Slobin, 1976). Inevitably, this phenomenon is reflected in *Landay*, the two line poems common in Afghan oral culture (Schuster & Shinwari, 2020) and frequently composed by anonymous women (Griswold & Murphy, 2014). Migration, whether to the next valley, to the big city or across porous borders has for centuries been an important survival strategy for the poorest (Monsutti, 2005) and a source of wealth for rich merchants and traders. For some, like Tagore's *Kabuliwala* (2005), these were seasonal journeys, from which men would return every winter having sold dried fruit, and the carpets woven and shawls embroidered the previous winter by members of the family. They would bring back money for a bride price, or goods to sell in the market, enjoying an affectionate return:

مسافری نه په خیر راغلې
اول خوله درکړم که دې جیب ولټومه

Welcome, my beloved migrant,
Shall I kiss you first or search your pockets?
(Laiq et al., 1982, p. 444)

Men would write Landays complaining of the loneliness of exile, while women wrote of missing their beloved, urging him to return, complaining of being left to wait. For the less fortunate, *gharib kardand* (becoming an itinerant work or trader) meant years in exile, separated from all that was familiar, from those who depended on them, and surrounded by strangers who neither knew nor cared for them. The 'separation from family [that] is an expected consequence of migration' (Khosravi, 2010, p. 22) was felt as keenly, if not more so, by the women left behind, one of whom distils her yearning into this short verse:

روح مي په تن کي څکه پايي
زه ورته وايم اشنا نن سبا راخېنه

I sustain my soul in my body by deceiving it
that my beloved will come today or tomorrow
(Benawa, 1958, p. 49)

While a minority of the verses by women urge her husband to leave to show his courage by leaving to bring back riches and gifts (Schuster & Shinwari, 2020), many more urge the return of the wanderer. While this may be a son, it is most often a husband, and the many verses promising to be faithful and modest are designed to reassure those who leave that their honour will not be besmirched, that their wife will remain covered and unseen by other men:

په هندوستان خوشاله ګرزه
زه به دا توری سترګی ستا په نام ساتمه

Freely wander in Hindustan
For I shall keep these black eyes for you
(Laiq et al., 1982, p. 47)

مېينه خه الله دي مل شه
زه شينکی خال او زلفي تالره ساتمه

O' my beloved, go in the protection of God
For I will keep my face tattoos and hair for you
(Laiq et al., 1982, p. 454)

In these verses, which according to Laiq et al. pre-date the Soviet invasion, the singer promises to remain veiled and avoid the gaze of other men as demanded by social norms such as those encoded in *Pashtunwali* (the code that governs honourable conduct among Pashtuns). Until the 1970s, it was relatively rare for women to go abroad (to the next village, much less another country) and hundreds of verses describe the period of waiting and attest to the expectation that the male migrant would go and return home, and that women would wait modestly, watching for the moment he will appear, always prepared to welcome him home.

زلفي ول ول که سترګی توری

د مسافر لالی د غږ دی راښینه

Smooth your hair and beautify your eye
There are rumours that your migrant beloved is returning
(Laiq et al., 1982, p. 304)

Social norms that persist today specify that a bride moves to her in-laws' home, even if her husband is abroad, and leave some of these young women feeling very vulnerable. In the interviews, daughters-in-law whose husbands are abroad, described how they were expected to do an unfair share of the household chores and had to tolerate abuse and harassment since their husband was not there to defend them (in these cases, migration offered the promise of freedom from the scrutiny of in-laws determined to ensure their daughters-in-law worked hard at home and did nothing to sully the family reputation). Some older *Landay* reflects the vulnerability of these wives, cursing the husband for leaving her alone:

چي مسافر شي ما به پریږدي

بیا به د بل په کور کې ژوند څنګه کومه

He will leave me to migrate
How shall I pass life without him in a stranger's home?

مسافری ته دي څان جوړ کړ

له کنډو واوښتی راپري دي ټول دل غمونه

You migrate freely
You crossed the mountains and left the worries to me
(Laiq et al., 1982, p. 443)

This norm of sole male migrants, and families left behind, changed following the Soviet invasion, as whole families and whole villages were displaced to neighbouring countries (Safri, 2011; Centlivres & Centlivres-Demont, 1988; Centlivres, 1993). Those who went to Iran were initially welcomed and largely self-settled. Though men and boys had sometimes to travel to find work, or left their families to fight in the Iran–Iraq war, on the whole, Afghan families stayed together.

In Pakistan, the Afghan refugees were at first settled in camps, where many of the men were armed to return to fight in Afghanistan (Dupree, 1988), leaving their wives among strangers and without a *maharam* (a close male family member).

خما وطن کې بمباری شوه
جانانه لاړې زه دې چاته پرېخودمه
There is bombardment in my homeland
O' lover you have gone and now who will care for me
(Majruh, 2003)

For those women left in Pakistan while the men returned to Afghanistan as *Mujahedeen* (warriors for their faith), the practise of *purdah* (the demand that women keep themselves apart from men who are not members of their immediate family), made life in the refugee camps where people were crowded together, extremely difficult (Dupree, 1988). Dupree, and later Khattak have noted that women left behind in Pakistan by their husbands were effectively "'incarcerated' in their new 'homes'" (2007, p. 576). Khattak argues that the international community reinforced the subordination of women in these camps, by delivering aid through 'a particular vision of the Afghan family' (2007), one which could not be headed by a woman, so that widows, of which there were many, were forced to remarry.

Life on Hold

At different points over the past decades, driven to an extent by the discrimination and hostility described by many contemporary Afghan poets (Jafarai & Schuster, 2019), Afghan men have also returned home from Iran and Pakistan, not to fight but to see whether a more permanent return to Afghanistan would be possible. Alternatively, they have travelled onwards to Europe and elsewhere, often leaving their families in exile in Iran or Pakistan (Safri, 2011). As a result, women headed households in the Afghan diaspora are becoming more common, and some of these 'left behind' Afghan women share similar experiences with their sisters in Mexico (de Synder, 1993; Aysa & Massey, 2004), the Philippines and Vietnam, as they take up employment and take charge of decision-making. Nonetheless, it is important to understand the socio-economic context of women's lives in Afghanistan (rather than in the diaspora), where social norms, insecurity and economic instability make them and their children highly dependent on their husbands, or in his absence, his family.

Among the families in our project there was an understanding that remittances, or the repayment of debts incurred, would not happen quickly, and that those left behind would be dependent at least for an initial period on the income-generating activities of younger brothers or on the extended family. Where the men in the family were abroad or ill, women's roles did evolve. Although economic opportunities for women are extremely limited in Afghanistan, two young women in our study had made it into the labour market. One of these was Zahra, the eldest daughter in the Ahmadi family. This family, which included elderly parents and six children, offers an example of how sometimes a woman's role can grow into the space left by a father and or older brothers, but not always. Five years previously Mr Ahmadi had a stroke from which he had not recovered. The eldest son was in the army, posted to one of the most insecure provinces in the country, and could only return very rarely, while the second son, who had initially taken over his father's business, had left for Germany with his wife and children. Zahra, the eldest daughter, her two younger sisters, Shabnam and Neda (whose fiancé had left two years earlier for Germany), and Saudeq, their 16-year-old brother, lived at home.

Saudeq was desperate to follow his older brother abroad, but his mother and sisters needed a 'man' at home. It was Saudeq who was expected to fetch bread and groceries, and accompany his sisters on visits or to family events such as weddings. However, halfway through the fieldwork, in spite of his mother and sister's refusal to allow him to leave, Saudeq had run away to Iran (a decision he later regretted). His departure created problems for the four women left behind. The father's declining health and the absence of two, then three, sons meant that the responsibility for family decisions had shifted to Zahra's mother, and especially to Zahra, since her mother was not literate and rarely left home. At twenty-four years old, Zahra took her family responsibilities seriously, but was frustrated by her inability to persuade her younger siblings to study. She had enjoyed studying computer science, but her brothers had decided it was not suitable work for a woman, so she trained as a nurse.

Zahra told Hossaini that she enjoyed her work at the hospital, but found the stress of travelling to work challenging—not just the harassment, but the risk of attacks and explosions. However, it was her salary from two jobs that supported the family. Her older brother did not earn very much as a soldier and there were periods when he was not paid at all. Her brother in Germany was in a reception camp and not allowed to work. The family fretted over the length of time he was waiting for papers and unable to work (two years at the start of the fieldwork). Certainly, over the seven interviews conducted with the women of the family, it was clear that Zahra's role as breadwinner was respected and gave her authority. Shabnam and Neda explained that they consulted Zahra on everything, though they did not wish to be like her.

Although encouraged to study, Neda explained that she gave up school when she got engaged, expecting to marry relatively quickly. Her fiancé's abrupt decision to leave for Germany in 2015 had taken his family and Neda by surprise, but she was unwilling to go back to school despite Zahra's pushing. Neda told Hossaini that her fiancé's family had not wanted him to leave, and that they felt guilty because of what his absence would mean to her:

> They told him "you have put this girl's life on hold, her life depends on you, she cannot do anything now", but he just said I am not coming back. There is no job for me there, no future. (Hossaini interview, Ahmadi family, 5th visit, 2017)

Nonetheless, Neda's family were happy for her to continue studying. But she and Shabnam preferred to remain at home, frustrated only that the absence of their brother meant that they could not leave home. Towards the end of the fieldwork, Zahra and her family were traumatised by the attack on the hospital in the centre of Kabul where she worked (BBC, 2018), and finally the rest of the family persuaded her to give up her job at that hospital, keeping only the one at a local hospital. The absence of the brothers in this family gave the eldest daughter an opportunity that she seized, and offered her younger sisters an example to follow, one they rejected.

Literacy among Afghan women remains low at about seventeen per cent,[3] as does employment.[4] Though there is some work available in teaching or nursing (as with Zahra), and housekeeping (often the profession of widows or wives with husbands abroad), this is almost exclusively in Kabul or Mazar. Aside from the social norms that privilege the male breadwinner model, and the desire to protect women from the high levels of street harassment, the physical risks of being caught up in an attack or an explosion have severely curtailed women's movements outside the home, while men have no choice but to continue working in order to support the family (Hussaini et al., 2020). Hossaini and Rezaie, who interviewed family members (and as educated, employed women, were themselves objects of fascination as they visited homes across Kabul), were told repeatedly, by all the women they spoke to, that their days were spent waiting for the safe return of family members from work or from school—'we cannot go to Kote Sangi or Shar e Nau. It is like being in prison' (Razaie interview, Bishno family, 3rd visit, 2017). But among those whose fathers, husbands or brothers were abroad, the confinement was worse, as without male companions they could not go to weddings, funerals or even the bazaars.

Scholars have described the waiting inflicted on people seeking asylum (Conlon, 2011; Mountz, 2011), and argued that this waiting is not just passive. Brun (2015) speaks of active waiting and women working in the fields and caring for children and elderly relatives. Sakina, whose lament introduced this paper, was one of those women who in the absence of

---

[3]There is high variation in literacy among women, indicating a strong geographical divide. The highest female literacy rate, for instance is 34.7%, found in the capital, Kabul, while rate as low as 1.6% is found in two southern provinces of the country (2017 http://www.unesco.org/new/en/kabul/education/youth-and-adult-education/enhancement-of-literacy-in-afghanistan-iii/).

[4]Since 2016, the overall figure is 40%, but there are no reliable figures for female participation in the workforce https://www.tolonews.com/afghanistan/unemployment-rate-spikes-afghanistan.

her husband and eldest son, had grown in social stature and enjoyed an autonomy she may not have had in the presence of her husband. His remittances, though irregular, allowed her to support the five remaining children and her mother, and after her brother-in-law's death, her sister and her disabled nephew and his wife and child. This, and her own strength of character meant that she had significant authority within the family. But this status did not compensate for the absence of her husband and son, as the extract from field notes at the top of the paper indicates. In urban contexts with limited employment opportunities and high levels of existential fear, the time spent in waiting is most often experienced as imprisonment.

Among the families, there were also two young men engaged to women abroad. Although these young men had much greater freedom than the women we encountered, nonetheless they were disempowered and to a certain extent, emasculated by the 'waiting'. One in particular saw no point in continuing his studies, since his qualifications would not be recognised in the US. Instead, as his mother explained 'his feet are bound while he waits – he cannot move forward'. Finally, unable to live with the waiting and uncertainty (and afraid that his bride would expect him to stay home in the US) he broke his engagement. For the left behind, there is a strong sense of time wasted, '"paused", "interrupted", "on hold"' (Brux et al., 2019, p. 19), especially when the absence of husbands stalls the normal markers and rewards of time passing such as the birth of children.

Time and the 'Left Behind'

د هندوستان سفر دی خار شه
زما په تور اوربل کې سپین اولګېدنه
The journey to India shall be cursed for you
My black hair turned grey waiting for you
(Laiq et al., 1982, p. 263)

As described in Landays, and during fieldwork with Afghan families, during this period of waiting, life is suspended as wives, mothers and daughters, fiancées (and more recently, fiancés) focus their hopes and plans on an uncertain, unknown future. But as Brun points out, hope is a double-edged sword, sustaining people in the here and now, but also preventing them from moving on (2015). In this future- and elsewhere-orientated present, the young people see no point in investing in their own future or that of Afghanistan, and so an engagement to someone abroad as described in the previous section led in some cases to young people abandoning their studies. Such engagements and marriages create expectations of opportunities to leave, of remittances, or of a fiancé returning with a passport that allows for travel to a safe country if that should become necessary.

It is understood that there will be a period of waiting, but it is expected that this will be a year, or two at the most. *Aya qabuli grifti?* (have you the papers yet?) is a question posed urgently during each telephone call. Sakina's husband had left seven years before, and never made further than Italy for a short period. He had been deported from there to Greece, where he spent some years working as a smuggler, before fleeing arrest back to Turkey where Schuster interviewed him and where he continued 'helping those European governments would not help' (in his words). So Sakina understood very well that the expectations associated with a husband or fiancé abroad were not always fulfilled. In spite of that, she had made a decision:

> Pule Khumri, Baghlan Province. 2012
> 'I want Latifa to marry Ali. Tell him he should ask for her'. I looked at Sakina, Latifa's mother and Ali's aunt. 'Ali doesn't have his papers yet. Do you want Latifa to end up like you – alone, waiting for a husband you haven't seen for seven years? Bringing up children who don't remember their father?'

Ali had left Afghanistan in 2008 and arrived as a minor in France in 2010 when Schuster met him. Through Ali she met his family in Pule Khumri, including his cousin, a young woman a little older than him with her mother's determination. Without *qabuli* (papers) Ali was unable to leave France, but was in regular contact with his aunt, who persistently brought up the proposed marriage.

Finally, in 2015 the French authorities had decided to give him a student visa rather than refugee status. He received a one-year residence permit and like many Afghans, immediately returned home to see the family he had missed and visit his father's grave. For some Afghans, a combination of duty and homesickness causes them to travel to Iran or Pakistan and cross the frontier without papers, since refugee passports issued by European states permit travel anywhere but to the country from which one has fled. However, consciousness that loved ones are waiting pushes some to risk being trapped at home and losing their status. And like many young Afghan men returning after years away, during his month at home, Ali got married to Latifa.

For the family back home, the different statuses and the range of rights to which they gave access were incomprehensible. When Ali called to say he had his paper, for his parents and aunt, this meant one thing, that he would soon be able to come home to see them and that he would be a catch for his cousin, able to bring her abroad too. However, as time passed after his return to France, doubts grew about Ali's commitment to bringing his wife to Europe. Ali had trained as a carpenter in France, but was unable to earn enough to send money back and pay for a large enough apartment to meet the family reunion criteria.

> Paris, 2019
>
> They think I have a girlfriend here, that I don't want to bring her. They don't believe me about the rules and problems. They say "look at Bilal – he brought his wife after two years". My aunt is complaining that she has no grandchildren. Latifa is complaining that she cannot go out, that her life has stopped. Please, go and explain to them that I am doing everything I can, but it is difficult. You know how it is. We have to wait, but inshallah, she will come next year. (Schuster Fieldnotes)

At the time of writing (2020), Latifa is still waiting to join Ali and he is still trying to meet the criteria for family reunion while supporting his mother, brother and wife in Pule Khumri.

And yet though life is suspended, 'everyday time' (Brun, 2015) continues to pass as those waiting see their peers have children, live a 'normal' life, while their youth fades and they age.

شیرین اشنا می مسافر شوو
تر گلاب سره ووم له لارنجه زیره شومه

My sweet beloved migrated
I was redder than rose and now I am yellower than a lemon
(Laiq et al., 1982, p. 342)

This resentment among women that their youth and beauty is wasted can be found in the older Landays collected by Benawa, Laiq and Shaheen, which speak of red lips now white with dust, and black hair turned grey.

تا د دکن سفر قبول کړو
خما په تور اوربل کی سپین اولګیدنه

You decided to leave for Decca
Waiting has turned my hair from black to gray
(Shaheen, 1994)

Clearly, just as migration has been part of Afghan culture for centuries, so too has women waiting for men to return, and many of the constraints experienced by Afghan women left behind in the twenty-first century are similar to those of women left waiting a century before. But now the waiting is complicated by the need for documents and a certain level of income, and the capacity to negotiate hostile bureaucracies.

Latifa, and thousands of young Afghan women married to migrants in Europe, hear the promise 'soon I will bring you…' often as they wait for husbands and fiancés to negotiate bureaucracies determined to keep family reunion to a minimum, and to ensure these young women and their children (potential or actual) do not become a burden on the state. When Schuster began working with young Afghans in Paris in 2009–2010, it was not uncommon to meet young Afghan men who had cut off contact with their families because they were unable to bear the weight of expectations from home. It is difficult to convey the anguish and guilt experienced by these young men at their inability to fulfil the hopes of those left behind, especially when their journey had been financed at great cost to their families. On the other hand, this anguish was matched by that of families who could not understand why their sons, now 'safely in Europe' and posting photos on Facebook were not working to repay their debts and support their families. Moving between Kabul and Paris for the first project, Schuster was quizzed by mothers and older brothers about the activities of young men in Europe: 'is he taking drugs? Does he drink alcohol? Has he taken a girlfriend? Why does he not call? Why does he not send money?'. During the second project, families told Hossaini and Rezaie of those who had left and as time passed, changed and became emotionally cold.

Then and Now

In our research, we found that the pain caused by separation from loved ones was a constant motif, whether in poetry, songs, or interviews and from whatever era. We also found that in the past and the present, the lives of women left behind by Afghans forced to migrate was curtailed to a greater degree than that of men. So there was a significant degree of continuity. However, we also noted a significant discontinuity. While the analysis of oral poetry, mostly from the pre-war period, revealed many pleas from the 'left behind' for the migrant to return home, in our interviews with families, all of whom had family members abroad, the pain of separation was ameliorated by the knowledge that those family members were safe, that they had survived the journey and they were no longer at risk in Afghanistan. In contrast to the voices in the poetry, the families in the project were unanimous in urging family members not to return home. Mamelekat, for example, told us 'whenever my brother calls me from Sweden and tells me how much he misses us, I tell him 'don't worry. At least, you are safe there. Try not to be sent back to Afghanistan' (Hossaini interview, Nasiri family, 4th visit, 2017).

All of the authors, throughout the research and in our personal lives, heard family members in Afghanistan use the phrase 'at least you are safe there' in response to complaints about how difficult life is in exile. Having someone abroad who is safe, means one less person to worry about and someone who may be able to 'work hard there for your family back in Afghanistan' (Hossaini interview, Nasiri family, 4th visit, 2017). Inevitably though, this increases the burden on those who are forcibly returned. In that case, all of the waiting, as well as the resources invested by the family, are wasted.

Two other novelties emerged: the switch from granting refugee status to granting subsidiary protection, as mentioned above, and the increase in forced return, whether through deportation or so-called 'voluntary' return, which means all the waiting and resources invested are wasted, and the individual returns to a situation of uncertainty and risk. This brutal and expensive process (Schuster, 2005) is more likely to target single young men—once they have wives and children, or elderly parents, expulsion is that much harder. The impact of deportation on these families is often catastrophic. Elliot describes how the promise of being able to take someone 'out' is a part of the bride wealth in Morocco (2016, p. 107), so too in Afghanistan, when parents negotiate a match, a son (or a daughter) who is in Europe is considered a catch, and deportation robs the individual, his family and his bride of all the potential invested in their imagined future.

During the first piece of research on which this work was based, the issue of shame and the stigma of failure were important themes (Schuster & Majidi, 2015). What made the waiting bearable was the expectation that it would be for something—when someone is returned with nothing but a plastic carrier bag, the tears shed, the years of confinement, the humiliation of neighbours and extended family asking 'did he send money? When is he coming back to see you (and by implication bring gifts and fetch his wife)?' are for nothing. All the money, time and waiting, the house not built and the children not born, are wasted. In 2016, the EU and its member states, signed the EU–Turkey deal, which rewarded Turkey for taking back those trying to get to Europe and for deporting Afghans to Afghanistan, and the Joint Way Forward, which rewarded the Afghan government for accepting deported Afghans and discouraging irregular migration. As a result, the number of Afghans deported (overwhelmingly, though not exclusively, men) has increased, and made the time the 'left behind' spend waiting much more uncertain and precarious.

Conclusion

In this chapter, we have seen that migration imposes costs on those left behind, as well as those who leave. The costs are of course financial, as the family pools its resources or indebts itself to pay for the journey and support those in the asylum system who are not allowed or are unable to find work. They are also emotional, as those left behind miss and worry for those who are abroad, and fret that they are losing their sons or husbands or fiancés to 'Europe'. However, at least in the Afghan case, there are additional costs to the women left behind who find themselves imprisoned in their homes both by the fear of being killed or injured, and by social norms that require a male companion when leaving home.

We also noted that calls for migrants to return have been superceded by calls for them to stay away and to stay safe, just as the states hosting them are plotting to both return those who have left and prevent others from leaving. Given what the absence of a man or older boy means in an Afghan household, this shift is significant and tells us that migration remains an important survival strategy for households, whatever the cost.

'Nation-states advance their own politics of location by imposing immobility on others' (Mountz, 2011, p. 394), and not just those confined in camps, reception centres or hostels, but in homes around the world, in Kabul and Ghazni and Laghman. As Griffiths et al. note 'there exists a strong relationship between power, the state and time' (2014), as receiving states dictate how long wives and children wait to join husbands and fathers.

References

Aysa, M. & Massey, D., 2004. Wives Left Behind: Labour Market Behaviour of Women in Migrant Communities. Dans: *Crossing the Border: Research from the Mexican Migration Project.* New York: Russell Sage Foundation, pp. 131–144.

BBC, 2018. *Kabul Mourns 100 Dead After Ambulance Bomb.* Available at: https://www.bbc.com/news/world-asia-42850624. Accessed 19 April 2020.

Benawa, A. R., 1958. *Landaye*. Kabul: Askari.

Boccagni, P. & Baldassar, L., 2015. Emotions on the Move: Mapping the Emergent Field of Emotion and Migration. *Emotion, Space and Society*, 16, pp. 73–80.

Brun, C., 2015. Active Waiting and Changing Hopes: Toward a Time Perspective on Protracted Displacement. *Social Analysis*, 59(1), pp. 19–37.

Brux, C., Hilden, P. K. & Middelthon, A. L., 2019. "Klokka tikker, tiden gar": Time and Irregular Migration. *Time and Society*, 28(4), pp. 1429–1463.

Centlivres, P., 1993. *A 'State of the Art' Review of Research on Internally Displaced, Refugees and Returnees from and in Afghanistan*. Oxford: Report prepared for the Planning Committee of the Fourth International Research and Advisory Panel Conference on Forced Migration.

Centlivres, P. & Centlivres-Demont, M., 1988. The Afghan Refugee in Pakistan: an ambiguous identity. *Journal of Refugee Studies*, 1(2), pp. 141–152.

Conlon, D., 2011. Waiting: Feminist Perspectives on the Spacings/Timings of of Migrant (Im)mobility. *Gender, Place and Culture*, 18(3), pp. 353–360.

de Synder, V., 1993. Family Life Across the Border: Mexican Wives Left Behind. *Hispanic Journal of Behavioural Sciences*, 15(3), pp. 391–401.

Dreby, J., (2007). Children and Power in Mexican Transnational Families. *Journal of Marriage and Family*, 69(4), pp. 1050–1064.

Dupree, N., 1988. The Afghan Refugee Family Abroad: A Focus on Pakistan. *Afghan Studies*, 1(1).

Elliot, A., 2016. Paused Subjects: Waiting for Migration in North Africa. *Time and Society*, 25(1), pp. 102–116.

Eurostat, 2019. *Almost 20 000 Unaccompanied Minors Among Asylumseekers Registered in the EU in 2018*. Available at: https://ec.europa.eu/eurostat/doc uments/2995521/9751525/3-26042019-BP-EN.pdf/291c8e87-45b5-4108-920d-7d702c1d6990. Accessed 19 April 2020.

Freedman, J., 2016. Sexual and Gender-Based Violence Against Refugee Women: A Hidden Aspect of the Refugee "Crisis". *Reproductive Health Matters*, 24(27), pp. 18–26.

Fuller, H., 2017. The Emotional Toll of Out-Migration on Mothers and Fathers Left Behind in Mexico. *International Migration*, 55(3), pp. 156–172.

Griffiths, M., Rogers, A. & Anderson, B., 2014. Out of Time: The Temporal Uncertainties of Refused Asylum Seekers and Immigration Detainees. *Journal of Ethnic and Racial Studies*, 40(12), pp. 1991–2009.

Grima, B., 1992. *The Performance of Emotion Among Paxtun Women*. Karachi: Oxford University Press.

Griswold, E. & Murphy, S., 2014. *I am the Beggar of the World: Landays from Contemporary Afghanistan*. New York: Farrar, Straus and Giroux.

Hoang, L. A., & Yeoh, B. S. A., (2011). Breadwinning Wives and "Left-Behind" Husbands: Men and Masculinities in the Vietnamese Transnational Family. *Gender & Society*, 25(6), 717–739. https://doi.org/10.1177/0891243211430636.

Hussaini, R., Hossaini, M., Rezaie, R. & Schuster, L., 2020. The Gendered Nature of Migration Decision-Making in Afghan Families. *Seminar paper, Department of Anthropology Series, University of Stockholm*. Stockholm.

Jafari, B. & Schuster, L., 2019. Representations of Exile in Afghan Oral Culture. *Crossings: Journal of Migration & Culture*, 20(2), pp. 183–203.

Jafari, B., Schuster, L. & Shinwari, M. R., 2017. *Pa Afghan Shefahi culture ky deh Muhajirat anzor: nangawani aoh taglaree" Migration in Afghan oral culture: Approaches and Gaps*. Kabul: Afghanistan Centre at Kabul University.

Jehan, S., 1993. *Pa Pakhtu Adab keh da Mermano Barkha [Women Contribution in Pashtu Literature]*. Lahore: Pashtu Academy.

Khattak, S. G., 2007. Living on the Edges: Afghan Women and Refugee Camp Management in Pakistan. *Signs*, 32(3), pp. 575–580.

Khosravi, S., 2010. *Illegal Traveller: An Auto-Ethnography of Borders*. Oxford: Palgrave Macmillan.

Khosravi, S., 2018. Stolen Time. *Radical Philosophy*, 2(3), pp. 38–41.

Laiq, S., Momand, M.A., Ziaran, S., Patwal, M. M., Saraban, M. I., Gorbuz, M. A. & Wiar, H. M., 1982. Pashtu Landays. Research project of Department of Oral Literature and Folklore, Academy of Sciences Kabul.

Leutloff-Grandits, C., 2017. New Pasts, Presents and Futures: Time and Space in Family Migrant Networks Between Kosovo and Western Europe. In: H. Donnan, M. Hurd & C. Leutloff-Grandits, eds., *Migrating Borders and Moving Times: Temporality and the Crossing of Borders in Europe*. Manchester: Manchester University Press, pp. 121–139.

Majruh, B., 1994. *Le suicide et le chant*. Paris: Gallimard.

Majruh, B., 2003. *Songs of Love and War: Afghan Women's Poetry*. New York: Other Press.

Monsutti, A., 2005. *War and Migration: Social Networks and Economic Strategies of the Hazaras of Afghanistan*. London: Routledge.

Morokvasic, M., 1984. Birds of Passage Are also Women. *International Migration Review*, 4, pp. 886–907.

Mountz, A., 2011. Where Asylum Seekers Wait: Feminist Counter-Topographies of Sites Between States. *Gender, Place & Culture*, 18(3), pp. 381–399.

Phizacklea, A., 1983. *One Way Ticket*. London: Routledge and Kegan Paul.

Rahimi, F., 2017. Landay as the Voice of Pashtun Women's Passion and Social Life. *Journal of Research Initiatives*.

Safri, M., 2011. The Transformation of the Afghan Refugee: 1979–2009. *Middle East Journal*, 65(4). https://doi.org/10.3751/65.4.11.

Schuster, L., 2005. A Sledgehammer to Crack a Nut: Deportation, Detention and Dispersal in Europe. *Social Policy and Administration*, 39(6), pp. 606–621.

Schuster, L. & Majidi, N., 2015. Deportation Stigma and Re-Migration. *Journal of Ethnic and Migration Studies Special Issue: Deportation, Anxiety and Justice*, 41(4), pp. 635–652.

Schuster, L. & Shinwari, M. R. K., 2020. Migration Reflected Through Afghan Women's Poetry. *Soundings*, 76, pp. 111–123.

Shaheen, S., 1994. *Rohi Sandaree [Pashtu Songs]*. Peshawar: Pashtu Academy.

Slobin, M., 1976. *Music in the Culture of Northern Afghanistan*. Tucson: University of Arizona Press.

Tagore, R., 2005. *Selected Sort Stories*. London: Penguin Classics.

2

Journey and Encampment Observations: Liminality and the "Protracted Refugee Situation"

Karam Yahya

Introduction

Discussing experiences of crossing borders inevitably creates one of two frames: criminality, or victimization and vulnerability. There is little space in between to consider agency and existence, experience and personal reality. For those of us who have crossed borders and survived, we are often talked *about* rather than taking platforms to talk ourselves. What we are left with is a gaping hole in experiential knowledge that, when filled, leads us to think differently about migration and mobility, and in particular time and temporality.

This hole is gradually being filled, and the narratives of people who migrate becoming more centralized. In this chapter, I will further this exercise in outlining temporality and uncertainty when crossing borders. I describe a liminal area in the process of migration that is *betwixt and between* (Turner, 1967). It is after one leaves their home, but before

K. Yahya (✉)
Humboldt University of Berlin, Berlin, Germany

© The Author(s), under exclusive license to Springer Nature Switzerland AG 2021
M. Bhatia and V. Canning (eds.), *Stealing Time*,
https://doi.org/10.1007/978-3-030-69897-3_2

becoming a citizen of another country or gaining rights as a refugee. It is when you are stuck in an uncertain position: when you are seen and referred to as "illegal migrants" by people and in media and press. You are without status, and therefore largely without rights. When I crossed the sea, I was going somewhere that I had no idea about. When I recall the experience, I often question myself as to why I took one path and not another. The closest image I can relate it to is a bird following a flock, following a pre-designed pathway. Surrounding me were doctors, experienced travellers, mothers, and other people you trust. As the chapter outlines, no such recognition of these complex identities is afforded to those of us who cross borders and seas.

To Cross or not to Cross: Reflections on Bordered Mobility

Through recounting my own experiences as a migrant, aid worker, and scholar, this chapter will explore the notion of liminality: the in-betweenness that refugees experience during their journey after being thrust onto a pathway and assigned identities that they have not chosen. The status of being *without* status, of being undefined both legally and socially, has long-standing impacts on a person even after the initial migration is over.

The term liminality was first introduced by Arnold Van Gennep in 1961, and expanded on by Victor Turner in 1967. Turner described liminality as being "characterized by structural invisibility, which means that the subject is, if not physically, then structurally invisible, as it cannot be defined within any existing categories, which creates a certain level of ambiguity for both the ritual subject and those surrounding it" (1967, 5–6). To be in a liminal period, then, is to be in a space of in-betweenness, existing without defined identity or category.

Barbara E. Harrell-Bond and Eftihia Voutira are perhaps the first to use "liminality" in describing the refugee experience, arguing that "refugees are people who have undergone a violent 'rite' of separation and unless or until they are 'incorporated' as citizens into their host state (or returned to their state of origin) find themselves in 'transition', or in a state of 'liminality'" (1992: 7). Since Harrell-Bond and Voutira, a considerable body of research on this in-betweenness that refugees experience has been developed. Malkki expanded on the notion of "liminality" in describing the refugee experience, arguing that "refugees can be seen as liminal in 'the national order of things' as they do not fit into existing categories based on nationness" (1995, 1–2). This experience of liminality extends past just legal status, including social, economic, and psychological status as well.

To write about these experiences necessitates that I recall them. Several times during the process of writing this chapter, I would give up, saying to myself "I will write this story at some point, but without me being in it". Despite being at this late stage of asylum, the process of migration has continued to cast a shadow on life after migration. After traveling by foot, boat, taxi, and truck, where only spaceship remains as an unutilized method to enter the European territories, the social spiral that occurs after migrating is impossible to anticipate. In this way, the experience of migrating continues to steal time from you long after the fact; the long-term impacts of the uncertainty and lack of control experienced during the migration period still cast a shadow now, despite no longer being in that suspended, uncertain period.

Recollections from Za'atari Camp, Jordan

In 2011, demonstrations erupted in Syria. Like others, I was waiting to see what would unfold: would the Assad government lose their position in the Syrian regime after so many years? Many casualties occurred in response to the demonstrations—it was not surprising. We expected repressive responses from the Syrian regime, but what was less anticipated was mass migration. I never expected that Syrians would leave their homes to take refuge in neighbouring countries, so when the news began to talk about Jordan building a large camp for Syrian refugees who may flee from Syria in 2012, I received this information with some scepticism. But with the construction of Za'atari Camp, Syrians, especially from the south of Syria, began coming to the camp and Jordan in general, which (perhaps unsurprisingly) led to a gradual change in the ways that Syrians were regarded and treated in Jordan.

For me, this change was difficult to understand. Radio stations and general discussion began talking about "refugees", and about how Jordan will not be able to bear any substantial population increase due to lack of resources and poor infrastructure. This is a very fair concern: Jordan is a small country and is the fourth poorest country in terms of water resources. What was most surprising, however, is the substantial change in how Syrians were regarded by the Jordanian government and bureaucratic institutions. Before the war, being Syrian had little impact on my life in Jordan. Now, however, it was as if Syrians were facing accusations of wrongdoing by nature of their presence.

As is often the case in host countries, the positive effects that refugees had on society also went unmentioned, despite their clear impact. For example, cities in the north of Jordan witnessed considerable economic growth. In general, cities outside of Jordan's capital, Amman, had been witnessing population loss as people left to pursue better economic options in the capital. The opening of Za'atari Camp and influx of Syrians actually helped to re-stimulate the economies in the north or Jordan and replace some of the population loss that these cities had been experiencing.

In 2012, after graduating from university, I began working in Za'atari Camp. I watched as hundreds of thousands of Syrians streamed into Jordan, many of whom would end up at Za'atari. It was the arrival point in the journey from what is known to what is unknown. It was here, in Za'atari, that the arriving Syrians will first encounter their new identities, ones that they did not choose. The hierarchy of presenting yourself in a new society is usually a challenge, but presenting yourself with an identity of which you know nothing and did not choose adds an additional layer of difficulty. You are caught in a liminal stage not only physically and legally, but in your identity as well. Dealing with people was dependent on another social contract, and your presence as a refugee on any land makes social interactions change. This can be shocking to experience at first, as all of your expectations, thoughts, and feelings about the world were formed in a normal life, not in a camp. Now, you are seen as either a tired victim or as a ruthless violator and societal danger. Both are identities that you have not chosen.

Working in Za'atari Camp, it was difficult to see my own community leaving Syria and making the decision to come to the camp. As an aid worker, what you do never feels like it is enough—you try to help and do everything you can, but it is never enough. People began to forget the root cause of the migration. Importantly, public discourse focused on victimizing or criminalizing the people coming. It did not, however, ask about the root cause of the people coming here. You are criminalized based on the place that you come from, and now, as the person occupying the lowest rank of social order, as the weakest link in the new societal chain, the blame for societal problems tends to fall on you.

The refugees arriving in Za'atari were entering a new period of liminality; their legal statuses were undetermined, their pathways were unclear. So, too, were their identities caught in this in-betweenness: you are not what you were, but you still are not yet what you will become. Turner described this very phenomena in his study of ritual passage, writing that "a ritual subject is neither a boy nor a man, as long as he is in the liminal phase, but somewhere both between and outside of the categories" (1967, 5–6). Refugees, too, are caught in between their past identities and their future ones, but simultaneously are neither.

The Right to Return? The Lived Complexity of Borders Closing

Two years after working in Za'atari, I travelled to Turkey, this time as a so-called "refugee". It was the summer of 2014, and Jordan's borders closed behind me. I stayed in Turkey for several months before making the decision to cross the Aegean Sea, uncertain of my final destination. Physically you are crossing the sea. Legally, you are perforating bordered territories of the European Union. But psychologically, you are crossing between the known to the unknown, crossing into a new and unfamiliar system. Leaving Turkey during the winter would mean that I would cross the sea during the most dangerous time of year. I felt, however, that I could not afford to waste more time—I needed to go, and go quickly.

Generally, I observed that people who are crossing the sea have a lack of awareness about the true dangers of the crossing, and what they will face once they arrive. They may make the decision to cross the sea out of hope, perseverance, or unknowing, only to find themselves in a similar or worse position than they were in before once touching shore in Europe. In the worst of cases, as Iliadou's chapter in this collection shows, people do not make it to the shore at all. Even with correct information, there is no way to prepare someone to understand the absolutely horrifying experience of crossing the sea as a migrant. The boat ride was terrifying. I truly believed, without exaggeration, that I would die. The waves of the cold Aegean Sea kept smacking the side of the boat; the freezing water slapping our faces with each wave. People had begun fighting with each other. The reality of the danger settling in, paired with desperation, was taking hold. When the Greek coast guard arrived and extended the life preserver, I no longer felt like I was living the experience. Rather, I was watching it from the outside, a witness to my own rescue and my own life. The sense that I had reached a point of no return had settled in, that my own pathway forward was narrowing and my control over my future was diminishing.

When you are on the boat, your focus is only on reaching the shore, on grasping the second chance that migration represents. When I arrived on the Greek Island of Samos, I was first happy to touch earth again. I felt flooded with a feeling of gratefulness and relief, but simultaneously, I felt that I was moving across the threshold of an invisible door that would shut behind me. Syria, Jordan, and Turkey were becoming my past—past meaning something that I could not return to, something that is only reserved for memories stored in the back of your head. I felt that same feeling looking out over the Turkish Islands on which I stood only a few hours before. I felt that something was different- a system I had never encountered before. The problem with the European system is that once you arrive, you feel that you have to continue—because of legal papers, because of the feeling that you can't just quit in the middle of the mission. You have to finish it. When you are on your way to Europe, you have the space to think about any possible survival path. Anything could happen, as long as your aim is to survive. But when you finally reach the shore in Europe, you step into a framework that is decided for you.

Now your path is defined. And when that path is in a detention camp and your identity is now a refugee, you begin to feel as if you are walking into something that you have not—and could not have—prepared for. Your time, your identity, and your future are no longer yours to decide.

These thoughts come to many refugees when they are in a very vulnerable situation; they have just survived crossing the sea and live in the most minimal of circumstances in a detention camp. In the moments when they are having the most difficult thoughts they have ever faced, they are also living within a brutal context and in a place where they lack identity, where they cannot exert their own will over their lives. They are suspended in a system that is *designed* to keep them suspended, reminding them that they do not have power. Bordieu writes, "The all-powerful is he who does not wait but makes others wait [...] Waiting implies submission" (2000: 228). To be subject to this waiting is to be forced to submit yourself to a convoluted and unclear system.

After leaving the detention camp in Samos, I spent around twenty days finally relaxing in Athens before deciding that I would continue. I thought that if I was able to survive the boat, I would certainly survive the walk. The people around me warned of the dangers of taking the Balkan route during the winter, suggesting that I wait in Athens until Summer. But I was consumed by a sense of not wanting to lose *more* time. I didn't know exactly what that feeling was, but I knew I couldn't lose time because I would feel worse and felt I must move on as fast as possible. Now, I recognize that I was trying to avoid being caught in the liminal space of in-betweenness and uncertainty.

I had made the decision that I would not use a smuggler. Firstly, I felt that I would be better off and more inconspicuous trying to cross the border on my own. Secondly, I was afraid of the loss that would come with using a smuggler—both financially and time-wise. I wanted to maintain control over my own journey, and, notably, over my time. I was able to make my way through Greece and cross the Macedonian border with little more than the advice of friends who had already made the journey. Back then, nobody batted an eye.

In March of 2016, as a result of negotiations between the EU and Turkey, the Greek border was closed off, leaving fifty thousand people stranded beyond the border. When I had crossed, the imaginary line separating the two countries had been porous, permeable. Now, this imaginary line had turned into an impenetrable wall. The narrative and verbiage used to discuss the people stuck in Greece had changed almost overnight—they were no longer refugees and had become "illegal migrants". This change prompted not only a massive backup of nearly 50,000 people along the Greek–Macedonian border, it also prompted a change in how they were treated. The pathway that I had followed had been closed, and now the only option for these migrants was to wait.

A month after the border closed, I came back legally to Greece, ironically to exactly the same place where I had entered Macedonia illegally before, a village called Idomeni. There I was, with legal papers, assisting people who lacked legal papers, just because I had come a year earlier. I felt the inherent contradiction within this strongly. On the one hand, I was glad to be back in a place where I had really suffered but this time completely legally, with no need to be afraid of the police. This time, I felt safe. I was the same person, just with recognized refugee status. On the other hand, I knew very well that there were people in the Idomeni camp who had suffered more than I had. I knew that there were families who deserved to be in a better place. But I also knew that there was no justice in this process of legal recognition.

The situation had changed, police now had more authority, and using violence against migrants was becoming more and more justified both in the eyes of the law and the eyes of the public. When people asked me in Greece "should I cross the border?" I had told them no, that I didn't think it was safe. At the same time, however, I recognize that I was in a not-so-different position as them only a year prior, where I was being warned against making the journey along the Balkan route.

Greece 2016: Illegality and Waiting

The closing of the Greek border had created a bottleneck of movement in Idomeni. The refugees in the Idomeni camp had effectively been indefinitely stranded in Greece, without there being any clear pathway forward, just because they had come a month too late. The only thing that they were now able to do was wait powerlessly while the European Union debated over their ultimate fate.

After a few days staying in the village with a group of translators, we entered the Idomeni refugee camp. The atmosphere of the camp was one of desperation. On top of the destitute conditions, there was also a desperation to not be stuck in this in-between phase, unable to continue forward but also unable to return. The people in the camp had begun demonstrations in order to try to convince the EU into opening the border and allowing them to continue forward. People were at the end of their ropes—one protestor had set himself on fire out of desperation. To protest was an attempt to exert what little agency they had left in their own lives.

While in the camp, our group met a Syrian doctor who had recently escaped from Aleppo. We asked him why he had fled and what had happened on the way, and surprisingly, he began speaking with the Macedonians in their Slavic language, and with the Germans in German and English. Why did he speak all of these languages? He explained that he had worked in all of these countries before, but had ultimately decided to go back to Syria to be with his family. At some point in 2015, he had to flee Aleppo due to the heavy bombing. Now, he was a refugee in the same place that he previously was a doctor. Perhaps the greatest irony in all of this was that he was in a camp where they really needed doctors, but he wasn't allowed to practice. Even with all of his experience, his several languages, he wasn't allowed to help even those in the camp with him, because he was a refugee, confined to liminal legal status. His expertise and knowledge were therefore irrelevant to government authorities and organizations present. His only option was now to wait—either for an opportunity to continue forward, or a forced deportation backward.

Elsewhere in Greece, the first deportations of people back to Turkey had begun. I travelled with a group of aid workers and journalists to the distant island of Chios to document the first deportation of refugees according to the new treaty between the EU and Turkey. The deal requires new arrivals to be deported back to Turkey, considering Turkey as a safe country, instead of being allowed to continue on in Greece.

This legal change has created a major gap in migrants' journeys: if they are not deported to Turkey, they must remain on the Greek island for at least one year before they can continue with their asylum application. The problem with this waiting period is that families must put their lives, school, and careers on hold with no subsequent prospects. Children from the detention camp are not permitted in public schools, so their time in the camp is completely filled with waiting and isolation. During this waiting period, people question whether they should return to Turkey or continue with the application process.

After watching the first deportation from Chios to the Turkish side, I met a fresh graduate and a former rescue worker who was in Chios as a journalist. After just a few minutes of talking, he found out I was from Syria and said, "Come with me". He took me to the Souda camp. When we arrived, I saw random tents and children playing on the seashore, with a long line of people waiting to receive food. He told me, "We are going to build a school here", as those refugees living there would be stuck for a long time with nothing to do. I came back to Germany already planning to work with him in the school in Chios.

A year later, in 2017, I decided to return and help build the school in Chios. The school was already set up in two different buildings. The teachers were volunteers from many European countries, Australia, and the United States. In the primary school, we had kids under eight years old. Those children had never been to school before. They had only learned how to speak from their parents. They had no routines. Not only were they learning how to read and write for the first time, they were also learning how to be in a school environment.

One of these kids, Qais,[1] was an interesting case. Qais gets up at night sleepwalking, leaves the tent, and stands on the shore. He had a traumatic journey, but a child's trauma, affecting him without him knowing how and why, bearing the effects of something that he does not necessarily fully understand. Moreover, the process of growing up and transitioning between youth and adolescence and adulthood is already rife with liminality—to experience these transitions while already in a space of uncertainty and in-betweenness may further compound its effects on that child's future and development.

---

[1] This name has been changed.

The voluntary school in Chios, built by Action for Education, served as more than just a place to deliver education to the youth living on the island. It was a source of routine and normalcy in an otherwise very undefined period in the students' lives. Its goal was to not only provide students with the education that they were missing out on by nature of their migration, but also give them a sense of purpose.

Why Do We Rescue?

In November 2016, I participated in a rescue mission on the Mediterranean Sea south of Italy. We received a call from MRCC Roma with coordinates for a rubber dinghy packed with approximately 120 people, around ten miles away from the Libyan shore. We prepared our boat and launched the search party. When I saw this dinghy for the first time, to my surprise, I noticed that it was completely different from the one that had taken me from Turkey to Greece. This boat had twice the number of passengers. Most were from African countries, while in the case of boats launched from Turkey people are primarily from Syria and Iraq.

The smuggling route through Libya is much more dangerous than the one through Turkey. People face the danger of getting caught by slavers and trapped there possibly for years, while in Turkey you are usually "free", at least until you embark on your boat journey. Though both routes are dangerous, it's difficult to compare between these two pathways.

Knowing all of this, I was waiting with the crew to take the dinghy's passengers aboard. Helping them with life jackets and informing them about their rights, reassuring them that they are safe on our rescue ship: that was our role. We were giving them another chance, as I had been given. This was my motivation for doing such work—everyone has the right to that second chance. But the likelihood to receive that second chance has been significantly reduced for people by the changing policies and increasing militarization of EU borders. The practice of sea rescue, now, has substantially decreased, and laws that criminalize humanitarian sea rescue missions have been introduced across the EU and in Italy in particular. Since 2014, over 12,000 people have died trying to cross the Mediterranean Sea (IOM, 2020).

After the passengers boarded, their relief and temporary joy was clear. They felt as if they had made it, and finally arrived at a better life in Europe. But looking back to my own experience in Europe, I couldn't tell them that they had just begun. They had just arrived on a boat, surviving so many (illogical) problems, that it was difficult to tell them about a structured system that might still place them in the midst of violence. It was not something I could just tell them about. The best I could do was inform them about their rights, and tell them that they have another chance. I did not want to place barriers in front of the passengers. Each of the refugees I met would go on to face different challenges integrating into European society. I wondered if they would regret the entire journey. At the same time, you can't share that with them, seeing how happy they are just to be alive. You want them to have their moment of relief and happiness before they must face what will inevitably come.

The passengers on the ship thought they had opened a window, their chance at survival. But they had no idea how big the window was. As someone who had already done it and gone through being fresh in Europe, I knew that they could never anticipate how great the challenge would be. Often coming from poor countries, they may have no idea how confusing and bureaucratic European systems function. They would have to stand in a long queue, take a number and wait for hours or days, live in a *Sporthalle*, as is termed in Germany, get tired of waiting. Most would not obtain asylum. All would face racism and the palpable sense of feeling unwanted.

More broadly, each of them faced a liminal stage. When you graduate from university and enter the first step of your career, you also face a liminal stage, but at least in the context of your own society, and in one way or another, the decision is in your hands. But being in a liminal stage as an asylum seeker means that you are not only transitioning, you are doing so in a society and system that is entirely unfamiliar to you, towards a future that is completely unknown to you. Moreover, the length of that period of transition is undetermined and unstandardized—you are truly trapped in an indefinite limbo.

Conclusion: Tomorrow, Tomorrow

To migrate is to be trapped in an in-between space where one is undefined. Identities, futures, and legal status all remain unclear. You are trapped in a stage where you are neither what you were before, nor what you will become. The liminal period experienced by a refugee strips them of agency, forcing them into a period where they are unable to continue their lives—unable to work, study, or make forward progress. They are told only to wait.

This period of waiting can vary substantially. It is sometimes experienced in the process of the migration itself—being told "tomorrow, tomorrow". It is sometimes experienced through the endless hoops of bureaucracy that must be jumped through in order to acquire legal status. And it is sometimes experienced through being held at a border detention camp, with no sense of when you will be able to move forward. In all of these instances, however, this waiting is a theft—for each day that you must wait, for each day that you are stuck in this liminal period is a day where you are placing your life, your forward progress, on hold. You might feel you are unable to exercise the identities that you previously held nor develop new ones, such as a doctor unable to practice medicine, or a young boy unable to experience childhood.

I often get asked if I regret crossing. The answer: I don't know. I don't think I regret it, but at the same time, crossing the sea and coming by boat places you under a certain social pressure and assigns an identity to you that you do not choose. You are now one of the refugees who came by boat whose right to be here has been hotly debated in European politics. Your story *before* you made the decision to migrate will never be mentioned.

I don't accept that a person sitting behind a desk in European parliament can tell me that I should have done things a different way, that I shouldn't have come or should have done it differently. What is their experience of fleeing their country and home? They do not understand what could potentially happen if you *don't* leave—torture, kidnapping, and worse. But crossing the sea by boat is not a decision that you truly get to make—it's not an option, it's a necessity. To leave a dangerous place for a safe one is human instinct at the most fundamental level: survival.

The borders, visa applications, and bureaucracy are all that is unnatural. Migrants enter a system that is entirely unfamiliar to them, where ultimately we are treated as a guilty party and expected to be accountable for our supposed crimes. The crime in question? Being born in the "wrong place", and wanting to secure a safe future for ourselves and the people we love.

References

Bourdieu, P. (2000). *Pascalian Meditations*. Stanford: Stanford University Press.

Gennep, A., Vizedon, M. B., &Caffee, G. L. (1961). *The Rites of Passage* (First ed.). Chicago: University of Chicago Press.

Harrell-Bond, B., & Voutira, E. (1992). Anthropology and the Study of Refugees. *Anthropology Today*, Vol. 8, No. 4: 6–10.

International Organization for Migration (IOM). (2020). *Missing Migrants Project*. Available at https://missingmigrants.iom.int/region/mediterranean. Last Accessed 28 July 2020.

Malkki, L. (1995). Refugees and Exile: From "Refugee Studies" to the National Order of Things. *Annual Review of Anthropology*, Vol. 24: 495–523.

Turner, V. W. (1967). *The Forest of Symbols: Aspects of Ndembu Ritual*. Ithaca, NY: Cornell University Press.

3

Micropolitics of Time: Asylum Regimes, Temporalities and Everyday Forms of Power

Isabel Meier and Giorgia Donà

Introduction

In this chapter, we discuss the micropolitics of time: the ways in which different temporalities are used to articulate and negotiate state power in the context of everyday bordering experiences of subjects engaged within and against the asylum regime. We do so by bringing together the empirical work of Isabel Meier with individuals who are seeking or have gone through the asylum system in London or Berlin and that of Giorgia Donà with forced migrants in London and Calais. The chapter draws attention to the subtleties of how power is maintained and challenged through temporal structures, practices and experiences. Everyday encounters with power, for example at the Post Office in London, the Jobcentre in Berlin, the asylum substantial interview in the UK, as well as in the realities of poverty and financial hardship, all of which

I. Meier (✉) · G. Donà
University of East London, London, UK
e-mail: isabel.meier@tuni.fi

illustrate the importance of exploring temporal forms of power across different spaces, experiences and subjectivities, to accurately capture the nuanced micropolitics of time. Moreover, by following several everyday encounters of migrants, we show temporalities as sites of struggle and possibility. Our fieldwork in London, Berlin and Calais revealed how migrants challenge temporal regimes by re-claiming temporal experiences and practices, counter-temporalising spaces, and thereby regain some level of autonomy and emotional well-being.

In addition to locating temporal forms of power in the every day, the chapter draws particular attention to the affective dimension of temporal experiences and practices. Temporalities can produce anticipation, desire and hope as much as discomfort, chronic stress, fear and despair. By looking at the affective and emotional nature of the micropolitics of time, this chapter builds on a longstanding interest of making visible emotional and embodied negotiations of power (Butler, 2015; Ahmed, 2004; Lorde, 1981; Fanon, 1970).

Asylum regimes have become one of the main stakes in the global geopolitics of migration control (Tazzioli et al., 2018) and everyday bordering (Yuval-Davis et al., 2019). We use the term *asylum regime* to refer both to the power enacted through the asylum system as well as the wide range of differently situated subjects and bordering practices engaged within the asylum regime. Politicising the asylum system beyond its institutional and juridical framework allows us to capture everyday experiences and practices of migrants that are shaped by the anticipation and the legacy of the institutional asylum practice beyond the official waiting time for an asylum claim to be processed. This includes the experiences of those whose claims have been refused, those who have received temporary leave to remain but are still subject to illegalisation, securitisation and criminalisation, as well as those of people waiting at European borders in the anticipation of entering the asylum system. The asylum regime allows us to capture the plurality and entanglement of actors, practices and agencies that make up the asylum borderscape not only as a site of violence and harm, but also as a place of multiple possibilities (Rajaram & Grundy Warr, 2007) where new subjectivities and agencies are shaped.

Scholars within migration studies (Cwerner, 2001, 2004; Griffith, 2014, Fontanari; 2017; Andersson, 2014; Lilja et al., 2018), border studies (Little, 2015; Reitel, 2013) and geography (Tazzioli, 2018; Thorshaug & Brun, 2019) have attended to different temporalities mobilised in the context of the asylum regime. Martina Tazzioli (2018) introduced the term *temporal borders* in the context of the EU migration management to describe the establishment of an accelerated temporality of control through deadlines and time limits which impact on asylum seekers' lives. According to Tazzioli, time is "not only object of mechanisms of control - control *over* time- but also a mean and a technology for managing migrant - control *through* time" (p. 14).

From protracted waiting at state borders, refugee camps or so-called reception centres, or long periods spent in detention centres while asylum claims or deportations are being processed, states mobilise slowness as a bordering technology that demands migrants wait patiently, often without recourse to public funds. These spaces of waiting (Rotter, 2016; Turnbull, 2016) function to keep asylum seekers in a state of uncertainty (Griffiths, 2014) and limbo (Donà, 2015). On the other hand, politics of speed (Cwerner, 2004) are used to further restrict access to the right to seek asylum and to make the asylum experience as uncomfortable as possible. Fast-tracking measures, such as faster decisions on asylum claims and appeals, and lists of so-called "safe countries", produce deadlines and streams that decrease people's possibilities to access legal support and obtain the right to remain. Through such temporal politics, states silence and delegitimize asylum experiences and highlight the tension between the formal guarantee to the right to asylum and its (in)formal deferral. However, these temporal regimes even as they are forced upon migrant subjects, are also constantly negotiated and subverted. As such, migrants counter-temporalise spaces and practices through mobilising specific temporal modalities—political agencies that can be located within temporal politics that allow migrants to reclaim temporalities, autonomy and emotional well-being, as well as wider narratives. These agencies highlights how, even though states make constant claims on bordered subjects' time, time is subject to both ongoing claims and counterclaims.

This chapter explores the relationship between temporality and power; the ways in which negotiations over access to rights and belonging take place in and through specific temporal structures, experiences and practices. The chapter reveals tactics of state bordering through time as well as migrants' everyday practices of negotiating temporal regimes. We highlight three different temporal forms of power: the pace of the asylum regime and its fast and slow tactics, the politics of continuity and affective rhythms. For analytical purposes we distinguish these three temporal forms of power, all of which reveal ways in which temporalities are used to control and border migrants. The aim of this chapter is threefold: (1) to reveal some of the coexisting temporal structures, experiences and practices of the asylum regime, (2) to illustrate how migrants negotiate temporal regimes in their everyday lives, (3) to examine the affective dimension of temporalities. Overall, we argue for the importance of developing an understanding of temporalities of power beyond a linear understanding of time.

Time, Temporalities and Asylum Timescapes

Following a large body of literature (Robertson, 2014; Babalola & Alokan, 2013; Beyaraza, 2004; Adjaye, 1994) we argue for the importance of investigating time as socially and culturally constructed, rather than a linear and abstract given. Fusing solely on chronological time renders subjective, affective and situated temporalities invisible. Time needs to be considered in its multiple forms. Similar to other work (Sharma, 2014; Stubbs, 2018; Thomas, 2017), this chapter highlights the coexistence of different temporal structures, experiences and practices through using the term "temporality" in its plural form. Furthermore, temporal structures, experiences and practices are also always embedded in the social and cultural dynamics of power and inequality (Sharma, 2014). Temporalities are used to articulate state power and specific organising and controlling temporal forces can rule over other temporalities, as the invention of the "enlightened subject" illustrates. The notion of modernity produced a secularised, naturalised and spatialised temporality of the "primitive" who by definition has no future (Fabian, 2014).

Therefore, attending to temporal forms of power is essential to the study of *borderscapes*. We conceptualise the asylum regime as a "timescape" (Adam, 2003), a key site of bordering in which states regulate, allocate and occupy temporalities. Within the asylum timescape, multiple everyday temporalities unfold through administrative, economic and affective practices and experiences. However, the temporal performance of borders is also constantly contested, de-ordered and re-claimed through disruptions of those struggling within and against the asylum regime. The notion of the "timescape" allows us to explore multiple coexisting temporalities unfolding in the asylum regime such as the ways in which time is lived, embodied, felt and organised, as well as time patterns (rhythms), duration and continuity.

The term *timescape* incorporates thus both the representation of multiple temporalities as well as individual and collective practices of time-making, and in doing so highlights the ways in which time is always plural and affords certain sets of reproductive practices. Looking at the temporal dimension of power, as well as subversions and resistances, the notion of *asylum timescape* offers a nuanced analytical tool. While the European border regime uses temporal experiences and practices to govern the bodies of those seeking asylum, the notion of *asylum timescapes* allows us to read contemporary borders not only in terms of exclusion but also through power negotiations among multiple actors, spaces and temporalities. Exploring *asylum timescapes*, therefore, also allows us to observe political agencies that would otherwise remain unnoticed.

In the European context of the asylum regime, the temporal imaginaries of an asylum or refugee story often follow linear trajectories: a person flees a country due to persecution, is at present caught in temporary uncertainty while waiting for their asylum claim to be processed, and finally then supposed to be moving towards a better future. However, research with people in search of protection show much more non-linear, disrupted and sometimes circular temporalities, suggesting that a chronological ordering of time cannot account for the multiple coexisting temporal experiences and practices of migrants (Kallio et al., 2020).

Some migrants live and work in European countries for long periods of time before entering an asylum system (Dwyer et al., 2016). Others are illegally deported from one country to another in the hope of gaining access to another status (Majidi & Schuster, 2019). Even within one particular administrative event, such as the substantive asylum interview[1] in the UK, multiple temporal experiences and practices take place simultaneously. While the interview may take place at a specific chronological time following a bureaucratic asylum schedule, for many forced migrants, distinctions between past and present momentary collapse when they are asked to recall their most traumatic experiences in front of an asylum case interviewer from the Home Office.[2] These coexisting temporal experiences can result in inconsistencies or disjointed autobiographical accounts during the interview and are exacerbated in repeated interviews (Herlihy et al., 2002; Paskey, 2016) strongly affected asylum seekers possibilities of acquiring a legal status.

Methodology

The chapter draws from ethnographic material collected by the authors between October 2015 and July 2018. It brings together the empirical work of Isabel with individuals who were seeking or had gone through the asylum system in London or Berlin and that of Giorgia with forced migrants who, at some point on their journey have engaged with the European asylum regime while on the move, at the border in Calais, in the North of France or upon arrival in the UK.

Isabel's field research explored migrants' political agencies in and around spaces of anti-border struggles. The research was based upon observation, ongoing conversations with 40 people registered as asylum seekers, and participation in activist communities in both locations.

---

[1] The asylum interview in the UK is a two-stage process; the asylum screening interview and the substantive interview. The substantive interview is the lengthy, detailed interview, in which people are asked about their reasons claiming asylum.

[2] The Home Office is the department responsible for determining asylum claims in the UK. The asylum process is governed centrally across the four nation states—England, Wales, Scotland and Northern Ireland—but with varying policies and approaches.

Isabel contemplated the construction of contemporary political spaces as well as the role of affect and emotion within them. Extensive field notes were taken and while some interviews were recorded and transcribed, most conversations were reconstructed from fieldnotes.

Giorgia's fieldwork was conducted as part of a civic engagement project run by the University of East London (UEL) between 2015 and 2016. Staff and students delivered an accredited short University course on "Life Stories" to migrants residing in the so-called Calais Jungle, the name of the informal camps formerly located at the UK–French border. The UEL team organised workshops on life narratives, which included reflections on refugees' own journeys. Forced migrants who were also students wrote their own testimonies of their lives, which were published in the book *Voices from the Jungle* (Godin et al., 2017). Participant observation, life narratives and informal conversations with (then) residents of the Jungle took place in Calais. Since 2016, ethnographic work and ongoing conversations have continued with a sub-group of (former) migrant students and residents of the Jungle who now live in the UK and France. Additionally, we used research conducted by Nuria Targarona and Giorgia on the impact of the 12 months "Prohibition to Work" policy for asylum seekers in the UK, which consisted of interviews and group discussions with fifty-two asylum seekers, migrants and practitioners.

While many quotes used in the chapter are from migrants based in London, we include material from Berlin and Calais to draw attention to the transnational modalities through which temporalities are forced upon and lived by people encountering the asylum regime. Understanding the complex and ambiguous micropolitics of time in the context of the asylum regime requires methodological approaches that overcome methodological nationalism (Wimmer & Schiller, 2003) and a perspective that considers temporalities produced beyond nationally defined territories to identify European-wide tendencies and changes. The methodology integrates fieldwork across three European sites that are locations of context-specific temporal negotiations. Across different field sites in Europe, different asylum regimes operate, yet temporal forms of power are similarly mobilised across these spaces.

We proceed firstly by examining different temporal forms of power: the pace of the asylum regime and its fast and slow tactics, the politics of duration and continuity and affective rhythms.

The Pace of the Asylum Regime: Slow and Fast Tactics

One key form of temporal experience is pace—the way everyday lives are slowed down or accelerated to articulate or negotiate state power. Accelerated pace as well as slowness can be experienced as violent temporal regimes, which are not "ordinary" temporal experiences but rather a form of governing, punishment and control that aims to regulate the life (Foucault & Ewald, 2003) and death (Mbembé & Meintjes, 2003) of the migrant other.

Pace is often captured through the notion of times of waiting (Rotter, 2016; Turnbull, 2016). The lives of people who seek asylum are characterised by long periods of waiting—in detention, reception and registration centres, in the Home Office, waiting for their claims to be processed. John,[3] a 36-year old man from Uganda who had to report at the Home Office in London every Thursday while waiting for his asylum claim to be processed, describes the temporal and emotional precarity that the slow tempo of the event creates: "the purposes of that waiting is to frustrate you, because sometimes you'd be waiting in the cold, other times you'd be, there'd be very many people. So the predicament was always how to handle the time. You would never know when you're going to finish. So you cannot say, you remember, I never make any plans. It had little to do with reporting and more to do with wasting time". John describes waiting at the registration centre as an affective tool of punishment and control disrupting and claiming his autonomous time. Handling time and feelings of frustration, as his story communicates, is hard emotional work. John goes on to say: "and then four hours have passed. All of that time is to just get someone to tell me when I'm coming back. And that is all the person does, the person writes when you're

---

[3] All names used in this paper are pseudonyms.

coming back". John captures many migrants' experiences of their time being "wasted". His story also reveals the role of administrative spaces and practices in producing differential time and inequalities experienced at the level of time.

Next to these administrative spaces and times of waiting such as the Home Office, slowness is also more indirectly enforced through financial precarity. The majority of migrants mentioned about using slower modes of travelling, such as buses. In spring 2016, Mary, a 33 year old woman from Cameroon, described her journey to the Home Office in London: "I would take the bus because it is cheaper, but the journey is longer, because there were three buses I would take instead of one train. I would take the 90, okay I would take the 282 to Northolt, then the 90 from Northolt to Feltham and then another bus, I think it was the 312 or 132 to Hanslow, towards the centre, towards Lunar House[4]". Similarly, in summer 2017, Mina, a 23-year old woman described her journey to a local Jobcentre, processing benefits and employment advice, in the south of Berlin: "I often walk, sometimes it takes me two or three hours. Your feet get so tired... and then when you arrive at the centre you have to wait, sometimes for a long time. A whole day goes by and the only thing I did was have a short conversation about my benefits... and most of the time I need to come back. I often ask myself: why are they doing this to me? I'm sure they would not treat other people like that..."

Mary and Mina's stories reveal how the slow pace of the asylum bureaucracy affects their everyday lives. Both describe, in many conversations, time being taken from them as "wasted". Elina Fontanari (2017) calls this "temporal injustice", that deprives individuals of control over and access to decisions that influence their everyday time. Mary and Mina's accounts illustrate different capacities and powers of states and individuals to slow down everyday experience.

John's expression, "the purposes of that waiting is to frustrate you", and Mina's contemplation, "why are they doing this to me?", show how, according to them, these temporal experiences are mobilised to trigger

---

[4]Lunar House is an office block in Croydon, South London, that houses the headquarters of the UK Visas and Immigration division of the Home Office.

certain affective responses. In several conversations, John and Mina articulate the distress generated through the pace of the asylum regime as "stressful", "frustrating", "messing with you" and "everyday torture", highlighting the affective dimension of these temporal forms of power.

Next to slowness, accelerated pace is used as a tool of governing migrants. According to Cwerner (2004), temporal politics of speed synchronises and controls migrant and refugee movements in the name of bureaucratic efficiency. While people seeking asylum often wait for months and sometimes years, for decision letters as well as requests for information and evidence, when these letters arrive, they often evoke an intense sense of urgency and resulted in immense stress and worry. Felix, a 31-year-old Rwandan man who had sought asylum in the UK, described in 2019 how upon the arrival of a negative decision on his asylum case and his attempt to submit a new claim, he was "working tirelessly" and needed tasks to be accomplished "as soon as possible".

Another example of how states use accelerated pace as a tactic to govern and control migrants is the 28-day deadline people face in the UK after they have been granted asylum. Once somebody's asylum claim has been decided upon, they cease to receive their allowance of £37.75 per week and have to move out of their provided accommodation. They have 28 days to find a new home, apply for housing and unemployment benefits and/or find a job. Jasmine, a woman in her thirties from Cameroon, described her experience in spring 2018, two weeks after she was granted the right to remain: "I don't think I have ever felt so much stress! … You realise that what happens after you get asylum is more stressful than waiting for the decision. At least then you are cared for, you have somewhere to live and get a little bit of money. But now? Nobody cares… I'm so worried I will end up homeless, that I have nowhere to go and no money left".

Jasmine's story describes the ways in which slowness and speed affect her life as she transitions from being registered as an asylum seeker to being granted temporary right to remain. It exemplifies one of the ways through which states articulate power through "stretched" temporalities, followed by the need for immediate action. The letter confirming the new status comes not with an end to uncertainty but instead brings a sense of accelerated pace and precariousness, which demonstrates how temporal experiences of slowness while waiting are followed, sometimes unexpectedly, by experiences of speed and urgency. Jasmine expresses her disappointment after realising that the phase after the successful outcome of her application is yet another space of waiting and control, rather than bringing resolution and lasting emotional relief. Jasmine's story also foregrounds the radical instability and inconsistency of demarcations drawn between different figures of migration (Tazzioli et al., 2018, p. 244); even though she received temporary leave to remain, Jasmine is still subject to migration control.

For Jasmine, the accelerated pace brings about a strong affective response of intensified stress, loneliness and financial precarity. She worries about not being able to find a house and becoming homeless. In a conversation in summer 2018, Jasmine explained, "Even if I would have tried very hard, showed up at the Jobcentre every day, called every day, the system would have still not been able to help me in time". Jasmine's account highlights how the slowness and inefficiency of the welfare system bureaucracy means that even if she tried her best to accelerate her pace accordingly, she would still have struggled to get everything sorted in such a short period of time. During a conversation in a cafe in London in 2018, Jasmine mentioned "I'm sure they know that this isn't working. Even then they show you that they really don't want you to be here".

Jasmine's particular experience is also marked by the fact that unlike other individuals seeking asylum we spoke to, she does not have a wide social network of family and friends that she can rely on. The solitary nature of Jasmine's experience intensified her fear of homelessness and isolation associated with these temporalities. Jasmine's account further illustrates how, depending on a person's social position, accelerated pace mobilised by the asylum regime is experienced and navigated differently.

Having examined the micropolitics of pace and how it is used as tactic of punishment and control, the next section explores experiences and practices of duration and continuity. As we will show, similar to pace, the experience of duration and continuity is used as an affective technology of bordering.

The Politics of Duration and Continuity

By duration we mean the lengths of an experience, event or practice. This section explores practices and experiences of duration and continuity and illustrates the ways in which they create and exacerbate stress, fear and discomfort, but also open up political possibilities. Ansems de Vries and Guild (2019) developed the notion of a "politics of exhaustion" to speak to the duration and consequent accumulated effects over time and across space in the context of today's asylum, migration and border governing. Other scholars have discussed how governments mobilise a politics of slowness, duration and waiting over time as slow violence (Nixon, 2011; Hage, 2009; Puar, 2009), slow death (Berlant, 2007) and affective border violence (Meier, 2020). Affective technologies of bordering such as precarity and "unlivabilty" (Butler, 2006, 2012) force migrants to live within conditions that slowly wear them out.

In the context of the asylum regime, the politics of duration are mobilised everywhere. One example is the many years migrants spend in temporary accommodation centres, often in isolated areas, waiting for a decision on their case. Even though the Home Office in the UK states that asylum applications will usually be decided within 6 months, by the end of 2017, 53% of asylum claimants had been waiting longer than 6 months for a decision (Refugee and Asylum Seeker Voice, 2018). Between 2015 and 2017, there was an increase of 178% in the cases of applicants waiting for longer than 6 months (Bulman, 2017). Another example is the changed UK policy that confines migrants applying for asylum to an enduring temporary status not only during but also after their asylum claim has been accepted. In 2005, the UK government decided to replace permanent leave to remain for asylum seekers who were granted refugee status with a five-year leave to remain (Refugee Council, 2010). This change in policy has drastically shifted the duration in which migrants are forced to navigate their temporary right to stay. In the past, the end to the waiting embedded in the official asylum system was marked by the bestowing of refugee status with indefinite leave to remain. However, now the undefined waiting during the asylum process is followed by more periods of fixed-term waiting (first the 28 days, followed by the 5 years leave to remain). The politics of duration are thus mobilised to permanently produce a non-citizen and migrant other, cutting across different figures produced through the migration regime, such as the "asylum seeker", "migrant" or "refugee". As a result, more and more migrants across different social, legal and administrative positions, are kept in a state of "permanent temporariness" (Vosko et al., 2014; Bailey et al., 2002).

When contemplating the politics of duration, two conversations with migrants in London came to mind. Both tell the story of how specific events related to the asylum process made them aware of the continuity of their experience as bordered and controlled subjects. The first conversation took place within a research project led by Giorgia exploring how the 12 months prohibition to work policy affects people seeking asylum in the UK (Targarona & Donà, Forthcoming). Abdo, an African[5] man, had been waiting for several months to hear the outcome of his asylum claim without working in London. When he received a negative decision, he decided to appeal. His case was to go to court at a specific time, yet it was postponed. Abdo's realisation that after all of the time he had already spent waiting, the appeal process would take an additional, unpredictably longer expanse of time, signalled to him the "endlessness" of being stuck in the asylum system. Abdo described the moment of finding out that his court hearing had been adjourned as a breaking moment full of intensity. Until then, he felt mentally strong enough to wait and cope with the situation. But when Abdo was informed that his court hearing had been adjourned and he had to, again, wait for an undetermined time, he felt he was not able to cope with the stress and fear of the ongoing uncertainty. After the psychological distress had settled, he decided to stop waiting and start working as a way to keep himself busy and distracted from the seemingly endless nature of the process.

The second example takes us back to Jasmine's story of transitioning from seeking asylum to gaining temporary leave to remain. Even after the successful outcome of her application, an event she had waited for nearly two years, Jasmine's experience of limbo continued. When she discovered that she would have to leave her provided accommodation,

---

[5]Abdo chose not to name his country of origin but the continent he moved from

she realised "it isn't over": "You receive the decision and it's a good decision. And you are happy, but then you realise that it isn't over. Maybe it's never over. I don't know". Similar to Abdo's story, Jasmine's account describes a key moment, in which the politics of duration and continuity that states mobilise become very vivid and clear. Her biggest fear, as she described in a conversation in summer 2016 was that her experience as a bordered, controlled and punished migrant might never be over, illustrating the distress but also claustrophobic bodily intensity evoked by the event. The letter confirming her new status came not with an end to uncertainty but with the realisation that she would still be subject to migration control and bordering. Jasmine and Abdo's stories reveal the affective politics of duration and continuity and the importance of attending to the relationship between temporalities and power to explore how different temporal forms of power, such as duration and continuity, fulfil specific state bordering interests.

After pointing at the importance of attending to the politics of pace and continuity, in the next section we explore affective rhythms—a temporal form of power enforced upon migrants through specific everyday rhythms.

Affective Rhythms

We define rhythms as the arrangement and order of different temporal experiences in time. While the temporal form of pace speaks to how states use different tempos as tactics of bordering, less is known about the more complex ways in which these different tempos are arranged in time and what interests are served by their particular arrangement. Here we want to pay particular attention to the affectivity of these asylum regime rhythms.

The asylum timescape is full of rhythmic temporalities, both bureaucratic and embodied. These rhythms can be regularly repeated and yet, sudden abrupt changes can also happen at anytime. One way of gaining a better understanding of the temporal order of events and temporal experiences in the context of the asylum regime is by examining the arrangement of events in official asylum processes: the screening interview, substantive asylum interview, decision, appeal and associated rhythms like the 12-month prohibition to work in the UK. In the following we want to illustrate the affectivity of rhythms through two events in particular: reporting to the Home Office and collecting money from the Post Office.

Many migrants described reporting to the Home Office as an extremely stressful experience, as there is the recurring threat of detention and deportation. John, the 36-year old man from Uganda, introduced earlier, described in 2017 his weekly visits to the Home Office in London: "Reporting structures my week. I go to report every Thursday morning. I get up really early and have to take three different buses to get there. Sometimes it takes me up to three hours. And that is only to get there. Usually, there are very long queues and often people are waiting for 3 h or more, sometimes in the cold. The reporting itself goes very quickly and it seems you wait all this time just to be told when to come back. You can feel the anxiety in everyone. People are looking around nervously but also trying to make each other more comfortable". John has heard several stories of people being detained when reporting: "It can always happen, you just know. Everyone knows and everyone is worried. Sometimes people get sick from worrying so much". John's story describes the affective rhythms that the repetitive reporting imposes on him and others and how these temporalities are collectively embodied.

A similar affective rhythm is visible in the weekly collection of the asylum allowance that created a lot of discomfort in the lives of people seeking asylum in the UK. Until spring 2017, most people seeking asylum in the UK had to collect their allowance in cash from a local post office, where they had to present their Application Registration Card (ARC) to confirm their identity and eligibility for support (this practice has since been replaced by the allowance being loaded onto debit cards each week, with which they can withdraw money from cash machines). The impact of this asylum seeker support practice has been explored and criticised as dehumanising by many others (Mayblin, 2017; Canning, 2017; Meier, 2020). In spring 2016, Cynthia described her weekly journey to a local post office in the North of London and how much discomfort she experienced. "If you go to the post office to pick up your money everyone is looking at you, and you feel so uneasy. I always feel so uneasy...". Similar to John, Cynthia describes the affective rhythms these routines create. Knowing that these uncomfortable and fearful events of reporting and collecting are regularly repeated for an unpredictable amount of time consumes a critical amount of emotional and mental space and time in their lives. John and Cynthia worry all week about being detained and consequently deported when reporting at the Home Office. These two examples show oscillations between long periods of waiting, filled with stress, anxiety and worrying, short moments of increased intensity when officially encountering the Home Office administration and gaps of relief and ease when leaving the Home Office and Post Office. These practices create a specific emotional and bodily rhythm for people encountering the asylum regime: the slow waiting and fearful anticipation is followed by a short phase of extreme distress and bodily tension, when encountering the formal spaces of administrative bordering, and it is followed by a short moment of release before worrying about the next visits. Many migrants we spoke to described these cycles as "traumatic" and "unhealthy". Mary (introduced earlier), concluded a conversation she had with Isabel in the winter of 2016 with "the problem is that there is never a break, you are always stressed. Of course you are more stressed on the day you report than on the day after but it never stops". It is worth noting that John, Cynthia and Mary are equally stressed about the rhythms continuing and the rhythm breaking as a visit to the Home Office, or any other official encounter with the Home Office administration can always lead to detention or deportation.

While these affective micropolitics of pace, continuity and rhythms shape migrants' lives in significant ways, they are also constantly negotiated, challenged and resisted by them. The asylum timescape is thus not only a space in which power is enforced but also constantly negotiated, subverted and re-ordered.

Negotiating Temporal Regimes

In this last section, we examine some of the ways in which migrants negotiate, subvert, re-order and counter-temporalise spaces, experiences and practices. In our research with people engaged within and against the asylum regime in London, Berlin and Calais, both slowness and speed were used to counter-temporalise spaces and organise collectively. In 2015 in Berlin, camp spaces accommodated 85% of all asylum seekers. Migrants who were involved in activist groups repeatedly organised pop-up protests within these camp spaces as a way of mobilising resistance without the police shutting them down. It was the accelerated speed and flexibility to respond to equally fast-changing state-bordering technologies that allowed the protests to take place.

Another example of how speed was used as a tool of resistance within these camp spaces was to prevent deportations from happening. Mara, a woman from Syria in her early 30s, explained how she helped a woman from Moldova and her daughter to hide when the police came to her camp: "You know we used to hide women in different rooms when we knew the police were looking for them. They don't have the time to search the whole camp so in the end they will leave again, and everyone is… There was this one woman from Moldova and the police came to deport her and she and her daughter were hiding in another room and the police didn't know. We had to act so fast! Often, we don't know when the police will show up but when the come… All the women in the camp work together - they run around sharing information and offering their rooms to hide in". Mara's story shows how migrants use speed to resist and delay deportations. As deportations are a key event in which states mobilise their tactics of acceleration of pace, the women in the camp negotiate these tactics through rendering the deportation unsuccessful.

Through delaying responses, absence or hiding, as outlined in Mara's story, asylum activists use slowness as a tactic to extend appeal processes or prevent deportations from happening. Asylum seekers and activists stopped deportations through acts of resistance, such as handcuffing themselves to objects and urinating in their pants with the result of a total of 1637 deportations in Germany in 2018 being called off at airports. We also observed individuals taking different actions to counter-temporalise spaces of control and migrant management. Firstly, we observed how camp spaces, often portrayed as wasted time of waiting (Bissell, 2007), were used to develop collective strategies of survival and political mobilisation. For example, a former resident of the Calais informal transit settlement originally from Afghanistan who chose the pseudonym "Refugee's Voice" explained how he came up with the idea of creating a Facebook page called "RefugeesVoice2015" when he was in the camp to help provide humanitarian assistance to residents, not only to help them in the camp, but also to travel safely to the UK: "I was a refugee volunteer. I realised that I saw many things being done from the volunteer's perspective but what would I do from a refugee perspective? I saw many social media pages, pages on Facebook and this is the time I realised I need to do something". He then decided to set up a Facebook page to create awareness about the conditions of people on the move in Calais and to provide information to enable safer journeys into the UK. Other residents in Calais "Jungle" documented the violence that French police and fascist groups used against them at the border and posted videos online to raise awareness (Godin & Donà, Forthcoming).

Similarly, Maria and John, introduced earlier, described how they used their time waiting at the Home Office in London to compare notes: "So if I met so-and-so and they told me, have you tried this? Have you done this? It was like a day to know, any information from anyone could be helpful".

Another way in which we observed migrants counter-temporalise spaces of waiting and slowness is by looking for work. In the UK, people seeking asylum are normally not allowed to work while their claim is being considered. Only if their claim has been outstanding for more than 12 months through "no fault of their own", can they submit a request for permission to work. Not being able to work generates uncomfortable emotions such as embarrassment, boredom, frustration, depression and anger (Kenny, 2002; Hartley & Fleay, 2014; Hennessy, 2017). Kamal, a Sudanese man describes the a/effects of a politics of slowness and continuity: "I had too much time to think about problems, things that happened back home and on the journey. I looked for a job to get rid of these bad feelings". Kamal describes how the slowness of the administrative procedure produces "bad feelings" that he thought he was able to manage better when keeping busy. Similarly, Suleyman, a 27-year-old Sudanese man, shared that his decision to look for work in the undocumented sector was driven by the desire to move on with his life: "I feel uncomfortable to stay all day in the house, I feel like I want something to do". These stories show how people seeking asylum navigate the affective precarity of slow tempo and waiting through employment and keeping themselves busy. Kamal and Suleyman negotiate the politics of slowness by turning wasted time into spaces of learning, development and self-care.

All three examples, the Calais camp, waiting at the Home Office and unemployment in the UK, show how people reclaim waiting as a liveable space. Regardless of whether the waiting is seen as a moment of stagnation or a political project, people are nevertheless pursuing multiple goals in their lives while waiting: they are learning languages, working (often illegally), getting education, starting families, etc. Through counter-temporalising spaces, people in the asylum regime negotiate the meaning of these spaces: from passive and unchanged (El-Shaarawi, 2015), to spaces of "transformation, movement and volatility" (Brun, 2016, p. 393).

Next to subverting and counter-temporalising the politics of slowness, people seeking asylum counter-temporalised practices and experiences of continuity. Godfrey, a 32-year-old asylum seeker from Uganda, who was detained several times while waiting for his asylum claim to be processed, described how doing little practical things to help others in need helped him to survive his time in detention. Doing what was possible within the very limited range of actions and possibilities within detention, allowed Godfrey to stay in the present and feel some kind of ease and relief, while not worrying about the uncertainty and endlessness of his days in detention. Through his focus on the present and the little practical things that were possible (Kallio et al., 2020), Godfrey re-claimed control over his time and subverted the politics of duration. As pointed out before, the politics of duration works by evoking intense emotions and affects through the lengths of which individuals in the asylum regime are exposed to temporal regimes. Individuals seeking asylum who were placed in detention often described their time in detention as "timeless" and "time stopping", illustrating the slow tactics mobilised within these spaces and how they impacted their well-being. By focusing on the present, Godfrey re-temporalised his experience in smaller daily units that he could observe passing by. Moreover, by helping others with little practical things such as making a photocopy, he experienced his time in detention as, at least to some extent, meaningful.

Finally, to illustrate how individuals engaged within the asylum regime negotiated rhythms, we return to conversations with John. He negotiates the politics of rhythms by searching for ways to extend the moment of relief following, and in-between, his mandatory and regular visits to the Home Office. On Thursdays, which was the day John used to report, directly after the Home Office, he used to visit a local community garden. He described multiple times how coming to the garden where he usually spent three hours weeding and watering followed by a lunch with other volunteers, quieted his mind and stopped him from worrying about the coming weeks, months and years. Seeking out spaces that bring about release and moments of happiness, while being engaged within the asylum regime, can be seen as a form of political agency, we argue, as it marks a small act of resistance to comply with the affective technologies of stress, worry and fear mobilised by states. John's story illustrates how rhythms can be mobilised by migrants to manage affects.

Conclusion

We started out by locating asylum politics not just in bureaucratic structures but within everyday, emotional and affective practice and experience of borders. Tracing multiple everyday encounters of migrants with asylum regimes in London, Berlin and Calais revealed the multiplicity of temporal forms of power: states and migrants mobilised pace, duration, continuity as well as affective rhythms in the every day. This highlights the importance of developing an understanding of the micropolitics of time that goes beyond a linear one-dimensional understanding of temporal experience and practice as either "slowing down" or "speeding up".

As a way of capturing the multiplicity and entanglement of these temporalities, we introduced the concept asylum timescape because it allows us to re-think time as plural, fluid and contested zone. The asylum timescape portrays temporality as a site of struggle and ongoing negotiation over rights and belonging but also a place where meaningful spaces of resistance and radical hope can open up. Our results show numerous examples of migrants subverting and counter-temporalising the politics of speed, slowness and continuity and thereby re-claiming temporal experiences and practices. Another form of political agency we observed was migrants counter-temporalising spaces such as refugee camps, Home Office visits or unemployment, through which they regained some level of autonomy and emotional well-being. Our findings emphasise the importance of locating not only governing but also resisting and emergent forces within a politics of time.

The chapter makes an important contribution to existing literature on the temporal politics of asylum and bordering (Thorshaug & Brun, 2019; Tazzioli, 2018; Fontanari; 2017) by locating these struggles in the every day and the body. Disclosing some of these otherwise invisible intensities of power condensed in the articulation of these encounters is essential to address and challenge these forms of power. Several examples from our research with people seeking asylum in London, Berlin and Calais revealed everydayness as an organised tool of governing unwanted migrants through routines and rhythms of normalised discomfort (Meier, 2020) and the deliberate infliction of harm (Canning, 2017). Everyday encounters with asylum regimes, for example at the Home Office, Jobcentre, in the realities of financial hardship produced through depriving people seeking asylum the right to work and an allowance of 37.75 per week to pay for food, clothes, legal support and travel, illustrated how states create and exacerbate fear, stress and worry through the temporal dimensions of pace, duration and rhythm.

Next to everyday encounters, the politics of time articulates itself through affective governmentality: the power to provoke discomfort, exhaustion (Ansems de Vries & Guild, 2019) and harm (Canning, 2019) as a tool of bordering and control. The chapter illustrated how temporal politic of duration further intensify the bodily life of everyday precarities and echoed what other scholars have discussed as slow violence (Nixon, 2011; Hage, 2009; Puar, 2009), slow death (Berlant, 2007) and affective border violence (Meier, 2020). In that sense, the micropolitics of time are material and embodied, states mobilise the affective nature of temporal experience against the migrant other. However, as the final section showed, migrants negotiate these affective techniques of governance through extending gaps of ease and comfort through practices of care, comfort, hope and solidarity.

References

Adam, B. (2003). Reflexive modernization temporalized. *Theory, Culture & Society, 20*(2), 59–78.
Adjaye, J. K. (Ed.). (1994). *Time in the Black experience* (No. 167). Westport, CT: Greenwood Publishing Group.
Ahmed, S. (2004). Affective economies. *Social Text, 22*(2), 117–139.
Andersson, R. (2014). Time and the migrant other: European border controls and the temporal economics of illegality. *American Anthropologist, 116*(4), 795–809.
Babalola, S. F., & Alokan, O. A. (2013). African concept of time, a sociocultural reality in the process of change. *Journal of Education and Practice, 4*(7), 143–147.
Bailey, A. J., Wright, R. A., Mountz, A., & Miyares, I. M. (2002). (Re)producing Salvadoran transnational geographies. *Annals of the Association of American Geographers, 92*(1), 125–144.
Berlant, L. (2007). Slow death (sovereignty, obesity, lateral agency). *Critical Inquiry, 33*(4), 754–780.
Beyaraza, E. (2004). *The African Concept of Time. A Comparative Study of Various Theories*. Kampala, Uganda: Makerere University Press.
Bissell, D. (2007). Animating suspension: Waiting for mobilities. *Mobilities, 2*(2), 277–298.
Brun, C. (2016). There is no future in humanitarianism: Emergency, temporality and protracted displacement. *History and Anthropology, 27*(4), 393–410.
Bulman, M. (2017). Number of asylum seekers waiting more than six months for decision rises more than 70% in a year. *The Independent*. Available at: https://www.independent.co.uk/news/uk/home-news/asylum-seekers-wait-six-months-more-decision-rise-80-per-cent-figures-home-office-refugee-council-a7755626.html.
Butler, J. (2006). *Precarious Life: The Powers of Mourning and Violence*. London, UK; New York, NY: Verso.

Butler, J. (2012). Can one lead a good life in a bad life? Adorno Prize Lecture. *Radical Philosophy*, *176*(9), 9–18.

Butler, J. (2015). *Notes Toward a Performative Theory of Assembly*. Cambridge, MA; London, UK: Harvard University Press.

Canning, V. (2017). *Gendered Harm and Structural Violence in the British Asylum System*. Oxford, UK: Routledge.

Canning, V. (2019). Abject asylum: Degradation and the deliberate infliction of harm against refugees in Britain. *Justice, Power and Resistance*, *3*, 37–60.

Cohen, C. J. (2004). Deviance as resistance: A new research agenda for the study of black politics. *Du Bois Review: Social Science Research on Race*, *1*(1), 27–45.

Conlon, D. (2011). Waiting: Feminist perspectives on the spacings/timings of migrant (im)mobility. *Gender, Place & Culture*, *18*(3), 353–360.

Cwerner, S. B. (2001). The times of migration. *Journal of Ethnic and Migration Studies*, *27*(1), 7–36.

Cwerner, S. B. (2004). Faster, faster and faster: The time politics of asylum in the UK. *Time & Society*, *13*(1), 71–88.

de Vries, L. A., & Guild, E. (2019). Seeking refuge in Europe: Spaces of transit and the violence of migration management. *Journal of Ethnic and Migration Studies*, *45*(12), 2156–2166.

Doná, G. (2015) Making homes in limbo: embodied virtual "homes" in prolonged conditions of displacement. *Refuge*, *31*(1), 67–73.

Dwyer, P., Hodkinson, S., Lewis, H., & Waite, L. (2016). Socio-legal status and experiences of forced labour among asylum seekers and refugees in the UK. *Journal of International and Comparative Social Policy*, *32*(3), 182–198.

El-Shaarawi, N. (2015). Living an uncertain future: Temporality, uncertainty, and well-being among Iraqi refugees in Egypt. *Social Analysis*, *59*(1), 38–56.

Fabian, J. (2014). *Time and the Other: How Anthropology Makes Its Object*. New York: Columbia University Press.

Fanon, F. (1970). *Black Skin, White Masks*. London: Paladin.

Fontanari, E. (2017). It's my life. The temporalities of refugees and asylum-seekers within the European border regime. *Etnografia e Ricerca Qualitativa*, *10*(1), 25–54.

Foucault, M., & Ewald, F. (2003). *"Society Must Be Defended": Lectures at the Collège de France, 1975–1976*. United Kingdom: Pan MacMillan.

Godin, M., & Doná, G. (Forthcoming). Forced migrants in transit: Mobile technologies and techno-borderscapes. *Journal of Ethnic and Migration Studies*.

Godin, M., Hansen, K. M., Lounasmaa, A., Squire, C., & Zaman, T. (Eds.). (2017). *Voices from the 'jungle': Stories from the Calais Refugee Camp*. Pluto Press.

Griffiths, M. B. (2014). Out of time: The temporal uncertainties of refused asylum seekers and immigration detainees. *Journal of Ethnic and Migration Studies, 40*(12), 1991–2009.

Hage, G. (2009). Waiting out the crisis: On stuckedness and governmentality. In G. Hage (Ed.), *Waiting* (pp. 97–106). Melbourne: Melbourne University Press.

Hartley, L., & Fleay, C. (2014) *Policy as Punishment: Asylum Seekers in the Community Without the Right to Work*. Centre for Human Rights Education, Curtin University. Available at: http://www.nwhn.net.au/admin/file/content101/c6/CHRE_PolicyAsPunishmentAsylumSeekersInTheCommunityWithoutTheRightToWork_Feb_2014.pdf. Accessed 6 April 2017.

Hennessy, M. (2017). The right to work for asylum seekers: Ireland's prohibition on Employment. *European Database of Asylum Law*. Available at: http://www.asylumlawdatabase.eu/en/journal/right-work-asylum-seekers-ireland's-prohibition-employment. Accessed 3 April 2017.

Herlihy, J., Scragg, P., & Turner, S. (2002). Discrepancies in autobiographical memories—implications for the assessment of asylum seekers: Repeated interviews study. *British Medical Journal, 324*(7333), 324–327.

Kallio, K., Meier, I., & Häkli, J. (2020). Radical hope in refugee political agency: Reaching beyond linear temporalities. *Journal of Ethnic and Migration Studies*.

Kenny, C. (2002). *Asylum seekers in Galway and the Right to Work*. Galway: Galway Refugee Support Group.

Little, A. (2015). The complex temporality of borders: Contingency and normativity. *European Journal of Political Theory, 14*(4), 429–447.

Lilja, M., Henriksson, A., & Baaz, M. (2018). (Re)thinking the precarity of Swedish migrants: Governing through decelerations and timescapes. *Journal of Refugee Studies, 32*(1), 144–161.

Lorde, A. (1981). The uses of anger. *Women's Studies Quarterly, 9*(3), 7–10.

Majidi, N., & Shuster, L. (2019) Deportation and forced return. In: Bloch, A. & Donà, G. (Eds.), *Forced Migration: Current Issues and Debates*. Abington-on-Thames: Routledge, pp. 88–105.

Mayblin, L. (2017). *Asylum after Empire: Colonial Legacies in the Politics of Asylum Seeking*. London, UK; New York, NY: Rowman & Littlefield.

Mbembé, J. A., & Meintjes, L. (2003). Necropolitics. *Public Culture, 15*(1), 11–40.

Meier, I. (2020). Affective border violence: Mapping everyday asylum precarities across different spaces and temporalities. *Emotion, Space and Society.*

Mezzadra, S., & Neilson, B. (2012). Between inclusion and exclusion: On the topology of global space and borders. *Theory, Culture & Society, 29*(4–5), 58–75.

Munt, S. R. (2017). *Queer Attachments: The Cultural Politics of Shame.* Oxford: Routledge.

Nixon, R. (2011). *Slow Violence and the Environmentalism of the Poor.* Cambridge, MA; London, UK: Harvard University Press.

Paskey, S. (2016). Telling refugee stories: Trauma, credibility, and the adversarial adjudication of claims for asylum. *Santa Clara Law. Review, 56*(3), 457–530.

Puar, J. K. (2009). Prognosis time: Towards a geopolitics of affect, debility and capacity. *Women & Performance, 19*(2), 161–172.

Rajaram, P. K., & Grundy-Warr, C. (Eds.). (2007). *Borderscapes: Hidden Geographies and Politics at Territory's Edge.* Minneapolis, MN: University Press of Minnesota.

Refugee and Asylum Seeker Voice. (2018). *The Waiting Game. The Impact of Delayed Asylum Decisions.* Available at: https://www.refugee-action.org.uk/wp-content/uploads/2018/03/Refugee-and-Asylum-Seeker-Voice-The-Waiting-Game-Report-1.pdf. Accessed 14 July 2018.

Refugee Council. (2010). *The Impact of Limited Leave on Refugees in the UK.* Retrieved, June 12, 2020, from https://www.refugeecouncil.org.uk/wp-content/uploads/2019/03/Limited_leave_report_final_September.pdf.

Reitel, B. (2013). Border temporality and space integration in the European transborder agglomeration of Basel. *Journal of Borderlands Studies, 28*(2), 239–256.

Robertson, S. (2014). Time and temporary migration: The case of temporary graduate workers and working holiday makers in Australia. *Journal of Ethnic and Migration Studies, 40* (12), 1915–1933.

Rotter, R. (2016). Waiting in the asylum determination process: Just an empty interlude? *Time & Society, 25*(1), 80–101.

Seitz, D. K. (2017). Limbo life in Canada's waiting room: Asylum-seeker as queer subject. *Environment and Planning D: Society and Space, 35*(3), 438–456.

Sharma, S. (2014). *In the Meantime: Temporality and Cultural Politics.* Durham, NC; London, UK: Duke University Press.

Stubbs, P. (2018). Slow, slow, quick, quick, slow: Power, expertise and the hegemonic temporalities of austerity. *Innovation: The European Journal of Social Science Research, 31*(1), 25–39.

Targarona, N., & Donà, G. (Forthcoming). Forced unemployment or undocumented work: The burden of the prohibition to work for asylum seekers in the UK. *Journal of Refugee Studies*.

Tazzioli, M. (2018). The temporal borders of asylum. Temporality of control in the EU border regime. *Political Geography, 64*, 13–22.

Tazzioli, M., Garelli, G., & De Genova, N. (2018). Autonomy of asylum? The autonomy of migration undoing the refugee crisis script. *South Atlantic Quarterly, 117*(2), 239–265.

Thomas, P. D. (2017). The plural temporalities of Hegemony. *Rethinking Marxism, 29*(2), 281–302.

Thorshaug, R. Ø., & Brun, C. (2019). Temporal injustice and re-orientations in asylum reception centres in Norway: Towards critical geographies of architecture in the institution. *FENNIA, 197*(2), 232–248.

Turnbull, S. (2016). 'Stuck in the middle': Waiting and uncertainty in immigration detention. *Time & Society, 25*(1), 61–79.

Vosko, L. F., Preston, V., & Latham, R. (2014). *Liberating Temporariness. Migration, Work and Citizenship in an Era of Insecurity*. Montreal and Kingston: McGill Queens University Press.

Wimmer, A., & Schiller, N. G. (2003). Methodological nationalism, the social sciences, and the study of migration: An essay in historical epistemology. *International Migration Review, 37*(3), 576–610.

Yuval-Davis, N., Wemyss, G., & Cassidy, K. (2019). *Bordering*. John Wiley & Sons.

4

The Weaponisation of Time: Indefinite Detention as Torture

Omid Tofighian and Behrouz Boochani

Introduction

On July 19, 2013, Australian Labour Prime Minister Kevin Rudd announced that anyone seeking asylum by boat from Indonesia will never be settled in Australia and will be removed to the recently reopened immigration detention centres on Pacific islands: Manus Island (Papua New Guinea) and the Republic of Nauru—a former Australian colony and a protectorate. Both now embody neo-colonial dynamics. Manus

---

O. Tofighian (✉)
School of the Arts and Media, UNSW Sydney, Kensington, Australia
e-mail: omid.tofighian@sydney.edu.au

Department of Philosophy, University of Sydney, Sydney, Australia

B. Boochani
Ngāi Tahu Research Centre, University of Canterbury, Christchurch, New Zealand

School of Social Sciences, UNSW Sydney, Kensington, Australia

© The Author(s), under exclusive license to Springer Nature Switzerland AG 2021
M. Bhatia and V. Canning (eds.), *Stealing Time*,
https://doi.org/10.1007/978-3-030-69897-3_4

was for men travelling alone. Nauru for women, unaccompanied minors and families. This inhumane and desperate policy was introduced only a number of years after Rudd's decision to end the previous Liberal government's practice and close the island facilities; carceral sites that the conservative government had originally set up. When Rudd first took power in 2007 he ended the offshore policy designed and maintained by Liberal Prime Minister John Howard in 2001 (known as the Pacific Solution). The detention centres were reopened in 2012 when Rudd was replaced by Labor Prime Minister Julia Gillard (2010–2013); phase two of the "Pacific Solution" began with Gillard and was reinforced when Rudd returned to power in 2013. Just months after the July 19 policy the Liberal Party, under Tony Abbott, won the Federal election; soon after immigration minister Scott Morrison (Prime Minister since 2018 and at the time of writing), followed by Peter Dutton, further militarised border controls by implementing and reinforcing 'Operation Sovereign Borders'.

Sixteen people have died as a result of indefinite detention on Manus, Nauru and Christmas Island (an Australian territory) since 2013. Thousands of lives have been destroyed and hundreds are still detained and in limbo after being transferred between various detention centres, community detention or granted temporary visas (although unreported, a number have died after being deported).

Behrouz Boochani—a Kurdish Iranian writer, journalist and cultural advocate—arrived by boat on his birthday (23rd July, 2013), four days after Rudd's ruling. Four days after the introduction of his exile policy. In the prison camp, the weaponisation of time was interconnected with multiple and multiplying forms of debasement, control and subjugation–together they constitute what he refers to in his book *No Friend but the Mountains: Writing From Manus Prison* (Picador 2018) as the kyriarchal system. This concept is a translation of the Farsi neologism *system-e hākem* which Boochani uses to describe the pyramidal system governing the detention centre, driven by an insatiable drive for domination, oppression and subordination (with roots in Australia's colonial history). The translation adopts the term 'kyriarchy', a neologism introduced by radical feminist theologian Elisabeth Schüssler Fiorenza which uses the term kyrios ("master" or "lord") in its construction, and which

4 The Weaponisation of Time

she applies in her critical biblical hermeneutics (1992, 2001; See also Boochani 2018a, fn. 124; Tofighian 2018).

This chapter provides insights into the system and how time is manipulated to torment and humiliate, and to strip hope, humanity and selfhood. Kyriarchal strategies are best explained through the narratives and the affliction suffered by the characters in the book. Engaging with the lived experience is the most effective way to communicate the interlocking systems of violence. Techniques within the kyriarchal system all exploit time in varying and perverse ways. They involve queuing for long periods for everything in degrading conditions (even for basic necessities), dysfunctional bureaucratic processes, the bad faith exercised by authorities, infantilisation and lack of control over one's routine and plans, and the indefinite nature of detention.

Behrouz spent over six years in the prison camp and challenged the system by producing journalism, art and literature using a smuggled mobile phone. In the context of indefinite detention, this system of domination and violence is obsessed with grinding people into submission, forcing them to return to the countries from which they fled, or to perish.

This chapter presents the reflections and critical analysis of Behrouz and his collaborator and translator Omid Tofighian. Omid is an Australian-based academic whose family left Iran during a different period (around the time of the Iranian Revolution) and came to Australia after over four years in the US. After experiencing difficulties in the US and unable to return to Iran for political and religious reasons, his family was accepted to immigrate to Australia—at the time (1982) the nation had an increasing immigration intake after recently abolishing the White Australia Policy. Behrouz and Omid forged an important and productive relationship based on their experiences, their academic training and mutual interests, their shared cultural vision, and commitment to resistance. Omid has collaborated with Behrouz on many artistic and political projects, has translated a large number of his journalism articles and also his multi-award winning book *No Friend but the Mountains: Writing From Manus Prison*.

This piece consists of excerpts that explore the experience of time while in indefinite detention and its weaponisation against refugees by the state and its corporate allies. This discussion is one element of what the authors refer to as "Manus Prison Theory" (Boochani 2018b; Tofighian 2020). The fragmented, disrupted and disjointed style and structure of the piece conveys the lived experience and stream of consciousness of Behrouz, the nature of his shared philosophical activities with Omid, and their work's mode of production. Contributions to the following article were written after 20 May, 2019; many of the entries here respond to the fallout from the Australian Federal Election (Morrison's re-election on 18 May, 2019), while Behrouz was incarcerated in Manus Prison and then transferred to the capital of Papua New Guinea, Port Moresby. In November 2019 he was able to escape to New Zealand; his application for asylum was accepted on the 23rd of July 2020, exactly seven years after his boat travelling from Indonesia was picked up by the Australian Navy:

> If I were to use one phrase to describe the situation in the Manus prison camps it is this: this prison is quite frankly a graveyard. A graveyard. A graveyard. Total silence Total silence (Behrouz, Tweet: 20 May 2019—the day after the Federal Election).

Time in Manus Prison: Reflections from Behrouz Boochani

Refugees have been captive to this system for over seven years. It is unbelievable. I know many of you, like the refugees, never thought that the Australian government could keep human beings here for more than seven years. I would like to analyse the barbaric policy we have been struggling against which has a long history of producing suffering by torturing innocent people. It has been going on for a long time, and I believe that in order to understand this system and the policy of exile we need to analyse it in relation to specific moments of its history; that is, we cannot understand it without considering the dimension of time. The policy must be interpreted in the context of different periods, and this needs a particular historical approach.

For example, our lives were different during the first six months of being imprisoned here, the treatment was incomparable to other time periods. After those first six months we were involved in a large-scale uprising in Manus Prison during which Reza Barati was murdered by G4S[1] guards, and in the aftermath we experienced a whole new kind of treatment. The physical violence remained, but as time went by most of the brutality morphed into more complex forms of psychological, emotional and spiritual torture.

After being imprisoned by the Australian government for eighteen months, we began a mass hunger strike which lasted a long time and resulted in the leaders being sent to a local jail. After spending some time there we were returned to the Australian-run detention centre. We had been held in Manus Prison for approximately three years when the PNG Supreme Court ruled that keeping us incarcerated in this prison camp for refugees was illegal. They opened the gates, but we were still in the prison camp; we had no documents and experienced obstacles when trying to travel to Lorengau—the main town on Manus Island—and find ways to engage in a society where we had no rights, no way of supporting ourselves and encountered an impoverished society struggling with the longstanding realities of colonialism. Therefore, we were still isolated from society and could not engage with any communities in meaningful ways.

Notions of History and Time

Behrouz

After four-and-a-half years the authorities relocated us by force to new prison camps in Lorengau. Until quite recently I was held in one of the three prison camps they set up for us in the main town. Not long ago I

---

[1] G4S term themselves as "the world's leading integrated security company. We offer a broad range of security services delivered on a single, multi-service or integrated basis" (G4S, n.d., https://www.g4s.com/en-gb/who-we-are). G4S was responsible for operating the Manus Island (and Nauru) detention centre during the early period when Reza Barati was killed during unrest in Manus on 14th February 2014. This generic description obscures the companies role in extraterritorial/extrajudicial sites, which has involved numerous instances of human rights abuses in which the company has been implicated; examples include Manus, Nauru, Palestine and in Guantanamo Bay. See Boochani (2019a).

was transferred to Port Moresby, the capital of Papua New Guinea, and I remained there with many others waiting for the authorities to determine our future.

I thought it was necessary to provide this overview here in order to expand on the central elements of the system later in this piece. But in order to understand the depths of this policy we should analyse the periods that break up our time here: before the 2014 uprising; after the uprising and up to the 2016 mass hunger strike; the 2016 Papua New Guinea Supreme Court ruling; the 2017 closure of the prison in Lombrum Naval Base, relocation to camps in Lorengau, and then transfer to Port Moresby. In 2019 hundreds of refugees from Manus and Nauru were moved to Australia as urgent medical transfers (under the now-defunct Medevac legislation), however they remain locked up onshore without having received medical treatment.

The history of this policy consists of distinct periods, but the system remains the same throughout. Even though the system has treated us differently, at certain times we have always known what we are facing—all throughout we have been up against the same system. This is a system that is still producing suffering, but inflicts punishment in different ways.

Thinking deeply about the notions of history and time are very important here. An interpretation of these factors assists in appreciating the collective movement of the imprisoned refugees and our connection with parts of civil society in Australia. Both groups are fighting against this system and its barbaric policies. What is to be done next?

First, we should ask the question: what has been taking place in Australia that makes it possible for a government to create something like Manus Prison? This is my central question. In fact, civil society in Australia should ask and answer this question—and think deeply about their response. I realise that all over the world, border politics has always been violent and now we are seeing a greater shift to right-wing parties in Western countries. However, Australia has been doing what other countries have been planning to do for a long time; we can see a trajectory of right leaning policies over many years and the expression of fascist ideology in the way Australia treats refugees on Manus Island and Nauru. This question needs serious engagement; the Australian government could never incarcerate people in Manus and Nauru without a network of support systems. Clearly, both the Labour Party and Liberal Party have support from various factions of society. Both parties accrue political benefits from maintaining this policy.

Another question for all of us battling this ruthless policy is this: why are refugees still imprisoned in Papua New Guinea and Nauru when so many people have been resisting, in so many ways, for so many years? This struggle has been taking place for over seven years in Australia, and among the imprisoned refugees. It is an important question. We must accept that we have made many mistakes along the way. Advocacy needs to change and new forms of resistance are necessary if we wish to dismantle this system. We need to form new strategies aimed at subverting the system and work out the best ways to succeed in advocacy. The government needs to be pressured into changing this policy; the political, intellectual and cultural work we have done needs to be leveraged in order to dismantle Australia's detention industry and create socio-cultural shifts and systemic change in relation to the treatment of displaced, exiled and incarcerated peoples. The refugees remain political hostages in Papua New Guinea, Nauru and in Australia because the right questions have not been asked and the right actions have not been taken; a better vision and better organising is necessary.

If only one refugee remains in either Papua New Guinea or Nauru (or onshore detention) it is still a defeat. Actually, after seven years, the deaths of thirteen inmates[2] and so many ruined lives, we need to accept that we have already been defeated.

I ask these questions and encourage reflection so that we can all think about what has happened, work to transform the situation, and do more research, organise and act to ensure it does not happen again:

> Manus & Nauru are part of the Australian imaginary. The violence inflicted on human bodies on these islands was initially political. But day by day it expands its psychological and sadistic dimensions. This is no longer state sanctioned hostage taking; this is unashamed fascism.

---

[2] The number of deaths related just to Manus and Nauru has now reached fourteen. However, this figure does not account for people who died after being deported.

Many are telling refugees on Manus to return to the countries from which they fled. This is a superficial interpretation of people who stand on the threshold of religious dictatorships and the re-emergence of Western fascism.

Since morning three people harmed themselves in Hillside camp of Manus and been transferred to local hospital. Since yesterday six people and since the election 26 people attempted suicide or self harmed. It is scary time in Manus (Behrouz Boochani, on Twitter, 28th May, 2019).

A Colonial Timeline and Transnational Resistance: Reflections from Omid Tofighian

In 2016, while illegally incarcerated in what he refers to as Manus Prison, Behrouz received an online request by Dutch Iranian filmmaker Arash Kamali Sarvestani to help make a film (Kamali Sarvestani 2019). Soon after Behrouz began filming shots for the 2017 co-directed film *Chauka, Please Tell Us the Time*. The movie is a meditation on time and the techniques of torture designed and implemented by the Australian government as part of their border regime. The film goes beyond presenting a critique of life in indefinite detention and the weaponisation of time; it situates the imprisonment of refugees within a history of coloniality (Galbraith 2019). Chauka is a sacred bird for Manusian peoples; for locals it represents—among other things—identity, morality and tells the time (Rooney 2018). Chauka is also the name given by Australian authorities to one of the solitary confinement cells within Manus Prison; for refugees it represents illegal detention, systematic torture and stolen time. In the film, the Chauka trope is a hologram—it is both a revered bird that symbolises temporality and identity, and an instrument of brutal punishment that distorts the prisoner's sense of time and self.

The making of the film is an example of how transnational resistance exposed the system by crossing borders, and how documentation of a short time during this phase of Australia's border regime somehow reclaimed time that was stolen (Elphick 2019). Time was stolen from the incarcerated refugees; also, information about the lived experiences of people held in this site during this time was stolen from the majority of the Australian public (and the world) through censorship and other silencing strategies (Olubas 2019).

After sharing shots over WhatsApp using a painfully slow internet connection, much of the film footage was smuggled out of Papua New Guinea by supporters and sent to the Netherlands from Australia. It was co-directed by exchanging 10,000 minutes of WhatsApp voice texts. *Chauka, Please Tell Us the Time* offers a nuanced, multidimensional and philosophical work of art that discusses themes often repeated in superficial ways within our mainstream news cycles. While the mainstream media portrays people seeking asylum by boat as a homogenous cluster of strangers espousing values incompatible with western liberal democracy, the film introduces us to individual intellectuals and creatives who give us unique insight into Australia's border regime. We understand how immigration officials, prison administrators and prison guards wield time as a weapon; when identifying and critiquing this dimension the filmmakers and refugees in the film create new knowledge. Incarcerated refugees are regularly accused of challenging Australian sovereignty, national culture and values and border control. However, the film shatters settler perceptions of themselves and situates Manus Prison within an extended, long-view colonial timeline.

In my study of the film, I expand on the multifaceted colonial dimensions of incarceration on Manus and foreground the importance of history and the continuities of violence. Reflecting on the notion of temporality in the film opens up for multidimensional historical and political critiques: it highlights and provides deeper insight into the island's geopolitical context and colonial legacy. The colonial history of Manus Island provides an indispensable contextual backdrop for analysing the multilayered political dimensions of the film, the situation of Boochani as an imprisoned refugee exiled by Australia, and the restrictions hindering the collaborations. The current refugee detention centre is part of a legacy of incarceration, colonial exploitation and geopolitical machinations. Manus Island (and Nauru) is the location for the first phase of Australia's Pacific Solution (introduced by the Liberal Howard government) and the second phase (reintroduced by the Labour Gillard and Rudd governments). Prior to this, for most of the twentieth century, the region now known as Papua New Guinea was an Australian colony.

As explained by Tofighian (2019a: 94–95): "In the 1960s Indonesia was preparing a military takeover of the former Dutch New Guinea, which was then recognised by many in the international community as part of Indonesia by 1969. Approximately fifty years ago Australia imprisoned West Papuan refugees (also known as West Irians) on Manus Island when they crossed into the then Australian colony for protection against the Indonesian takeover. The site was referred to as the Salasia Camp; remnants of this site remain in the same town as the three current Australia-run detention centres. During the fighting, Australia turned away many West Papuan refugees. But from among the small numbers who were permitted entry and then sent to Manus Island, some still reside there with their families (Papua New Guinea has only begun granting citizen status and rights). In the early twentieth century Australia seized control, the Japanese empire tried to invade the region and then they vied for control of several islands (including Manus) with Australian and US forces during the Pacific War. In the nineteenth century parts of the territory were controlled by the German and British empires. Papua New Guinea gained independence in 1975".

This extensive and endemic colonialist violence continued, as we can see through the formulations of time within Manus Prison:

September 2001:	Establishment of the Pacific Solution under the Liberal Howard government.
February 2008:	Manus Island and Nauru closed under the Labor Rudd government.
November 2012:	Manus and Nauru reopened under the Gillard government.
July 2013:	Rudd exiles refugees.
February 2014:	Reza Barati is killed by guards in Manus Prison.
September 2014:	Hamid Khazaei dies from medical negligence in Manus Prison.
2014–2015:	Mass hunger strike on Manus—leaders imprisoned in local jail.

4 The Weaponisation of Time

April 2016:	Papua New Guinea Supreme Court finds detention centre illegal—doors unlocked and mobile phone ban lifted.
August 2016:	Kamil Hussain drowns on Manus.
November 2016:	Prime Minister Turnbull and President Obama agree to resettle Manus and Nauru refugees in the US in exchange for resettling refugees from the US in Australia.
December 2016:	Faysal Ishak Ahmed dies from medical negligence in Manus Prison.
Good Friday 2017:	Drunk Papua New Guinea soldiers fire multiple shots into the detention centre.
August 2017:	Hamed Shamshiripour driven to suicide on Manus.
October 2017:	Rajeev Rajendran driven to suicide in Manus Prison.
October–November 2017:	23 day siege and forced eviction to 3 new prison camps in main town, Lorengau.
May 2018:	Salim Kyawning driven to suicide on Manus.
February 2019:	Medivac bill passed allowing ill refugees to be transferred to Australia for medical treatment.
May 2019:	Morrison government wins Federal Election resulting in over 100 incidents of self-harm and attempted suicide.
Post-election:	Refugees transferred to Port Moresby. Over 50 imprisoned in Bomana prison (those with negative determinations of claims and those who refused to apply through Papua New Guinea system).
October 2019:	Sayed Mirwais Rohani driven to suicide in Brisbane after transfer in 2017 for medical treatment.
December 2019:	Medivac legislation repealed.

2020: Hundreds remain incarcerated in Papua New Guinea, Nauru and onshore detention.

Horrific Surrealism and Indefinite Detention

Omid

Reflecting on the intervals of time while in indefinite detention, Behrouz considered the experience of being imprisoned in a tropical environment close to the equator. He remembers a time when life involved changing seasons. But in Manus Prison there is only one season—time somehow evaporates for people who have been exiled there and lack a spiritual and existential connection with the land and environment. There were also moments when Behrouz feels that time moves faster… the perplexity of indefinite detention. When communicating with each other and recollecting past experiences and events the incarcerated refugees use specific incidents as markers of time: "two months before Reza Barati [a man detained on Manus Island] was killed, just after the 23 three day siege, the day after the election… those first few months of being exiled to Manus".

Following Morrison's 2019 election win, Behrouz wrote about the atmosphere in the prison camp and makes reference to the death of Reza Barati in early 2014. His surreal reflections reflect the sense of hopelessness associated with stolen time and its reapplication as a weapon:

> Silence everywhere. The whole place … totally silent. A heavy atmosphere … terrifying. Exactly like a graveyard.

> No one is outdoors. It is as if no one lives here. Only a single dog walks through the camp, taking slow steps.

4 The Weaponisation of Time

I have never seen the refugees on Manus so depressed. Even when Reza Barati was killed, when that innocent man was sacrificed … that time when the other refugees were bashed and beaten.

I swear, it has never been like this. Not even on Good Friday in 2017 when soldiers rained shots into the prison camp.

Even at the height of the violence and when confronted with death, the refugees always maintained a sense of hope. However, the day after the election, everything sank into an abyss of darkness. The outcome of the last election extinguished the last glimmer of hope for freedom, it shut out any hope that remained after six years of purgatory. Overnight everything just slipped away (Boochani 2019b).

We use the term "horrific surrealism" as a schema and a way to describe the style, framework or attitude characterising his work. This notion also applies to the conditions, Behrouz's different relationships and external forces continuously impacting life in Manus Prison and Australia's border regime. The absurdity associated with all facets of the situation is captured in our analysis of surrealism here; this understanding highlights the disrupted, fragmented, disjointed and shattered nature of the experience. Behrouz's work, his intellectual standpoint and his formation of time in indefinite detention develop from the free flow of the subconscious—his creative work in particular involves dream visions; a sharp sense of satire; assemblages of objects and symbols from the built environment and natural environment; personification and anthropomorphism; a critical form of figuration and psychoanalytic explorations of himself and others (Tofighian 2019b).

Even my experience of engaging with him while translating the book was totally surreal: Behrouz is in indefinite detention in a remote island prison while I was crossing borders regularly, living and working in multiple cities and experiencing complex cross-cultural encounters. Also, consider the response to the book and how it enhances the surreal factor. Behrouz is given awards from the same political system that incarcerates and tortures him, and wins prize money he cannot access. In fact, so much about our relationship and the work we have been doing together is surreal. How does one interpret time within this surreal reality?

A horrific reality was created in Manus Prison. Hidden away from public view and with the application of strict censorship, Australia's border regime could experiment with forms of torture that leverage time in ways that amplify psychological and emotional violence. To understand the depths of this analysis, horrific surrealism must be interpreted according to its relationship with the many aspects of Behrouz's lived experience, endurance and resistance: horrific surrealism connects and informs (1) the identity of the author and his experiences of oppression and domination as a result of bordering practices in Iran and the border violence inflicted by Australia; (2) Australia's political situation in the context of global border politics and its role as a driver of forced migration; (3) the mode of production in the making of the book and Behrouz's other projects including the power dynamics between us, the use of technology, the uncertainty of his situation in contrast to my mobility, the three periods we were able to meet and work together on Manus and my subsequent deportation and blacklisting and (4) the heuristic spaces necessary for interpreting the style, content, structure and tropes used in his book and other works (Tofighian 2019b).

Considering space and time configurations regarding *Chauka, Please Tell Us the Time*, "In order to depict this connection, many scenes in the film blend open form and closed form visuals and thirdspace chronotopes: the sea and jungle/cages; open skies and jungle/dilapidated containers and rooms; the sea, sky and scattered coconut trees/closed-off roads, fences and vehicle enclosures; exits into jungle and open skies/guarded or fenced paths, corridors; children playing among nature/empty or sparsely occupied prison spaces. By using visual forms in this way the film enforces the notion that immigration detention and the island's natural environment are both under the dictates of coloniality.[3] This technique reduces the open spaces of the island to the claustrophobic spaces within the refugee prison; and, conversely, it projects the closed spaces inside the detention centre onto a larger, enduring colonial story. These spatial representations correspond with the temporal dimensions of the situation on Manus Island. For the refugees, time stands still

---

[3] "Coloniality" (sometimes phrased "coloniality/modernity") is a concept that describes colonialism not as an event but as a pervasive structure and perpetual process. Aníbal Quijano introduced the term and it was developed further by other decolonial thinkers

in the prison; and even though Chauka tells Manus locals the time, very little has changed on the island since independence. Both spaces exist outside of time and within the same colonial schedule" (Tofighian 2019a: 98).

Conclusion: Time and Death

A timeline of Behrouz's journalism functions as a critical history of the border violence established in Manus Prison. Through artistic expression and creative resistance, he confronts the weaponsation of time; the recreation of time for the purposes of survival and struggle has proven to be an effective counter and a vital contribution to history. It is worth ending with a particular example of Behrouz's writing which critically analyses the violence in the prison camp within pivotal moments in the history of Manus Prison and, at the same time, invites the reader to collaborate in ending indefinite detention, to end border violence (Giannacopoulos and Loughnan 2020).

As Behrouz reflects, in November 2017, the refugees on Manus resisted the extreme violence of the prison system for 23 days. On a number of occasions, the Home Affairs minister explicitly accused certain politicians and advocates of guiding the collective resistance, that the mastermind behind it resided outside the island. In reality, it was the refugees who rallied together and made decisions as a group about how to proceed. They were the ones who understood exactly how best to challenge the kyriarchal system.

...

For years our bodies have been made the subjects of politics and power. As such, they have become the last thing we have left with which to make a statement regarding the abuse of our human rights. Just imagine a young man battling many illnesses for six years only to be ignored by the system and refused treatment. What other option does he have?

A week never went by when we did not experience an instance of self-harm on Manus. And when someone self-harms here they do not only harm themselves—in fact, they perpetuate stress and a particular form of violence throughout the community around them. This is the cause of great suffering. It is extremely difficult to see a young man in agony. You soon realise both of you are suffering the same pain. Many people who have not self-harmed are still traumatised to a large extent by witnessing many self-harm incidents. When someone attempts suicide or self-harm, everyone is absorbed in the pain.

...

… we were not alone. During the campaign, and in its wake, I participated in dozens of events for my book, **No Friend But the Mountains**. Although I am only able to communicate with the Australian people using my mobile phone, the difference in mood before and after the election among Australian civil society was clear to me. Pre-election, the atmosphere was full of hope for change. Then came a climate of defeat and hopelessness.

...

Self-harm and attempted suicide are part of the reality of incarceration on Manus Island and Nauru. This is exactly what the Australian people and the politicians who represent them need to acknowledge.

The imprisoned refugees on these islands always feel the shadow of death hovering overhead. Death is as close as it possibly can be. The truth is that 13 people have lost their lives here in the past six years and hundreds of others injured themselves. Time is a weapon in this system for taking life (adapted from Boochani 2019c).

References

Boochani, B., 2018a. *No Friend but the Mountains: Writing From Manus Prison.* Translated by O. Tofighian, with translator's note and essay. Sydney: Picador.
Boochani, B., 2018b. Manus Prison Theory. *The Saturday Paper.* Translated by O. Tofighian. 11–17 August.
Boochani, B., 2019a. The Paladin Scandal Is Just a Drop in the Ocean of Corruption on Manus and Nauru. *The Guardian.* Translated by O. Tofighian. 27 February.
Boochani, B., 2019b. How many more people must die on Manus before Australia ends indefinite dentention. *The Guardian.* Translated by O. Tofighian. 3 June.
Boochani, B., 2019c. The Truth About Self-Harm in Offshore Detention. *The Saturday Paper.* Translated by O. Tofighian. 7 September.
Elphick, J., 2019. Cinematic Poetics and Reclaiming History: Chauka, Please Tell Us the Time as Legacy. *Alphaville: Journal of Film and Screen Media*, no. 18, pp. 199–204. https://doi.org/10.33178/alpha.18.18.
Galbraith, J., 2019. A Reflection on Chauka, Please Tell Us the Time. *Alphaville: Journal of Film and Screen Media*, no. 18, pp. 193–198. https://doi.org/10.33178/alpha.18.17.
Giannacopoulos, M. and C. Loughnan, 2020. 'Closure' at Manus Island and Carceral Expansion in the Open Air Prison. *Globalizations* 17 no. 7, pp. 1118–1135. https://doi.org/10.1080/14747731.2019.1679549.
G4S, n.d. Who We Are [Online]. Available at: https://www.g4s.com/en-gb/who-we-are. Accessed 15 August 2020.
Kamali Sarvestani, A., 2019. Looking for Chauka. Translated by O. Tofighian, *Alphaville: Journal of Film and Screen Media*, no. 18, pp. 188–192. https://doi.org/10.33178/alpha.18.16.
Olubas, B., 2019. "Where We Are Is Too Hard": Refugee Writing and the Australian Border as Literary Interface. *Journal of the Association for the Study of Australian Literature* 19, no. 2.
Rooney, M. N., 2018. The Chauka Bird and Morality on Our Manus Island Home. *The Conversation.* 2 February.
Schüssler Fiorenza, E., 1992. *But She Said: Feminist Practices of Biblical Interpretation.* Boston: Beacon.
Schüssler Fiorenza, E., 2001. *Wisdom Ways: Introducing Feminist Biblical Interpretation.* Maryknoll, NY: Orbis Books.

Tofighian, O., 2018. Translator's Tale: A Window to the Mountains. In B. Boochani, 2018. *No Friend but the Mountains: Writing From Manus Prison*. Translated from Farsi by O. Tofighian, with translator's note and essay. Sydney: Picador. pp. xiii–xxxvi.

Tofighian, O., 2019a. Displacement, Exile and Incarceration Commuted into Cinematic Vision. *Alphaville: Journal of Film and Screen Media* 18, pp. 91–106. https://doi.org/10.33178/alpha.18.07.

Tofighian, O., 2019b. In Conversation with Omid Tofighian. Vertigo. 20 October.

Tofighian, O., 2020. Introducing Manus Prison Theory: Knowing Border Violence. *Globalizations* 17, no. 7, pp. 1138–1156. https://doi.org/10.1080/14747731.2020.1713547.

5

Contested Dreams, Stolen Futures: Struggles Over Hope in the European Deportation Regime

Annika Lindberg and Stanley Edward

Introduction

Deportation denotes the 'forced removal of foreign nationals from a given national territory' (Drotbohm and Hasselberg 2015, 551). Rather than a singular event, deportation is a process that stretches across physical locations and through time, and it reflects and reproduces larger processes of global inequality and exclusion. Deportation is an instrument in states' nationalist projects, which seek to keep and to 'return' people to 'their' place—physically, socially and affectively—in the 'national order of things' (Malkki 1995; Walters 2002) and in global structures of inequality. As such, deportation relies on ethno-national notions of belonging (Brun and Fábos 2015) and on a hierarchical

---

A. Lindberg (✉)
Institute of Sociology, University Bern, Bern, Switzerland
e-mail: Annika.lindberg@soz.unibe.ch

S. Edward
Copenhagen, Denmark

sorting of humanity. It is therefore not only an act of corporal removal (Khosravi 2017a), but also a form of social regulation, which produces boundaries of belonging that benefit the few who are considered 'insiders' to the detriment of the many produced as 'others' (Anderson, Gibne and Paoletti 2011). As a tool of mobility control, deportation forms part of a system of a racialised global apartheid (Besteman 2019) that limits access to resources, mobility and life prospects for those who are classified as national and racial 'others'.

The deportation process subjects 'othered' people to various forms of state violence, including the direct violence of push-backs, criminalization, forced detainment and displacement (Gibney 2013), and the slow violence of deportability, marginalisation, destitution and exploitation (De Genova 2002). The violence of deportation also has a temporal dimension, as it keeps people waiting at the margins of state and society, subjects them to repeated cycles of displacement and immobilisation (Ansems de Vries and Guild 2018; Wyss 2019) and exposes them to constant stress (Griffiths, et al. 2013). Melanie Griffiths (2013) has captured how people living in a state of deportability are subjected to a 'dual uncertainty of time' (ibid., 1), including sticky or suspended time in the form of indefinite waiting, which is interrupted by 'frenzied', accelerated time in moments of sudden detainment or deportation. Sometimes, this temporal uncertainty is the result of complex bureaucratic procedures; at other times it is intentionally used as a governing strategy (Eule et al. 2019). By governing through time, states deprive deportable persons' lives of meaning in the present and of their hopes for the future, keeping them in a protracted present and preventing them from moving forward and building a life in the country they are to be deported from (Wyss 2019). Hence, deportation regimes not only dispossess deportable persons of the time they invested in migrating and settling in the country (Khosravi 2018), but also of their future life chances, hopes and dreams.

However, if deportation, as Susan Coutin (2015) suggests, is an expression of political 'fantasies' of controlling migration, deportable persons can challenge these political dreams by articulating their own hopes and aspirations against the deportation regime. Researchers writing on deportability have emphasised how hope enables people affected by states' exclusionary border regimes to reclaim a sense of ownership over the time, resources and relationships that states have stolen from them (Bendixsen and Eriksen 2018; Djampour 2018). Catherine Brun (2015) has argued that for people trapped in protracted, precarious conditions of displacement, hope allows them to transcend their physical, temporal and social marginalisation by orienting their practices towards the future (Brun and Fábos 2015). By envisioning alternative futures, they make their waiting time meaningful; even if it does not necessarily mean that their future will turn out as they envision.

In this chapter, we explore how such contestations over future time, hopes and dreams play out within deportation processes. The chapter evolves in two parts. First, we outline deportation agents' strategies for governing deportable persons' present and future time by manipulating their hopes, dreams and aspirations. For this purpose, we build on participant observation inside migration-related detention centres and deportation centres, and interviews with migration officials, police officers and NGO staff working with deportation enforcement in Denmark and Sweden, conducted by Annika between 2016 and 2018.[1] In the second part, we shift perspectives and build on Stanley's own reflections on how people who, like himself, live under threat of deportation navigate states' efforts to control their present time as well as their future hopes and aspirations. In this part, Stanley draws on activist engagement and collaborative research conducted with people subjected to European border regimes between 2015 and 2019, and his own decade-long experiences of seeking asylum and living in a condition of deportability in different European countries. In the concluding section, we discuss the ambivalent role of hope and future time in sustaining the marginality of deportable people in a protracted present, while also being a tool for challenging oppressive deportation regimes.

---

[1] The research has been conducted within the framework of Annika Lindberg's doctoral research project, *Governing the Deportation Limbo: State responses to non-deported migrants in Denmark and Sweden*. Building on ethnographic research conducted in detention and deportation centres in both countries, the project explores and compares the enforcement of deportation policies and their implications for the agents of enforcement and for the non-deported people targeted by these measures.

Manipulating Dreams and Stealing Futures: Annika's Notes on the Structures and Agents of Deportation Enforcement

In the past decade, states across Europe have stepped up their efforts to increase the speed and rate of deportations of people whose applications for protection have been rejected or who have been illegalised (Gibney 2013). In Sweden, the government announced in 2016 its intent to deport 80 000 rejected people seeking asylum within the coming three years (SVT 27 January 2016); in Denmark, the (now former) Danish government promised to make life so intolerable for non-deported persons that they would rather comply with their deportation order than remaining in Denmark (Suárez-Krabbe and Lindberg 2019). Both countries have renewed their investments in their deportation apparatuses, by expanding migration-related detention and introducing various deterrence measures, such as the 'departure' or deportation centres in Denmark (Freedom of Movements Research Collective 2018), and withdrawing social welfare for people whose applications for asylum have been rejected in Sweden (Kjellbom and Lundberg 2018). In this section, we explore the temporal aspects of these deportation policies. Drawing on Annika's research inside a Swedish migration-related detention centre, and in the deportation centres in Denmark, respectively, we trace state efforts to govern deportable persons present time and their aspirations for the future.

Enforcing Dis-Belonging in the Swedish Detention Regime

Swedish migration-related detention centres confine people who have had their asylum application rejected or who lack legal authorization to remain. In the six existing detention centres, people can be incarcerated up to 12 months while awaiting a decision on their residency status or the enforcement of their deportation. In cases where the deportation order has been issued by a criminal court, the detention order can be extended without time limit. The detention centres are administered by the Swedish Migration Agency and hosted in civil rather than prison facilities. Most detention custody officers have nothing to do with the deportation cases per se, but are supposed to tend to detained persons' daily needs—and to work on their 'attitudes towards returning' to their presumed countries of origin.

Detention centres are sites characterised by profound uncertainty. Detained persons are exposed to imposed boredom and idleness, while also facing significant anxiety and stress in face of the prospect of sudden deportation. Prior research has documented the drastic, negative effects of this temporal uncertainty on detained persons' mental and physical well-being (Griffiths 2013; see also Canning, this volume). Shahram Khosravi (2017a) has further noted that detention produces the spatial and temporal 'dis-belonging' of deportable persons from the country they are to be deported from. This is done not only by physical containment and social isolation, but also through various techniques aimed at governing their present time and manipulating their visions for the future. As William Walters (2016, 438) has argued, states' 'political dream' is that 'the migrant places themselves on the plane, without the need for guards, restraints or any spectacle of enforcement'. The job of the agents of deportation enforcement is to make deportable persons' dreams conform to this political fantasy (Coutin 2015), in view of ensuring a smooth, speedy deportation process (Canning 2019).

In the migration-related detention centre in Sweden where I conducted research, temporal governance took place through programmes designed to structure detained people's everyday time in ways that would 'keep their minds busy' and 'off the bad things', as Angelica,[2] a detention official, put it. For this purpose, staff had introduced a range of daily activities, including 'calming' yoga sessions, handicraft and quizzes on weekends (see also Canning 2019). By structuring detained persons' everyday time, governing their daily habits and monitoring and documenting any perceived changes in their attitudes, detention officials were supposed to prevent them from planning escapes, engaging in resistance attempts or resorting to self-mutilation, all of which might disrupt the deportation procedure. The activities

---

[2] All names of state agents are pseudonyms.

were also meant to create a daily routine that would 'help' detained people cope with the anxiety they experienced as a direct result of their confinement, and to create a 'homely' atmosphere. As Joseph, a detention caseworker, put it, guaranteeing that 'the vanilla yoghurt is on the breakfast tray' was equally important as making sure detained persons' asylum claims had been adequately processed before their deportation. The 'humane and dignified' detention regime (DeBono et al. 2015), which officials sought to perform, served to downplay the violent nature of detainment and to ensure smooth and frictionless deportation enforcement.

Strategies for managing detained persons' everyday time were coupled with efforts to assert their dis-belonging to Sweden (Khosravi 2017a) by manipulating their hopes and dreams for the future. Staff were trained in 'motivating' dialogue techniques, which were supposed to enable them to build trustful relationships with the people detained and to ensure their cooperation with authorities in the deportation process. As articulated by Joseph, 'detention is a graveyard for dreams. Here, we help them bury their dreams of a possible future in Sweden and plant a seed of a dream of another future elsewhere'. He continued, 'The prospects of return should be present throughout our conversations with them… if we come to discuss for instance passports, we can tell them that well, if you get your passport you will be out of here sooner' (quoted in Eule et al. 2019, 164). Motivating dialogues thus both served investigative purposes and to pressure detained persons to comply with the deportation order. Joseph described deportation as a way out of confinement, even as these measures were meant to reduce detained people's with 'choice' and agency in their deportation process (Webber 2011). Margareta, a senior Swedish border police officer, was blunter in her formulation of these 'choices': 'We have to niggle them down until they comply! And ask them, do you really think it's preferable to live as undocumented? Where will you get your money from?' As reflected in Margareta's account, the veritable choices presented to people threatened by deportation were between detainment and deportation, or illegalisation, destitution and potential criminalisation.

Still, many detained persons would use the time at their hands to contest and resist their deportation order, by filing appeals, drawing public attention to their case or physically resisting removal. Even if these attempts eventually turned out unsuccessful, they allowed them to disrupt the deportation process and buy them some time before the deportation was enforced (Eule et al. 2019; Griffiths 2013). Joseph explained that staff sought to preclude such attempts at resisting deportation in the so-called motivating dialogues they regularly held with detained persons. Staff would show statistics of the low turnover rates in the migration court to discourage detained persons from appealing, and try to 'steer the conversation in the direction of return'. This way, Joseph argued, staff 'helped them by preventing them from making stupid decisions (…) that they will anyway regret later on'. Indeed, like Joseph, many state officials considered speedy deportation to be not only more efficient but also more 'humane'. In their view, it was in the best interest of people awaiting deportation to abandon their hopes of remaining in Sweden, and instead align their dreams with the state's deportation fantasies as soon as possible, rather than maintaining 'false hopes' that their deportation order could be revoked.

Often, however, it was rather the political dream of 'voluntary' deportation cultivated by deportation agents that proved its falsehood. Several officials admitted that the authorities knew little if anything about the futures that actually awaited people after their deportation. Sometimes, this uncertainty would destabilise detention officials' own belief in the rosy future scenarios they were attempting to project onto detained persons. Mariam, another detention official, told me the following story:

> 'Some cases are extreme, people who have been rejected but keep trying for a long time, and they keep being sent back to Sweden under the Dublin Regulation. You can see that in their history of Eurodac hits. They try Sweden, then Germany, they abscond from there and there is a new hit from the Netherlands, then France, but they keep absconding and eventually Italy manages to deport them back here. And then I'm thinking fuck this, just leave them alone. I had one guy like that here, he said 'I know I have a decision on deportation but I will not comply, don't you understand?' …it was absurd, he didn't give a shit about what I said, and what should I tell him? Say something motivating like, 'Come on, you are going to Iraq! I'm sure you can get a job in Iraq?'—but of

course we both know he can't get that. 'No', he told me, 'leave me alone, I'm going back to Germany to work'.

In Mariam's case, the futility of her efforts to manipulate the detained man's aspirations for the future became evident to her as she came to realise the man's ability to navigate law enforcement and persistent plans to remain in Europe, and as she witnessed the absurd effects of his repeated deportations back and forth. Deportable persons' non-compliance with deportation orders regularly disrupt authorities' enforcement efforts, even if it does not always ameliorate their personal situation. Just like the man in Mariam's story, they might simply remain in detainment or in a highly precarious condition of deportability (De Genova 2002), or stuck in transit (Brekke and Brochmann 2015) in the Dublin system.[3] In such cases, where the deportation order becomes unenforceable, state authorities can resort to strategies of 'exhaustion' (Ansems de Vries and Guild 2018), which entail circumscribing deportable persons' access to rights, mobility, resources and membership. The next section details the Danish deportation centres as an example of such exhaustion strategies. While Stanley has direct experience of living in these centres, I will first outline their operation from the perspective of the agents of enforcement, before moving on to his account of how the deportation centres affect the people forced to reside there.

Stealing Futures in Denmark's Deportation Centres

The Danish 'departure centres' or deportation centres were inaugurated in 2013 to house people whose asylum applications have been

---

[3]The Dublin Regulation is a European law put in place to determine which signatory state is responsible for examining an application for asylum. While the Regulation is supposed to prevent situations where a person submits multiple asylum applications in different states, or where no country assumes responsibility for processing their claims, it has often been criticised for creating exactly the kind of 'orbit' or 'limbo' situations it was meant to prevent (Brekke and Brochmann 2015; Wyss 2019).

rejected and criminalised foreign nationals who await deportation. The two centres, Sjælsmark and Kærshovedgård, are geographically isolated in former military barracks and prison facilities with limited access to public transportation. They are run by the Danish prison and probation service, whose primary role in the centres is to monitor the coming and going of residents, and further staffed by the Red Cross, who run health clinics and offer limited activities. The deployment of prison officers to monitor the centres, where the majority of residents have not committed any crime, serves to symbolically criminalise residents; yet prison officers are, in fact, stripped both of their caring and controlling functions, as they lack the authority to use force—or to take measures to improve conditions in the centres. The Red Cross is permitted to perform a more social-oriented role, as long as their activities are aligned with the purpose of 'motivating' residents to leave Denmark. Neither prison officer nor the Red Cross have any part to play in residents' asylum cases.[4]

Politically, the deportation centres were setup to 'send a very clear message telling them [rejected asylum seekers] that this is the final stop in Denmark and that now you must go home' (Danish Ministry of Justice 2013); or to 'make life intolerable' for residents, as the former Minister of Immigration, Integration and housing has expressed it (see Freedom of Movements Research Collective 2018). Hans, a prison officer working in Sjælsmark, bluntly explained to me that they were supposed to 'take the meaning out of existence' for residents in view of making them comply with their deportation order—or to make them disappear out of sight and out of mind of Danish authorities. This 'intolerability' regime (Suárez-Krabbe and Lindberg 2019) was enforced through house rules designed to minimise residents' autonomy in their everyday life. Rules determined where, when and what residents could eat, how long they could be gone from the centres, and what activities were allowed. Residents were not allowed to cook their own food, nor were they, or any

---

[4]Since the research was conducted in 2016–2017, the prison officers in deportation centres have been exchanged for civilian 'centre workers' (*centermedarbejder*), although the Danish prison and probation service remains in charge of running the centres. The shift in personnel has been explained by a lack of prison officers in Danish prisons, which prompted the majority officers to return to prison. The Red Cross continues to run the centres' health clinics, and also run a kindergarten for the children in Sjælsmark.

NGO or solidarity network visiting the centre, permitted to arrange any regular activities that might risk making life more 'comfortable' in the centres. Daily, 'home-making' practices (Brun 2015), including arranging a space for oneself and doing other forms of housework, were also prohibited, as they risked encouraging residents to remain, which would contradict the isolation, deprivation and dis-belonging that the deportation centres were supposed to enforce.

As a result of these motivating schemes, Sjælsmark was a centre where lives were put on hold, and people were gradually worn down by idleness, anxiety, poverty and isolation (see Stanley's account in the next section). Prison officers, who were used to take active part in 'rehabilitating' and preparing imprisoned persons for the future that awaited them once they had served their time, were now supposed to *prevent* residents from building hopes and aspirations for a future life in Danish society. Yannick, one of the prison officers in Sjælsmark, noted, 'within the prison management, they assume our task is simple, because we are not doing anything with these people anyway'. When we discussed the visible, detrimental effects the centres had on residents' health and well-being, Yannick stressed that prison officers were not allowed to do anything to improve their situation: 'The negative consequences are an implicit part of the construction'. The only activities put in place to improve conditions for residents in Sjælsmark were, at the time of my research in 2016, English classes (Danish was prohibited as it might also induce 'false hopes' of a future in Denmark) and return advice, both offered by the Red Cross. If Sjælsmark was, as residents had put it, a 'centre of hopelessness', the activities were, in the words of Red Cross staff, supposed to 'inspire residents, make them happier, show them that there is a way out' (quoted in Lindberg 2019, 113). Similar to detention custody officers in Sweden, the Red Cross tried to manipulate residents' visions of the future and convince them that their only way out of their situation was to get out of Denmark.

The deportation centres were thus designed to deprive residents' present time of meaning and to create deliberately intolerable conditions that subjected residents to 'slow' suffering (Castaway Souls of Sjælsmark 2016). In addition, the centres exposed residents to profound uncertainty regarding their future. Residents of deportation centres were, because of their duty to reside and regularly register in the peripherally located centres, highly circumscribed in their freedom of movement, yet they were not considered legally detained (Freedom of Movements Research Collective 2018). Therefore, and in contrast to migration-related detention (which also exists in Denmark), the deportation centres had no time limit for how long residents could remain there. As the director of one of the centres told me, the ultimate implication of this was that a resident could remain there for the rest of their lives—unless they 'gave up' and complied with the deportation order, or embarked on precarious onward journeys elsewhere in Europe. In combination with the everyday degradation of not being in control over their present time, this potentiality of foreverness can be understood as another form of temporal violence, which confines deportable persons in indefinite waiting under harmful conditions. It also demonstrates how deportable persons' 'stuckedness' is as much temporal as it is spatial (Jefferson et al. 2019). Even though many residents defied the house rules and established their own, daily routines in the deportation centres, or found ways to circumvent or overcome the imposed constraints to their mobility and partake in social life outside the centres, the intolerability regime would slowly extinguish their hope—and their desire—to have a future in Denmark. This did not, however, necessarily mean that they cooperated with authorities in the deportation process. Prison officers working in the centres readily admitted that the centres simply 'did not make sense' as they did not enhance deportation rates, but only made deportable people stuck in a marginalised condition. Still, they maintained that state authorities could not be attributed responsibility for this. The prison officer Hans told me:

> 'Many say, I can't go back home. And I just say that I don't know anything about that, but that the fact is, that the door is open. Nothing is locked. You can just go. If you're unsatisfied with the food, the company, the bed, with me; you can just leave, you don't have to accept it. You can take your destiny in your own hands, like all of us have done, in one way or the other. At some point, they have done that on several occasions and that has made them end up here. So, this is not the final opportunity, the last chance to take your destiny in your own hands has not yet been used. I cannot say what that is and I can well understand that the fact that you have received a rejection, means that it also holds in Sweden, and in

Germany, so you cannot just take off to there and start over. What you should do, I cannot tell. But it is possible, either way. The door is not locked'.

Hans' attitude allowed for state authorities to ignore how residents' condition of stuckedness and lack of de facto future options were the direct result of the policies explicitly designed to deprive them of any way forward. Still, Hans contended, 'many residents here, when they get to speak, they always end by saying that I hope that they will reopen my case one day... that will not happen. But they still hope for it'. This persistent hope caused irritation among prison officers, as it directly challenged the exhaustion logic underpinning the deportation centres, while it also risked prolonging the time residents spent waiting there under precarious conditions. In the next section, we explore the ambivalent role of future hopes and dreams among the people who navigate states' efforts to exclude, exhaust and expel them.

Hoping Against the Deportation Regime: Stanley's Reflections on Living in Deportability

Hope can be a necessity in order to survive and endure hardships and marginalising conditions (Brun 2015). As we learnt from the prison officer in the Danish deportation centres, retaining hope against the deportation regime can also be a way for people threatened by deportation to challenge their temporal, spatial and social exclusion—and a source of irritation for authorities. Can we consider hope to be a subversive practice, a tactic for challenging the deportation regime? In this part of the chapter, Stanley builds on his own experience as well as collaborative research and activist engagements with people living under threat of deportation in different places across Europe, and reflects on how hope and dreams can be used to navigate oppressive deportation regimes, the risks this dreaming entail.

Hope as an Instrument of the Oppressor and the Oppressed

Hope is something necessary for us to find a way to navigate and to survive. If you are caught in a bad situation today, the best you can do is to give yourself hope that the nightmare will come to an end tomorrow, even if you do not know how. Ever since being a kid in Nigeria, hope has enabled me to dream and hope that things will change; it has encouraged me to look for solutions. In some respects, the situations have changed, but the reality is that the problem that keeps you in the bad situation you are in still remains in place. The hope just encourages you to continue; it does not change the basic issues you are facing.

Time is stolen from people already before they go on their journeys to Europe. Historically, European states have—and are still—benefiting from stealing time, resources and dreams from people in the Global South. Therefore, when you leave your home for Europe, you spend your time searching for a future in the same system that has already stolen your past, and deprived you of your dreams as you grew up in your country. We are told that we do not have the right to be in control of our own time, that we cannot have different dreams. Deportation is an expression of the false hope of states that they can control migration. This is what European states hope, but no matter how they do it, this project will fail, because people will always try to find ways to improve their unbearable situation. They will maintain hopes that they can escape the forces that are oppressing them, even if it takes their life. Therefore, hope is a mechanism used by both sides: The oppressor and the oppressed. It keeps them both going and engaging in the same cycles and struggles.

The oppressor tries to control your dreams by different means. The borders are in place even before you begin your journey, you encounter them already in your home country. First, you will have to wait for months or even years for a visa application to be processed; and even if you get it, you are likely to become held up in transit, where you will have your visa scrutinised and you risk detainment or deportation even before reaching your destination. Those who are unable to obtain a visa will have to extend their journeys even further, and will be systematically delayed at the borders, transit zones and in camps along the way.

Upon arrival, they risk illegalisation, even if they apply for asylum, and will then be held waiting in asylum camps; or, they might risk facing the Dublin Regulation, in which case the borders extend your timespan once more and force you to move on and to find a new goal. This way, your dreams are continuously stolen and you have to invent new ones. It is important to underline that this systematic delaying and prolonging of people's journeys take place throughout their migration process, and extends to the detention and deportation centres, and to when people are deported.

The detention and deportation centres are other examples of how the border system steals your time. And this is exactly the point of these places: to take away your future and your hope. The staff working in those centres—like the Swedish detention custody officers, and the prison officer in Sjælsmark, quoted earlier—even say that you should not have a future in this place, and you know this is their intention. They are meant to let you know that you should not dream of being here, we are sorry, but your dream will now be reconstructed. When I lived in Sjælsmark deportation centre in Denmark, life was put on hold. When they say that life is put on hold and dreams are stolen (see Khosravi 2017b, 2018), it is not an over-statement but the reality. In the deportation centre, the body is just there; meanwhile, your mind is thinking and dreaming of being somewhere else. They become two distinct entities: the body is one thing, and the dream and life aspiration another. In the deportation centres, they used motivational measures and return advice to manipulate people's hopes. They were aware that people hope that someone in the government, or the immigration service, will look at their case again and the intention was to try to convey to the people that this would not happen. Their job was to make you realise that your dreams would not work out. They offered you English courses and counselling, and tried to rework your idea of the future, arguing that once your asylum case has been rejected you will not have it reopened. Their counselling was about how nice it would be if you would go home. They said: 'Even though you didn't find it safe when you left, we will tell you how safe it is. You don't need to be in a rich place to be safe. You must not dream of Denmark being a safe place for you; the sooner you accept that going home should be your new future, the better; and it is our job to make you realise it. If you stay here, things will only get worse for you'. In my case, they said: 'We recognise that there are problems in Nigeria, but you can live in Cameroon'. And to Afghans, they say, 'We know Kabul is bad but there surely are some parts of Kabul where you can live'.

Even when they try to prevent us from dreaming, we are made to believe that if you make the effort, you can change your situation. Hope can then be a negative thing, because it urges you to endure the misery in which you are forced to live. Reality tells you differently, but hope keeps you believing that there is a chance that things will change. Even in the Danish deportation centres, Sjælsmark and Kærshovedgård, where they do not put a gun to your head, you are still subjected to a slow killing process. You make up fantasies that things will change. This hope makes some people blind. Each person you talk to, from Somalia, Afghanistan, or elsewhere, who has been detained in different places—in Australia, Libya, Denmark, Germany—even though their reality is different, these people keep putting their lives on the line, hoping *their* case will be different. Each of us with migrant or refugee experience maintains the belief that even though thousands of people before us have not been treated fairly, *we* will get the exceptional opportunity to explain our problems, the daily terrors we have experienced in our countries, and we believe the authorities will respect *our* human rights. We all want to believe we are the exception.

For this reason, and because of the general hostility towards refugees and migrants in Europe at the moment, some of us do not want to be referred to as refugees or migrants. This way, we try to disassociate ourselves from the system, even though we all silently suffer from it. Other people who fled from the same regions, who lost their lives on the way or were deported, each of them told their stories, and still, they were deported. The problems that made them leave were directly created by Western powers—so why would these countries recognise our problems and recognise us as human beings if we go there? Yet still, people maintain the illusion that there is justice. We tell ourselves this in order to maintain hope.

Still, any change can generate new hopes. If your situation changes, if it only means you move from one room to the next, that at least constitutes a change, which will keep motivating you. If you leave from one community to another, that's a huge step. It does not mean everything changed, or that you will not encounter the same problem; but even if the same pattern and structures of oppression remain, it gives you a sense that there is change. For instance, when people leave from the deportation centres in Denmark to another country, maybe they will find that their fingerprints are not recognised and they get a new chance. Or, they might still have to live in a new camp in Germany but over there they have more freedom to move around, and that's a big change compared to Sjælsmark and Kærshovedgård where you are subjected to curfews, and where you cannot decide what you eat. You might have to risk a lot and cross many borders to get away from there, out of the camp, to change your living conditions. But it might still give you a new motivation, even though the change of space does not mean that your problems disappeared. You might be in an equally or even more precarious situation, where you do not have healthcare, you might experience abuse or end up in jail if you are caught by the police, so some might say, why not go back to the camp?—but on the other hand, you can make your own food, go to bed when you want, and talk to people who are not crazy like you in the deportation centres like Sjælsmark and Kærshovedgård. This gives hope, instead of living like a zombie. It might not solve your problem but it constitutes an upgrade compared to what you had, so why not give it a try.

However, after many years of navigating the border regimes, of living in different camps and in prison, you realise that you are back to ground zero, and that your time has been stolen from you. You cannot get this back, so you have to leave it behind. As Shahram Khosravi (2017b, 2018) writes, when people are deported, a lot of time and hope, has been stolen from them. The hopes and time they invested in changing their conditions have been wasted. The knowledge and experience they have acquired is useless for the society they will be deported to, and you have to start over from the beginning, either in the society you left from, or by moving on. You are back to the same situation you once left from, but are even more confused than when you started. For instance, it is difficult for me to imagine returning to Nigeria after eleven or twelve years, considering how much and how fast things have changed there— it is a completely different society. I would have to invent a new dream, like any foreigner, would have to find a new way to navigate and build a new life in a new society.

I have by now accepted defeat in struggling against the deportation regime. It is a waste of time and energy to keep trying to believe you can change your situation. But I give myself a sense of hope that I can still find a way to live. It's a way of dealing with the defeat. So, to be honest… the recipe is still the hope. At the end of the day, even though reality shows something different, I still have to motivate myself by being involved in activism, by trying to educate and change this society's way of thinking; what motivates me to continue is the hope that there is somebody out there who will eventually recognise that this is completely wrong and inhumane. We always hope society will come to its senses, respect human rights and dignity. This is somehow the hope. If we consider the climate today, it is a false hope; but perhaps as a compromise, if you do some things that will make them understand it is not right, that can be a reason to hope. We need hope, but also to be realistic. The small changes are a deception, a false reality, but they keep you going. In my case, while I am still afraid of the police and of deportation, I still live precariously and with anxiety, I nevertheless feel positivity in the everyday life because of the small changes. Today I can live freely, and at the very least, I can go out and enjoy the sun in the park if I want to, whereas in the Danish deportation centres, you would have to walk 40 minutes to get out of there. The small changes still give you a sense that you are *moving on*.

To conclude, hope is a tool used by the oppressor and by the oppressed. The oppressor hopes to continue to oppress, and they want you to accept the kind of dream they created for you: that you cannot live in Denmark, in Europe, that you will stay in your country. At the same time, the counter-action, the resistance, is that people also express their hope. Which is what I'm doing now; it's good for me to believe that I'm resisting by having hope it will one day change. So, it becomes a tool for both sides. One to take away, one to keep it alive.

Conclusion: Struggles Over Hope in States' Deportation Regimes

In this chapter, we have focused on how border, detention and deportation regimes operate through the systematic manipulation and theft of deportable people's hopes, dreams and aspirations for the future. We have also shown how hopes and dreams for the future can be mobilised to navigate and resist oppressive deportation regimes. The stealing of deportable people's time by the European deportation regime begins already with the processes of colonisation and exploitation that push some people to leave for Europe in the first place. States' efforts to decelerate and disrupt their journeys and to steal the time, resources and relations they have since invested in their migration continue throughout the migration process, and further extend into the future, as deported persons are denied the opportunity to search for security and a livable future. The archipelago of border zones, detention and deportation centres, which is mobilised to contain, decelerate and deter unwanted migration, thus become tools for sustaining global inequalities (Besteman 2019; Khosravi 2018).

The chapter has detailed the techniques used by state authorities to extinguish deportable people's hopes of challenging these inequalities and of remaining in the country they risk being deported from. In the first part of the chapter, we detailed how officials working in Swedish migration-related detention and Danish deportation centres sought to manipulate the future dreams and hopes of deportable persons and align them with the intentions of deporting states. Here, the role of deportation in sustaining structures of global injustice become visible: when state officials who told Annika that deportable persons must abandon their 'false hopes' or dream of a future in a wealthy country, they asserted deportable persons' dis-belonging and indicated that they must accept 'their' place in a system of global apartheid (Besteman 2019). The example illustrates how this global system is not only sustained via militarised border enforcement but also through symbolic and affective governing techniques, which are not less violent. This is perhaps most starkly demonstrated by the Danish deportation centres, where residents were exposed to 'intolerable' living conditions and deprived of their autonomy over both their present and future time. With no time limit to their stay, residents risked becoming indefinitely stuck in conditions that were 'killing them slowly' (Castaway Souls of Sjælsmark 2016)—even though many residents eventually defied the government's deportation fantasies by staying put or moving on to seek new opportunities elsewhere in Europe. We have witnessed how the stealing and manipulating people's hopes cause direct, physical and emotional pain and suffering. We therefore consider state practices that systematically deprive people of hope as violent acts of domination.

Nevertheless, in spite of state authorities' strategies to ensure their physical, social and affective expulsion, many deportable persons find ways to renew their hopes and new tactics to pursue them. In the second part of the chapter, we explored the ambivalent role that hope plays for those who seek to navigate and resist repressive deportation policies. Stanley highlighted that hope is necessary for finding the motivation to *wait out* and endure precarious conditions in the present (Hage 2015), or to move on. During this waiting time, people articulate new hopes and dreams for things to change. As Stanley notes, these hopes might only translate into minor changes, which do not radically alter or improve their situation. Still, they might allow people to regain a sense of autonomy and find a new direction forward. By taking small steps to improve their situation, by creating daily routines inside or outside the camp, people living under threat of deportation are able to reclaim some control over their daily lives that the deportation regime has stolen from them (Brun 2015). Moreover, by denouncing the stigmatising labels it imposes on them, engaging in political activism, or moving on to seek better life chances elsewhere, deportable people directly challenge states' efforts to exclude them. We concur with Canning (2017, 156) that when state borders and deportation regimes create hostile conditions that are intentionally designed to make life intolerable for deportable persons, the very act of surviving is in itself 'an indicator of resistance'.

Still, hoping also entails severe risks. As Stanley points out, hope might induce the false belief that the injustices produced by the European border and deportation regime are exceptional, rather than systemic. While persistent hope might eventually result in an improvement of a deportable person's legal status, the hope that migration law will deliver 'justice' also risks reifying its exclusionary logic and obscuring the systemic inequalities that the law produces and sustains. Moreover, the person hoping for justice might ultimately still face deportation, and find their time, hopes and dreams wasted when they are deported 'back to zero'.

To conclude, hope serves an ambivalent role in the enforcement and contestation of deportation regimes. On the one hand, the manipulation and deprivation of hope is used as an instrument of oppression to smoothen deportation enforcement and to sustain global inequalities; on the other hand, hoping and dreaming against deportations can be acts of defiance, used by the oppressed to navigate and challenge states' deportation fantasies. In the worst case, hope exposes illegalised and unwanted travellers to protracted marginalisation, precarity or even death; in the best case, it is a source of motivation that can disrupt states' political dreams of sustaining global injustices, and produce alternative visions that challenge them.

References

Anderson, Bridget, Matthew J. Gibney, and Emanuela Paoletti. 2011. "Citizenship, Deportation and the Boundaries of Belonging." *Citizenship Studies* 15(5): 547–63.

Ansems de Vries, Leonie, and Elspeth Guild. 2018. "Seeking Refuge in Europe: Spaces of Transit and the Violence of Migration Management." *Journal of Ethnic and Migration Studies* 0(0): 1–11.

Bendixsen, Synnøve, and Thomas Hylland Eriksen. 2018. "Time and the Other: Waiting and Hope among Irregular Migrants." In K. Janeja Manpreet and Andreas Bandak. *Ethnographies of Waiting: Doubt, Hope and Uncertainty.* New York: Bloomsbury.

Besteman, Catherine. 2019. "Militarized Global Apartheid." *Current Anthropology* 60(19): 26–38.

Brekke, Jan-Paul, and Grete Brochmann. 2015. "Stuck in Transit: Secondary Migration of Asylum Seekers in Europe, National Differences, and the Dublin Regulation." *Journal of Refugee Studies* 28(2): 145–162.

Brun, Cathrine. 2015. "Active Waiting and Changing Hopes: Toward a Time Perspective on Protracted Displacement." *ResearchGate* 59(1): 19–37.

Brun, Cathrine, and Anita Fábos. 2015. "Making homes in Limbo? A Conceptual Framework." *Refuge* 31(1): 5–17.

Canning, Victoria. 2017. *Gendered Harm and Structural Violence in the British Asylum System*. Oxfordshire: Taylor & Francis.

Canning, Victoria. 2019. "Keeping Up with the Kladdkaka: Kindness and Coercion in Swedish Immigration Detention Centres." *European Journal of Criminology*: 1477370818820627.

Castaway Souls of Sjælsmark. 2016. "Asylum Seekers in Denmark: Manifesto—For the Right to Have Rights." Available at: https://alice.ces.uc.pt/news-old/?p=5492. Accessed 30 July 2019.

Coutin, Susan. 2015. "Deportation Studies: Origins, Themes and Directions." *Journal of Ethnic and Migration Studies* 41(4): 671–681.

Danish Ministry of Justice. 2013. "Udrejsecenter skal få flere asylansøgere til at rejse hjem". Available at: www.justitieministeriet.dk/. Accessed 4 September 2019.

Djampour, Pouran. 2018. *Borders Crossing Bodies: The Stories of Eight Youth with Experience of Migrating*. Malmö University.

DeBono, Daniela, Sofia Rönnqvist, and Karin Magnusson. 2015a. *Humane and Dignified?: Migrants' Experiences of Living in a "State of Deportability" in Sweden*. Malmö Institute for Studies of Migration, Diversity and Welfare, Malmo University.

De Genova, Nicholas. 2002. "Migrant 'Illegality' and Deportability in Everyday Life." *Annual Review of Anthropology* 31: 419–447.

Drotbohm, Heike, and Ines Hasselberg. 2015. "Deportation, Anxiety, Justice: New Ethnographic Perspectives." *Journal of Ethnic and Migration Studies* 41(4): 551–562.

Eule, Tobias G., Lisa Marie Borrelli, Annika Lindberg, and Anna Wyss. 2019. *Migrants Before the Law. Contested Migration Control in Europe*. London: Palgrave Macmillan.

Freedom of Movements Research Collective. 2018. *Stop Killing Us Slowly: A Research Report on the Criminalization of Rejected Asylum Seekers in Denmark*. Roskilde: Roskilde University.

Gibney, Matthew. 2013. "Is Deportation a Form of Forced Migration?" *Refugee Survey Quarterly* 32(2): 116–129.

Griffiths, Melanie. 2013. "Frenzied, Decelerating and Suspended: The Temporal Uncertainties of Failed Asylum Seekers and Immigration Detainees." *COMPAS Working Papers*, No. 105.

Griffiths, Melanie, Ali Rogers, and Bridget Anderson. 2013. "Migration, Time and Temporalities: Review and Prospect." *COMPAS Research Resources Paper*. Available at: https://www.compas.ox.ac.uk/fileadmin/files/Publicati ons/Research_Resources/Citizenship/Report_-_Migration_Time_and_Tem poralities_FINAL.pdf.
Hage, Ghassan. 2015. *Alter-Politics: Critical Anthropology and the Radical Imagination*. Melbourne: Melbourne University Press.
Jefferson, Andrew, Simon Turner, and Steffen Jensen. 2019. "Introduction: On Stuckness and Sites of Confinement." *Ethnos* 84(1): 1–13.
Khosravi, Shahram. 2017a. "Deportation as a Way of Life". In Rich Furman (Ed.) *Detaining the Immigrant Other: Global and Transnational Issues*, 169–181. Oxford: Oxford University Press.
Khosravi, Shahram (Ed.). 2017b. *After Deportation: Ethnographic Perspectives*. London: Palgrave Macmillan
Khosravi, Shahram. 2018. Stolen Time. *Radical Philosophy* 2(3).
Kjellbom, Pia, and Anna Lundberg. 2018. "Olika rättsliga rum för en skälig levnadsnivå? : En rättskartografisk analys av SoL och LMA i domstolspraktiken." *Nordisk socialrättslig tidskrift* 17–18: 39–71.
Lindberg, Annika. 2019. *Governing the Deportation Limbo: State Responses to Non-deported Migrants in Denmark and Sweden*. University of Bern.
Malkki, Liisa H. 1995. "Refugees and Exile: From 'Refugee Studies' to the National Order of Things." *Annual Review of Anthropology* 24: 495–523.
Suárez-Krabbe, Julia, and Annika Lindberg. 2019. "Enforcing Apartheid? The Politics of 'Intolerability' in the Danish Migration and Integration Regimes." *Migration and Society* 2(1): 90–97.
SVT Nyheter. 2016, January 27. "Ygeman: Uppemot 80.000 asylsökande kan utvisas." Available at: https://www.svt.se/nyheter/inrikes/tiotusentals-asylso kande-ska-avvisas.
Walters, William. 2002. "Deportation, Expulsion, and the International Police of Aliens." *Citizenship Studies* 6(3): 265–292.
Walters, William. 2016. "The Flight of the Deported: Aircraft, Deportation, and Politics." *Geopolitics* 21(2): 435–458.
Webber, Frances. 2011. "How Voluntary Are Voluntary Returns?" *Race & Class* 52(4): 98–107.
Wyss, Anna. 2019. "Stuck in Mobility? The Interrupted Journeys of Migrants with Precarious Legal Status in Europe." *Journal of Immigrant and Refugee Studies* 16(1): 77–93.

6

Compounding Trauma Through Temporal Harm

Victoria Canning

Introduction: Temporal Harm and Bureaucratic Thievery

> I have always despised waiting. Waiting is a mechanism of torture in the dungeon of time. (Behrouz Boochani, survivor of indefinite offshore detention on Manus Island, 2018: 62)

In 2018 I visited Faiza in a Danish asylum centre. We had first met in early 2017, by which stage Faiza—a survivor of domestic violence—had been moved six times around asylum centres, soon to be twice more. She had already 'lost' almost two years of her life, as she had put it, awaiting the outcome of an asylum claim. Those two years did not include the

---

V. Canning (✉)
School for Policy Studies, University of Bristol, Bristol, UK
e-mail: victoria.canning@bristol.ac.uk

many others she felt she lost with her controlling and coercive former husband.

Faiza had managed to endure this loss of time with almost boundless vigour. Although she had both threatened and attempted suicide the year before, she fought relentlessly since, 'as a mother I have seen my kids and I have seen there is no one who is going to care about my kids and the people who are sitting here, Danish Immigration, they don't care the condition of the mother, so then I make strong my willpower that no, I have to live and I have to take care about my kids because I gave birth to them, these are my responsibilities'. By the second place I visited her—in Sjælsmark[1] deportation centre in 2017—and before her move to a departure centre, she felt that, 'My life is just like a joke. It's priceless. Life is so costly, one life, but no one here takes care about even if I died or if I get suicide, no one can … I don't think so, people don't care'.

Seeing Faiza on this particular day later in 2018 was a stark reminder of the human costs of temporality when conditions are bureaucratically reduced to create 'intolerable' living conditions, as the former minister of Immigration, Integration and Housing, Inger Støjberg, had promised. The vigour I had come to know had all but dissolved. It is difficult to convey the witnessing of exhaustion, and there is no space in social sciences to say that someone has 'lost their spark', and yet Faiza's face conveyed just that—a shift in demeanour, eyes tired and removed of hope. The daily reduction of autonomy through poverty, spatial control through the remoteness of asylum centres and the orchestrated nothingness of temporality in camps and centres—eroded through welfare reductions and diminishment of activities through increasingly restrictive state policies—all were taking their toll. I am not alone in this observation, and heard similar from practitioners and activists working in asylum-related support. As one outreach support manager synopsised:

---

[1] Denmark has two departure centres (*udrejsecenter* as a formal term meaning departure, or *udvisningscentre* as it is known to 'residents', meaning deportation). These are *Udrejsecenter Sjælsmark* in Zealand and *Udrejsecenter Kærshovedgård* in Mid Jutland. Banality is inscribed as a means to facilitate easier deportation, as the centre governor informed me: 'it's deliberately not trying to make people stay, so there weren't be concerts every Friday night so you have something to look forward… there are activities there but the whole reason of the centre is to make people leave by themselves.'

I've seen people just decline from week to week. I think that's something that you really notice because there's people who might've been coming for a year or you might not have seen them for ages and then they come back and they seem like a completely different person and I think their mental health just declines so rapidly, people don't have that support. (England, 2016)

Like many other people stuck in asylum systems, Faiza continued to fight for her right to refugee status in Denmark, and the resistance required for such a lengthy feat is not to be undermined. The sheer capacity for people to endure waithood (Khosravi, 2018) for such lengths is itself a form of resistance (Canning, 2017). The point, however, is that people should not have to.

Focussing on research and activist work in Britain, Denmark and Sweden, this chapter argues that time—and the bureaucratic harms inflicted during ones time in asylum systems—is recognised as a contributor to the deterioration of mental and emotional health. Nonetheless, states and state-corporate alliances continue to develop and embed policy and practice which knowingly reduces autonomy over time, and regularly leaves people unable to plan for their future. In it is this way that we can begin to see that people in Faiza's position do not 'lose' time: time is actively stolen.

Evidencing Temporal Harm: A Note on Methods

Evidencing harm can be a complex feat. Harm has multifarious definitions and is not experienced as a monolithic issue. Indeed (like crime) harm arguably has no ontological reality (Hillyard and Tombs, 2017). Instead it may be understood through social categories rather than hierarchies, pertaining to emotional and psychological harm, relational harm, cultural harm, physical harm or sexual harm (see Canning, 2017; Hillyard and Tombs, 2008; Pantanzis, 2004; Pemberton, 2015). In the case of people seeking asylum, these may be interconnected rather than standalone harms—part of a continuum situated in socially ascribed conditions of inequality, precariousness or uncertain legal status.

As such, recognising or defining harm becomes even more complex if and when it is made structurally invisible through processes of exclusion and spatial isolation. This is very much the case broadly where immigration is concerned, and specifically in relation to illegalised travellers or people awaiting the outcome of a claim to refugee status. Dispersal policies[2] in the United Kingdom, ascribed housing in asylum centres situated on spatial peripheries in Denmark and Sweden, and the practice of immigration detention, all lend themselves to reducing social connectedness for people seeking asylum or people detained. For survivors of sexual violence, torture or *torturous violence* (see Canning, 2016) this harm compounds impacts of historical abuses and a structural lack of support in surviving violence. In the context of seeking asylum, such harms are inflicted by processes which arguably intentionally are created to bolster hostile environments (as former British Prime Minister Theresa May advocated) or intolerable living conditions (as outlined earlier).

As such, evidencing harm requires a multi-method approach, drawing in structural and institutional actors at macro and meso levels and situating these alongside every day, micro level insights. For this research, the latter included women seeking asylum and—as an activist academic—refection from ethnographic activism. It is based on research across four periods: reflections from a decade of activist participation and ethnography with women seeking asylum in the North West of England[3] (2008–2018); interviews with 19 psychologists and psychotraumatologists working with survivors of torture in Denmark[4] (2013); interviews with 74 sexual violence counsellors, psychologists, social workers, lawyers, immigration detention staff and medical doctors working with

---

[2]The policy of dispersal of those seeking asylum in the UK was introduced by the ***Immigration and Asylum Act 1999***. The legislative intention was that by distribution across the country no one area would be overburdened by the obligation of supporting asylum seekers.

[3]See Canning (2017) for further information on this aspect of work, activism and method.

[4]Funded by Liverpool John Moores University and working in conjunction with the Danish Institute Against Torture.

people seeking asylum in Britain,[5] Denmark and Sweden[6] (2016–2018); and oral histories with women seeking asylum during this period.

Unearthing the Mechanisms of Stolen Time

Unlike any other given materiality, time cannot be regained. Its value is reflected in how well time is spent: enjoyed or pained, fulfilled or emptied. For people seeking asylum, temporality is inherently and inextricably linked to legal processes—from application for asylum, to acceptance or refusal, to detention or deportation (Girma et al., 2014). Although there are pinnacle points in asylum processes, it is in the everyday that time is central and autonomy often structurally reduced, so even if individuals exercise agency in 'filling time', the intention of states does not change. Wellbeing and civil liberties are instead diminished by the structures within which people wait whilst their futures are decided upon. As Antonia, a survivor of trafficking living in a Danish asylum centre, so clearly articulated:

> Why do they keep us here? They start bringing papers: you have to wait for assistance; you have to wait for five months; you have to wait for three months; you have to wait for four months. I was thinking the last year, December, they are going to make the decision for me. The final decision. No, the next thing I expect, I get they bring again in four months' time. Which is last month, complete the four months. I did not get a letter from them! They told me last month on 18 they will write to me. They did not write, they did not do anything, they just abandon us here in the camp, here. When is immigration going to write? I have to know my footsteps, I have to know where I'm going, I have to know where I'm coming. My child cannot have a camp only life. (Denmark, 2017)

---

[5]Note that the terms 'Britain' and the 'United Kingdom' are included in this book chapter. The research area did not include Northern Ireland, but the UK is referred to when discussing aspects of border controls and asylum which affect Northern Ireland.
[6]Funded by the Economic and Social Research Council, project reference ES/N016718/1.

This is thus intertwined with socio-political decisions: decisions to reduce the right to access refugee status; decisions to change laws so that time can be sped up to easier facilitate deportation (or 'frenzied time', see Griffiths, 2013); and to make the time spent between application and refusal or granting status as hostile as possible. As one LGBTQ refugee rights organisation manager reiterated, 'they are not allowed to do a lot of things and then they lose their motivation to do anything so they just waste their time' (Sweden, 2017).

This time is littered with uncertainty and anxiety, where even the banal and every day are linked to immigration status, legal papers and unbelonging (Cassidy et al., 2018 see also Whyte, 2011). For example, many women I have spoken with over the years speak of increased anxiety when post is being delivered in case it is a refusal letter or deportation orders. Asma—a woman seeking asylum in England—sums up concerns for her child every time she has a meeting at the Home Office, the body responsible for determining the outcome of asylum claims: 'I was very scared when I go to Home Office because they can detain with children as well. Oh yeah, I feel very, very scared'. Likewise, as a refugee women's case worker reflected:

> The very fact that they've got a letter from the Home Office has put them in a complete panic… those letters are a direct reminder that when you're an asylum seeker you're not in control of your own life. The Home Office decides where you live, they decide how much money you get, they decide where you can and can't go, they pretty much delineate where your children go to school and most importantly, they decide whether you can stay in the country or not. (England, 2017)

A temporal period where autonomy over one's present or future is so heavily reduced is *harmful*. As the clock ticks on, fears over the threat of detention exacerbate, particularly for those who have already experienced detention and who regularly still recall, for example, the sound of keys (see Canning et al., 2017). For people awaiting family reunification—the right to which has also been reduced across all three countries—stories of border deaths or conflict-related deaths in their country of origin perforates time and emotional wellbeing (Khosravi, 2016).

As Melanie Griffiths points out, 'Time is a challenging concept to discuss. It is at risk of meaning both too much and too little, and is simultaneously over-analysed and taken for granted' (2013: 2). For people seeking asylum, time is dualistically a friend and an enemy: for as long as an asylum claim is under review a person can only gain a short term sense of safety from whatever it is that one has fled from.

The Infliction of Harm Through Temporal Insecurity

Many aspects of the asylum system take an incredibly long time. Indeed, 'The asylum system itself is often a slow process, one beset with bureaucracy, applications, appeals and judicial hearings' (Griffiths, 2013: 7). As has been highlighted so far, however, the point at which someone reaches a perceptively 'safe' country, time ironically becomes marred by unanticipated senses of unsafety. Uncertainty for the future restricts one's capacity to make plans, and the threat of detention and/or deportation remains a central aspect of temporal control. Adding to this is the length of time that protection is offered for, which has also been reduced in all three case study countries—and specifically since 2015 in Denmark and Sweden. As a social worker for refugee support in Denmark alluded, 'They are still terrified that they're gonna be sent home, they're still terrified… like their whole body is still like, kind of this crisis, and you can tell that. And I don't know how long they're gonna be in that kind of situation like this' (Denmark, 2017).

This particular period has thus the potential to exacerbate feelings of isolation or unbelonging (Yuval-Davis, 2006), and indeed compound earlier trauma or inflict new traumata, since safety and security are recognised as fundamental requirements for emotional and psychological wellbeing (Masmas et al., 2008; Women's Refugee Commission, 2016). As one international NGO co-ordinator put it, 'the isolation, the waiting, the uncertainty of whatever's going to happen to you and now the temporary protection, you not having access to getting your family to come here… all of these issues are making people more psychologically vulnerable than they were a few years ago' (Sweden, 2018).

However, isolation and uncertainty are engrained in the extended duration of asylum processes, which can take its toll on the health of individuals, including women with children who are disproportionately limited from travel or networks by school schedules and dependency (Women's Refugee Commission, 2016). As one psychologist working with people seeking asylum and undocumented migrants across the Skåne region of Sweden told me: 'Isolation—a *huge* problem. And the isolation tends to make people psychologically feel very much worse. We have people who have developed trauma by being at the asylum centres' (Sweden, 2017). Therefore what we can see here is that emotional and psychological harms are not only experienced prior to arriving in so-called safe countries, but that they can be central experiences during the process of seeking asylum.

It is no surprise then that the length of waiting is a central concern for people seeking asylum. It similarly remains a priority for further civil parties: for refugee advocates and support workers, the deterioration of mental health amongst clients and friends is recognisably problematic (as the following section shows). For state institutions, concern also lies with the cost[7] of lengthy processes. Since people are—with few exceptions—not allowed to work in Denmark or the UK, asylum applicants are usually, forcibly state dependent. This requires finances for housing, food allowance and—in Denmark—the infantilising term 'pocket money'.

Whilst time passes for us all, the legal restrictions placed on many people seeking asylum mean that there is uniqueness to the structurally designed reduction of *somethingness* in place of *nothingness*. Opportunities to engage in education or work are reduced both through temporal insecurity and—in the UK specifically—by unfeasible costs of higher education. In Sweden, qualified Swedish courses are only accessible *after* refugee status is granted, meaning adults 'have to wait maybe two, two-and-a-half years and then if they get positive, then they start with Swedish classes, so basically they waste their time here' (refugee youth support worker, Sweden, 2017). Since temporary protection is limited to a rolling 13 months, people I spoke to in refugee support networks

---

[7]This should, however, be considered in connection with the corporate franchising of border controls including in immigration detention through shares and other financiering. See Bhatia and Canning (2020) for full discussion.

were often also sceptical of spending time learning a new language if their future in the country could not be guaranteed.

As such, lengthy asylum claims are inherently detrimental to building futures, and to autonomy and wellbeing. Across the three case study countries included in this research, the length of time people wait for initial decisions for asylum claims on average has increased. In the UK, the time it takes for asylum seekers to receive an initial decision on their applications has increased somewhat in recent years. In the fourth quarter of 2012, 73% of applications received an initial decision within six months—compared with 25% in the last quarter of 2018 (Walsh, 2019). In Denmark in 2016, the average time of stay in the Danish asylum system was around 550 days, covering a span from one month to 18 years (Clante Bendixen, 2017). In Sweden, the average handling time for cases at first instance rose from 496 days or 16.5 months in 2017 to 507 days or 16.9 months in 2018 (Asylum Information database, 2018). Since research by Hvidtfeldt et al. (2019) demonstrates that long asylum decision waiting periods are associated with an increased risk of psychiatric disorders, to experience such suspended waithood with no temporal security in and of itself becomes a form of harm.

A key contributor to this lengthy process is that case decisions are often flawed or highly problematic, leaving people suspended in a kind of temporal limbo for years at a time. As one asylum support worker highlighted:

> I've been working with people seeking asylum for over five years; people have been seeking, in the same case, for nine years, ten years and on repeated cases and fresh claims and things because errors have been made for up to 15 years, which is ridiculous! So you don't really have a life. The waiting is a huge issue, you're completely in limbo, you haven't got any chance to really make roots and to really make a life, so instead you live in a weird cycle of drop-in centres and advice centres and groups instead of having a real life. (England, 2017)

It is this issue which poses a complex conundrum. If asylum claims are to be fairly and properly analysed, it is important that reviews *do take time*. As a member of the Queen's Counsel pointed out, 'there are some things you can't make quicker because it's inevitably a slow process, you need to get your material, you need to interview and everything else and we have quite a litigious system now, certainly an evidence-heavy system where you need experts and so on to give evidence' (England, 2017). As such there requires a balance between efficiency and quality. However, this should not detract from two key points. Firstly, cultures of disbelief regarding the narratives and claims of people seeking asylum (Bögner et al., 2010; Montgomery and Foldsprang, 2005; Smith, 2004) are central to undermining the credibility of claims in the first place, thus increasing the likelihood of rejections and subsequently increased (lengthy) appeals. Secondly, and as this chapter seeks to highlight, the deliberate reduction of autonomy over time is based on an architecture of exclusion that is built to create spaces of nothingness, and as such can be rebuilt. Instead, it is designed to be as bureaucratically complex and reductive as possible.

Surviving Stolen Time

Along with exacerbations in emotional or psychological harms, like the problem of stolen time as experienced by Antonia, Faiza and Asma, temporal harm becomes measurable in physicality of time when months or even years seep away. To give an illustration, the longest person I have personally known seeking asylum had spent 14 years stuck in the system, gaining refugee status eventually in 2014. In the same year, in a focus group with five women from four countries, I asked how long each had been awaiting a final asylum decision. One had been in the asylum system since 2013, one since 2012, one since 2009, one since 2010 and one since 2002. In just one small group, that is an accumulation of 24 years of waiting—hardly conducive to their time, or anyone else's.

It is no accident that unwanted bodies are often isolated or kept in temporal limbo, but a deliberate strategy to wear down one's resolve to the point that any alternative—including deportation—is preferable. To reiterate a message conveyed to me by Amina, a survivor of trafficking:

I've committed a crime of seeking protection in this country at the age of 18. I'll be 26 soon. So I have spent the most important stage of my age while completing the sentence of this sin. So even if I get status I'll still be a refugee for next five years. If life is all about running after papers… I don't wanna spend my rest of life to run after this fucking shit. Where I don't have a meaningful life at all… I don't want this kind of protection. Not more than a prison. (England, 2018)

That Amina refers to her own right to seek asylum as 'crime' and 'sin' is a testament to the invasive power of borders: the process treats her more like a criminal subject than a human or survivor. Whilst time goes by, people often reflect on losing important years of their life. As Asma reflected, 'I am here ten years now and my life has gone. I'm nearly 45. What I will do if I get status now? How I can do work? If ten years ago I got status, I would be able … I had to do the job, I was young, I could do everything'. What Asma identifies here is time as capital (Khosravi, 2018), when she otherwise had little else. Having left her abusive husband, Asma's status as a woman seeking asylum, now with a young child, has reduced her capacity to fulfil her own dreams or take part in life as she had planned it.

This was similarly felt at institutional levels. As the director of a national migrant rights organisation in Denmark highlighted, it is 'the uncertainty and the inability to make decisions for your own life and for your future' (Denmark, 2017) whilst a social worker specialising in refugee families surmised that 'people are just living in a kind of a limbo where they have no idea if they're gonna go home or if they're gonna stay and that just, pardon my word, fucks people up, being in that kind of situation'. Perhaps that which was attuned to the stripping of humanity was relayed by a first response NGO co-ordinator who pointed out that 'because of the temporary status that they have, they cannot settle in Denmark, they cannot fall in love or … some of they, they cannot start at university because of the temporary residency that they have. And even those who have five or three years of residency, they don't feel secure in the country' (Denmark, 2018).

This is the self-actualisation of socially induced degradation, where ones' own identity, freedom and self-worth are reduced by externalised processes of Othering and degradation (van Houtum and van Naerssen, 2002). As time goes by, self-worth reduces. This is not temporality: it is the infliction of temporal harm. It is the stealing of time.

When Harm Compounds Trauma

As this chapter thus demonstrates, people are subject to intersectional forms of temporal harm during migratory processes, in this case seeking asylum. These can have two effects: the development of emotional or psychological harms because of the complex bureaucratic systems embedded in such processes, and/or to experience the compounding of trauma if and when a person has been subjected to previous forms of violence. To pinpoint, as a refugee women's sexual violence counsellor summarised, 'not only have you been through whatever you've been through, now you're waiting for this' (England, 2016).

People seeking asylum who have fled conflict or persecution can be disproportionately affected by higher levels of extreme violence than general populations. To emphasise, this is not to say that broader populations do not experience extreme physical or psychological violence, but that people fleeing persecution face *disproportionately* high likelihoods both in their countries of origin and throughout the journey. This is also exacerbated through waiting at borders, such as in camps, as well as the time taken to move through borders as states expand externalisations and controls on illegalised routes of travel (Andersson, 2014; Infantino, 2015; van Houtum and van Naerssen, 2002).

Throughout the past decade I have spoken with women who have been subjected to rape, multiple perpetrator rape, being burned by cigarettes, scalding by water and oil, false imprisonment, forced pornography, sustained beatings, the breaking of bones, amongst many other coercive and psychological violences. Many of these have been at the hands of male partners, some at the hands of state or military actors. It is therefore important to highlight that the significant impacts of torture and indeed torturous violence[8] can be far reaching (see also Bhatia and Burnett, 2019, for examples of observations which correlate with these). As Green and Ward outline:

> The extent of port-torture suffering is extensive and involves somatic sequelae (gastrointestinal disorders, rectal lesions and sphincter abnormalities, dermatological disorders, organic brain damage, cardiovascular disorders, difficulties in walking etc.); psychological sequelae (anxiety, depression, psychosis, lethargy, insomnia, nightmares, memory and concentration impairment, hallucinations, sexual problems, alcohol intolerance etc.) and social consequences of the somatic and psychological sequelae (inability to work, impairment of social personality, negative self-image, inability to relax, inability to relate positively with family members etc.).
> (Green and Ward, 2004: 139)

Such impacts are also reflected in surviving sexual violence, as well as conflict-related trauma. In research examining the mental health of 7000 refugees living in Western countries, Fazel et al. (2005) found that people seeking asylum were five times more likely to have mental health needs than the general population and more than 61% will experience serious mental distress (2005). Moreover, survivors of sexual torture are more likely to experience multiple traumata—or increased emotional and psychological symptoms of trauma—than survivors of other forms of violence or trauma (see Kessler et al., 1995; Arcel, 2003; Kastrup and Arcel, 2004). This is compounded by the uniqueness of sexual torture which can lead to a level of stigmatisation and silence beyond other forms of torture (Canning, 2016, 2017; see also Dehghan, 2018; Freedman, 2016).

For some people then, particularly survivors of sexual violence, torture or other abuses, uncertainty can thus compound people's abilities to

---

[8] 'Torturous violence' (Canning, 2016) is a term which aims to move away from state-centric definitions of torture so that abuses which amount to torture—and which have similar or the same impacts thereof—are recognised more clearly as such. This specifically encapsulates forms of violence which are more commonly associated with domestic spheres than with the more publically political nature of state affiliated torture (see Green and Ward, 2004). It thus focuses attention on the impacts of violence, than the intention of the perpetrator.

engage in other aspects of everyday life, or indeed to access trauma-related support (Canning, 2016; Dehghan, 2018; Women's Refugee Commission, 2016). As a leading psychologist outlined, 'the lack of stability, the lack of knowing that you will stay, the lack of actually feeling safe in your environment and feeling that your environment is somewhat predictive is definitely very directly causing or exacerbating their symptoms of PTSD and other anxiety disorders' (Sweden, 2017). Thus, rather than facilitate healing, it can be time—waiting—that compounds the impacts of earlier trauma or traumata.

The importance of creating a safe space for survivors of trauma, torture and sexual abuse is well established in psychosocial and feminist literatures (Kinzie, 2011; Patel and Mahtani, 2004: 33; Sjölund et al., 2009; Women's Resource Centre, 2010). As Herman argues, 'The first task of recovery [from traumatic experience] is to establish the survivor's safety. This task takes precedent over all others, for no therapeutic work can possibly succeed if safety has not been adequately secured' (1992: 159). This should arguably be taken literally, in that space and time should be allocated to the development of rapport and trust with survivors seeking support, as well as structurally in that safety should be secured to avoid further future abuses or returning to harm. Whilst the former can be problematic in terms of resources, the latter is inherently embedded in socio-political limitations for people seeking asylum.

However, lengthy asylum processes, indefinite detention in some areas and the constant fear of forced deportation and repatriation are often at the forefront of asylum applicants' consciousness. Space is neither figuratively or literally provided in terms of a guarantee of safety, affecting people's temporality and capacity to deal with the past or plan for the future. Whilst this clearly differs for refugees (who may have some level of temporal protection through refugee status) as this chapter has highlighted permanent status has been reduced to the point of eradication in all three countries. Instead, people often find themselves reapplying for status after, for example in Sweden, every 13 months. Furthermore, as one asylum support worker highlighted in the British context, 'when they get their status… In some ways it's a bit of anti-climax because a lot of harm has been done in that seeking asylum period to their health, their mental health, their wellbeing' (Scotland, 2017). Thus survivors of violence are subject not only to physical border controls, but also the existential and psychological impacts of uncertainty and temporal stuckness which serve to inflict further forms of harm (see also Griffiths, 2014).

Temporal Barriers to Support

On the other end of this trajectory are the implications that temporal harm causes for both people seeking asylum and for those offering support. Where psychological support was available for people seeking asylum, practitioners working with survivors of trauma or sexual violence repeatedly raised concerns about the inability to focus on therapy or counselling programmes. People seeking asylum can be more concerned with pressing temporal issues arising in the immediate future, such as the threat of homelessness, fear of detention or deportation, or concern for family and friends still residing in areas of conflict or migrating across borders.

As such, some level of distinction can be made between supporting people who were awaiting a decision from the state on their legal status and those who had already gained refugee status and are living as legal subjects. For example, in the project undertaken in 2014 one organisation that provided psychological support and counselling to women, men and children living in Denmark *only* worked with refugee groups for reasons relating to permanency and people's capacity to 'move on' once they had more security (Canning, 2016). As one psychotraumatologist outlined:

> VC: What are the differences in trying to support asylum seekers in comparison to supporting refugees?
> Interviewee: The main thing is that they are not secure, they don't have a secure place. So much of their daily worry is attached to whether they can stay or not, so there is very little room for working on trauma or working on other problems because this is the main problem. Can we stay here or can we not.
> VC: Does that have any particular impacts?

> Interviewee: Oh yeah, huge impacts. It's very difficult to do things about mental health problems in that [living in asylum system] circumstance. You need to establish some kind of secure place before you can deal with certain kinds of problems. So it becomes more kind of supportive help rather than working through trauma. And that's the reason why we don't work with asylum seekers.
> (Denmark, 2014)

This security thus relates to the immediate future and the longer-term future if one is to receive protection. Similarly, a trauma counsellor specifically indicated that uncertainty—compounded by destitution and homelessness—limited her ability to support survivors, and that this was based on the Danish states' lack of caring for people who were seeking asylum:

> The state does not care. That is a total stressor for me.... How can we do therapy concentrated on that [previous torture] if the whole thing is, 'where am I going to sleep tonight?' If you don't know where you can sleep at night, even if you have horrible flashbacks, invading memories, you have very much pain, still survival is on your agenda and other things have to come later.
> (Denmark, 2014)

Given that conditions facilitating security have significantly reduced since this interview in 2014, particularly in Denmark and Sweden—which had much farther to fall than Britain in terms of the embedding of asylum rights—the potential for compounding further trauma through temporal uncertainty is exacerbated. Interestingly, and importantly, the gradual shift in increased bordering after the 2015 refugee reception crisis has created further barriers, not only to accessing trauma-related support, but in providing it. Indeed, one stark issue highlighted through interviews with psychologists and psychotraumatologists between 2016 and 2018 was that they felt their ability to effectively perform their own role well has been compromised. Some indicated increasing levels of stress and, in Sweden in particular, a decreased faith in state and state decisions. The impact of temporal harms were noted through people's psychological deterioration, which itself affects people working in support sectors.

As one manager at an NGO which provides psychological support to migrant groups highlighted, 'it is difficult to be witness to people who are deteriorating because of their circumstances and life conditions without being able to do anything about it' (Denmark, 2018).

Terms such as 'powerless' and 'stress' were included in responses to questions about the impacts of escalated internalised border controls—in particular that practitioners did not feel they could support people seeking asylum whilst they are being held in an indefinite state of uncertainty or crisis. As one leading psychologist emphasised, 'There are a lot of legal issues that keep requiring their focus and keep also presenting a threat, so that makes trauma treatment during the asylum seeking phase quite hard, because it keeps being interrupted or keeps just drawing the focus on an imminent situation that is not about the trauma taking place before' (Sweden, 2017).

The reality on the ground is that people seeking asylum who are survivors of violence or persecution face multiple barriers to obtaining support, but that practitioners themselves face barriers to providing support (see Canning, 2014, 2019; Herlihy et al., 2004). One outcome of this is that—with the exception of only a few notable organisations I interviewed at across any of the research periods—organisations are reluctant to work with people who did not have any confirmation of legal status, which effectively means people seeking asylum are side-lined for fear of inducing further trauma by providing counselling or psychotherapies when people survivors of violence are so deeply affected by other socio-politically driven problems. Moreover, if and when support *is* available, the increased stress placed on practitioners is in itself more likely to impact negatively on the forms of support provided.

Conclusion: Avoidable Harm, Achievable Hope

Time is unique to any form of lived materiality. How it is spent determines whether we experience time as positive or negative, and whether we wish it away or wish to slow it down. Unlike many other things, time cannot be regained once lost.

Indeed, autonomy over what we do with our time is crucial to our own civil liberties in the everyday. As this chapter demonstrates, however, autonomy over time is not equally distributed. For people seeking asylum, time is strongly structured by control, threat—of detention or deportation—and bureaucratic barriers. This can be part of a trajectory of controls for people who have crossed various countries and continents, or ongoing controls through waithood in asylum systems.

In any case, the architecture of asylum systems in Northern European states—in these studies, Britain, Denmark and Sweden—have been increasingly scaffolded in ways which both inflict harm and compound the impacts of previous harms. Processes of social exclusion, such as deprivation, welfare and rights reductions, and spatial dispersal are bolstered by harmful shifts in access to permanency and security with regard to settled status. Lengthy asylum processes render people state dependent for months or years, thus structurally placing people in temporal limbos. The outcome of this is twofold: asylum processes can both inflict emotional and psychological harm and, for survivors of sexual or domestic violence, torture, conflict and/or persecution, compound the impacts of previous trauma.

As this chapter highlights, the sense of unknowing or being able to plan causes serious harm and anxiety. Asylum centres, immigration detention, welfare and rights reductions: all are structurally and institutionally designed through policy, society and law. As such, they can be redesigned through increased forms of institutionalised resistance. To reiterate, then: the issues raised throughout this chapter are not simply by-products of poorly managed systems. They are direct outcomes of toxic policies which suspend autonomy, induce poverty and create temporally harmful conditions under which security for the future is increasingly dissolved for those who often most need it. This is the bureaucratised stealing of human time.

References

Andersson, R. (2014), *Illegality INC.: Clandestine Migration and the Business of Bordering Europe*. California: University of California Press.

Arcel, L.T. (2003), *Introduction*, in Arcel, L.T., Popovic, S., Kucukalic, A., and Bravo-Mehmedbasic, A., (eds) Treatment of Torture and Trauma Survivors in a Post-War Society, Association for Rehabilitation of Torture Victims.

Asylum Information Database. (2018), *Regular Procedure*, available at https://www.asylumineurope.org/reports/country/sweden/asylum-procedure/procedures/regular-procedure, last accessed 19 December 2019.

Bhatia, M., and Burnett, J. (2019), *Medical Power and the Culture of Disbelief*, in Perocco, F. (ed), Tortura e Migrazioni/Torture and Migration, Italy: Edizioni Ca' Foscari.

Bhatia, M., and Canning, V. (2020), *Misery as Business: How Immigration Detention Became a Cash-Cow in Britain's Borders*, in Albertson, K., Corcoran, M and Phillips, J. (eds) Marketisation and Privatisation in Criminal Justice, Bristol: Bristol University Press.

Bögner, D., Brewin, C., and Herlihy, J. (2010), *Refugees' Experiences of Home Office Interviews: A Qualitative Study on the Disclosure of Sensitive Personal Information*, Journal of Ethnic Migration Studies, Vol. 36, No. 3: 519–535.

Boochani, B. (2018), *No Friend but the Mountains: Writing from Manus Island*, Australia: Picador.

Canning, V. (2014), *International Conflict, Sexual Violence and Asylum Policy: Merseyside as a Case Study*, Critical Social Policy, Vol. 34, No. 1: 23–45.

Canning, V. (2016), *Unsilencing Sexual Torture: Responses to Refugees and Asylum Seekers in Denmark*, British Journal of Criminology, Vol. 56, No. 3: 438–456.

Canning, V. (2017), *Gendered Harm and Structural Violence in the British Asylum System*, Oxon: Routledge.

Canning, V. (2019), *Reimagining Refugee Rights: Addressing Asylum Harms in Britain, Denmark and Sweden*, Bristol: Migration and Mobilities Bristol, available at http://www.statewatch.org/news/2019/mar/uk-dk-se-reimagining-refugee-rights-asylum-harms-3-19.pdf, last accessed 19 December 2019.

Canning, V., Caur, J., Gilley, A., Kebemba, E., Rafique, A., and Verson, J. (2017), *Migrant Artists Mutual Aid: Strategies for Survival, Recipes for Resistance*, London: Calverts Publishing.

Cassidy, K., Yuval-Davis, N., and Wemyss, G. (2018), *Intersectional Border(ing)s*, Political Geography, Vol. 66: 139–141.

Clante Bendixen, M. (2017), *Case Processing Time, Refugees Welcome Denmark*, available at http://refugees.dk/en/facts/the-asylum-procedure-in-denmark/case-processing-time/, last accessed 19 December 2019.

Dehghan, R. (2018), *The Health Impact of (Sexual) Torture Amongst Afghan, Iranian and Kurdish Refugees: A Literature Review*, Torture Journal, Vol. 28, No. 3: 77–91.

Fazel, M., Wheeler, J., & Danesh, J. (2005), *Prevalence of Serious Mental Disorder in 7,000 Refugees Resettled in Western Countries: A Systematic Review*, The Lancet, Vol. 365, 1309–1314.

Freedman, J. (2016), *Sexual and Gender-Based Violence Against Refugee Women: A Hidden Aspect of the Refugee "Crisis"*, Reproductive Health Matters, Vol. 24: 18–26.

Green, P., and Ward, T. (2004), *State Crime: Governments, Violence and Corruption*, London: Pluto Press.

Girma, M., Radice, S., Tsangarides, N., and Walter, N. (2014), *Detained: Women Asylum Seekers Locked Up in the UK*, London: Women for Refugee Women.

Griffiths, M. (2013), *Frenzied, Decelerating and Suspended: The Temporal Uncertainties of Failed Asylum Seekers and Immigration Detainees*, Centre on Migration, Policy and Society, Working Paper No. 105.

Griffiths, M. (2014), *Out of Time: The Temporal Uncertainties of Refused Asylum Seekers and Immigration Detainees*, Journal of Ethnic and Migration Studies, Vol. 40: 1991–2009.

Herlihy, J., Ferstman, C., and Turner, S. (2004), *Legal Issues in Work with Asylum Seekers*, in Wilson, J.P., and Drozdek, B. (eds) Broken Spirits: The Treatment of Traumatised Asylum Seekers, Refugees and War and Torture Victims, Abington: Brunner-Routledge.

Herman, J.L. (1992), *Trauma and Recovery: From Domestic Abuse to Political Terror*, Philadelphia: Perseus.

Hillyard, P., and Tombs, S. (2008), *Beyond Criminology?* in Danny D., Dave G., Hillyard, P., Pantazis, C., Pemberton, S., and Tombs, S. (eds) Criminal Obsessions: Why Harm Matters More Than Crime, London: Centre for Crime and Justice Studies.

Hillyard, P., and Tombs, S. (2017*), Social Harm and Zemiology*, in Liebling, A., Maruna, S., and McAra, L. (eds) The Oxford Handbook of Criminology, Oxford: Oxford University Press.

Hvidtfeldt, C., Peterson, J.H., and Norredam, M. (2019), *Prolonged Periods of Waiting for an Asylum Decision and the Risk of Psychiatric Diagnoses: A 22-Year Longitudinal Cohort Study from Denmark*, International Journal of Epidemiology, Online First, available https://academic.oup.com/ije/adv ance-article/doi/10.1093/ije/dyz091/5491481, last accessed 19 December 2019.

Infantino, Frederica. (2015), *Outsourcing Border Control: Politics and Practice of Outsourcing Visa Control in Morocco*, New York: Palgrave Pivot.

Kastrup, M.C., and Arcel, L.T. (2004), *Gender-Specific Treatment*, in Wilson, J.P., and Drozdek, B. (eds) Broken Spirits: The Treatment of Traumatised Asylum Seekers, Refugees and War and Torture Victims, Abington: Brunner-Routledge.

Kessler R.C., Sonnega A., Bromet E., Hughes M., and Nelson C.B. (1995), *Posttraumatic Stress Disorder in the National Comorbidity Survey*, Archives of General Psychiatry, Vol. 52: 1048–1060.

Khosravi, S. (2016), *Deportation as a Way of Life for Young Afghan Men*, in Furman, R., Epps, D., and Lamphear, G. (eds) Detaining the Immigrant Other, Oxford: Oxford University Press.

Khosravi, S. (2018), *Stolen Time*, New Statesman, June/July: 33–34.

Kinzie, J.D. (2011), *Guidelines for Psychiatric Care of Torture Survivors*, Torture, Vol. 21, No. 1: 18–26.

Masmas, T.N., Møller, E., Buhmann, C., Bunch, V., Jensen, J.H., Nørregård Hansen, T., Møller Jørgensen, L., Kjær, C., Mannstaedt, M., Oxholm, A., Skau, J., Theilade, L., Worm, L., Ekstrøm, M. (2008) *Asylum Seekers in Denmark: A Study of Health Status and Grade of Traumatization of Newly Arrived Asylum Seekers*, Torture, Vol. 18, No. 2: 77–86.

Montgomery, E., and Foldsprang, A. (2005), *Predictors of Authorities' Decision to Grant Asylum in Denmark*, Journal of Refugee Studies, Vol. 18, No. 4: 454–467.

Pantanzis, C. (2004), *Gendering Harm Through a Life Course Perspective*, in Hillyard, P., Pantazis, C., Tombs, S., and Gordon, D. (eds) Beyond Criminology: Taking Harm Seriously, pp. 192–217, London: Pluto Press.

Patel, N., and Mahtani, A. (2004), *Psychological Approaches to Rape as Torture*, in Peel, M. (ed.) Rape as a Method of Torture, Freedom from Torture.

Pemberton, S. (2015), *Harmful Societies*, Bristol: Policy Press.

Sjölund, B.H., Kastrup, M., and Montgomery, E. (2009), *Rehabilitating Torture Survivors*, Journal of Rehabilitation Medicine, Vol. 41: 698–698.

Smith, E. (2004), *Right First Time? Home Office Asylum Interviewing and Reasons for Refusal Letters*, London: Medical Foundation for the Care of Victims of Torture (now Freedom from Torture).

van Houtum, H., and van Naerssen, T. (2002), *Bordering, Ordering and Othering*, Tijdschrift voor Economische en Sociale Geografie, Vol. 93, No. 2: 125–136.

Walsh, P.W. (2019), *Migration to the UK: Asylum and Resettled Refugees*, Oxford Migration Observatory, available at https://migrationobservatory.ox.ac.uk/resources/briefings/migration-to-the-uk-asylum/, last accessed 19 December 2019.

Whyte, Z. (2011), *Enter the Myopticon: Uncertain Surveillance in the Danish Asylum System*, Anthropology Today, Vol. 27, No. 3: 18–21.

Women's Refugee Commission (2016), *Falling through the Cracks: Refugee Women and Girls in Germany and Sweden*, New York: Women's Refugee Commission.

Women's Resource Centre (2010), *Power & Prejudice—Combating Gender Inequality Through Women's Organisations*, London: Women's Resource Centre.

Yuval-Davis, N. (2006), *Belonging and the Politics of Belonging*, Patterns of Prejudice, Vol. 40, No. 3: 197–214.

7

"Starting from Scratch?": Adaptation After Deportation and Return Migration Among Young Mexican Migrants

Alexis M. Silver, Melissa A. Manzanares, and Liron Goldring

Introduction

Sometimes it's still kind of hard...Having to meet my family, my friends, and everything. And having to completely turn your life around, you know? And adapt to a completely new country that you know you're from there, but at the same time you're not because you left when you were so little...I mean, having to adjust to a new school... and getting new friends, not knowing

---

This material is based upon work supported in part by the National Science Foundation Graduate Research Fellowship Program under Grant No. (DGE-1650116). Any opinions, findings, and conclusions or recommendations expressed in this material are those of the authors and do not necessarily reflect the views of the National Science Foundation.

A. M. Silver (✉) · L. Goldring
Purchase College, State University of New York, Harrison, NY, USA
e-mail: alexis.silver@purchase.edu

M. A. Manzanares
University of North Carolina, Chapel Hill, NC, USA

© The Author(s), under exclusive license to Springer Nature Switzerland AG 2021
M. Bhatia and V. Canning (eds.), *Stealing Time*,
https://doi.org/10.1007/978-3-030-69897-3_7

> *how to talk Spanish… in that way was kind of hard* – Belinda,[1] *young adult migrant who grew up in Atlanta, Georgia, USA*

Having spent her childhood and adolescence in the United States, Belinda described how moving back to her birth country, Mexico, meant building a new life. Like other young adult migrants who return to their countries of birth, Belinda struggled to find her footing. She did not feel comfortable speaking Spanish, and she faced a gauntlet of barriers when she attempted to enroll in school and find employment. Similarly, Rafael, a young migrant from Chicago, described moving back to Mexico after spending most of his life in the US as "starting from scratch."

Young migrants like Belinda and Rafael who were brought to the US by their parents never made calculated decisions to migrate away from their countries of birth. The term "return migration" suggests that migrants are returning to their homeland after a sojourn or long period of residence abroad. Though this is technically true for young migrants who spent their formative years in the US, their return journeys often bring them back to an unfamiliar birth country where they have few memories or social connections. Nonetheless, young migrants who were raised in the US are returning to Mexico in increasing numbers due largely to a hostile US climate that increasingly constrains their opportunities and endangers their safety.

Despite their embeddedness in US communities, young migrants find themselves vulnerable to detention and deportation, particularly as immigration enforcement has intensified since the mid-2000s (Golash-Boza 2015; Kanstroom 2012). Fears of deportation and lack of opportunity can bring chronic anxiety to the lives of unauthorized and liminally legal migrants (De Genova 2010; Gonzales and Chavez 2012; Menjívar and Abrego 2012). This "legal violence" (Menjívar and Abrego 2012) can compel young migrants to flee hostile surroundings in search of the security of citizenship in their countries of birth. Although these departures are technically voluntary, it is more accurate to describe them as "coercively volunteered" or "compelled" (Canning 2019a; Cassarino 2008). Others are returned forcibly through deportation. For both groups, the

---

[1] All names are pseudonyms.

transition to life in their birth countries is fraught with complications as they face substantial barriers to incorporation and lose precious time while attempting to establish a sense of normalcy.

Even with the benefits of citizenship, young adult migrants often lose time and money as they struggle to navigate their new surroundings, validate educational credentials from the US, and establish careers for themselves. Relying on interview data with 48 migrants who grew up at least in part in the US, this chapter examines adaptation among young migrants who felt compelled or forced to return, or were deported to their birth country of Mexico. We argue that in an era of "mass deportation" (Golash-Boza 2015), both compelled and deported migrants lose valuable time and money as they struggle to build new lives away from their foundations in the US. Although many gradually adapt, these migrants nonetheless suffer irrecoverable losses.

New Pathways of Return

Many young adults who spent their formative years in host countries never imagined migrating to their countries of birth, and only decided to return when faced with threats of deportation and limited opportunities for advancement due to their lack of authorized immigration status. Without access to higher education or formal job opportunities, many young migrants return under highly constrained circumstances.

For migrants with strong ties to origin countries, return migration ideally allows returnees to reunite with family members and regain a sense of comfort. However, research finds that return migration experiences are often more complicated, even for those who return voluntarily (Cassarino 2004; Gmelch 1980; Kuschminder 2017). Many return migrants feel disoriented upon return as they find that the communities they emigrated from have changed since their departures (Dumon 1986). This lack of familiarity is likely even more pronounced for young adult migrants who often have few memories, if any, of their countries of birth and returned under forced or constrained circumstances.

Despite culture shock and potential trauma surrounding their departures, young returnees and deportees may also find pathways toward adaptation. The ability of migrants to adapt in their country of birth is influenced by a set of factors including their preparedness, human capital, economic resources, the circumstances of their return and the context of reception (Cassarino 2008; Dingeman 2018). Additionally, the reintegration of migrants can also be impacted by the state contexts on both sides of the border as well as institutional and familial contexts in both places (Hagan and Wassink 2020). Finally, adaptation is also impacted by available opportunities in the local economies in the state of return (Hagan and Wassink 2020).

Young return migrants and deportees who grew up in the US are in unique social and economic positions. The length of residence in a host country is likely to influence whether migrants gain skills and resources abroad that can be utilized in their communities of return (Dustmann 2003; King 1986). Though some migrants may experience difficulty transferring skills gained abroad due to mismatched market opportunities or social or geographic limitations (Hagan, Hernández-León, and Demonsant 2015), migrants who grew up in the US generally return to Mexico with transferable capital in the form of English language skills and higher than average levels of education. However, they often lack formal job training due to their young ages during their residence in the US. Moreover, longer stays abroad also contribute to the attenuation of ties to migrants' birth countries as migrants orient themselves increasingly toward host countries (Dingeman 2018; Hernández-León et al. 2020; Waldinger 2015). Thus, while young migrants may be able to transfer valuable skills gained in the US, their lack of social and institutional connections in Mexico may slow their ability to apply those skills, achieve mobility, and experience social membership.

While return migrants can improve their prospects for successful incorporation by mobilizing resources prior to return (Cassarino 2008), not all migrants return voluntarily and thus are unable to prepare for the journey. In the context of mass deportation (Golsh-Boza 2015), return to one's country of birth exposes migrants, and particularly deportees, to alienation and poverty (Bhatt and Roberts 2012; Brotherton and Barrios 2011; Coutin 2016; Golash-Boza, 2015). Rather than finding comfort in their countries of birth, people who were deported can feel "exiled" to their supposed homelands (Coutin 2016). Moreover, they often find themselves exploited for global capital gain by providing cheap, exploitable labor to transnational corporations (Anderson 2015; Golash-Boza 2015). Research has powerfully indicated that the vast machinery of deportation strips unauthorized migrants of personhood rights by essentially positioning them as exploitable and removable workers with limited agency over their cross-border movements (De Genova 2010; Golash-Boza 2015).

For deported individuals, lack of autonomy can continue in their countries of birth as they find themselves facing limited opportunities for free development, movement, and work. Previous scholarship has termed this lack of agency as "autonomy harm," describing how the vast majority of working-class individuals face a litany of autonomy harms as they find themselves exploited by capitalist systems that alienate them from their own work and self-development (Pemberton 2016). Lacking agency over their movements and life trajectories indicate a lack of autonomy over time as well (Canning 2019b). Migrants, when forced or compelled to leave their intended state of residence, lose time that they had allocated to spend with family, earn money or develop skills and credentials.

Additionally, forcible removal robs deported individuals of valuable time and money that they had invested in their host countries. Khosravi (2018) argues that stolen time is similar to lost capital that cannot be recouped. Furthermore, returnees do not immediately start anew upon returning to their home countries, but generally undergo a period of paralysis wherein they recover from the trauma of forced or compelled return. Those who eventually adapt nonetheless mourn the time lost with family and friends, and also lose time that they dedicated to building human capital that does not seamlessly transfer across borders.

Previous research with young deportees and migrants who grew up in the US and moved to Mexico as young adults has demonstrated that they experience frustrating periods of waiting as they struggle to translate and validate transcripts necessary for enrollment in secondary and tertiary schools, and as they face discrimination and institutional barriers to the formal labor market (Anderson 2015; Silver 2018). Nonetheless, returnees do not necessarily remain in this state of paralysis indefinitely. Recent research indicates that deported migrants in Mexico often achieve economic mobility after a period of adjustment (Hagan, Wassink, and

Castro 2019). Moreover, young migrants who grew up in the US rely on each other to form communities of belonging and find a sense of membership (Anderson 2015; Silver 2018). However, even as young migrants create pockets of belonging within broader contexts of exclusion, they continue to suffer from stolen time and agency. Moreover, many feel ostracized from the larger Mexican society, only finding security and comfort among their migrant peers. Their journeys toward incorporation thereby remain suspended in time and even space as many young migrants traverse distinct social and occupational spaces than their non-migrant peers.

Data and Methods

We collected the data for this article in Mexico during the spring of 2015 and summer of 2018. Targeting localities where recent return migrants have concentrated (Masferrer and Roberts 2012), we conducted 48 semi-structured in-depth interviews with young return migrants and deportees who had spent their childhoods and adolescence in the US. Interviews lasted from 40 min to nearly four hours, with most lasting about 90 min. During our conversations, we asked participants about their lives in the US, the circumstances that precipitated their moves or deportations to Mexico, and how they have adapted since then. Specifically, we asked about their work and school experiences in both countries, their sense of belonging and identity, and their aspirations.

We used a combination of purposeful and snowball sampling to recruit young adults who had attended at least middle and/or high school in the US and spoke English fluently. To account for regional factors that may affect migrants' incorporation processes, we conducted interviews in 8 different locations thus capturing urban areas such as Guadalajara and Mexico City (n = 30) and tourist and colonial destinations such as Sayulita and San Miguel de Allende (n = 18).

In total, we interviewed 17 women and 31 men, which roughly reflects the gender breakdown of return migrants in Mexico more generally (Márquez, Ordaz, and Li Ng 2012; Hazán 2014). Respondents had returned to Mexico at various ages, but all were bilingual at the time of the interview and most had to work hard to improve their Spanish. The mean age of the research participants was 26 years old. Respondents had spent an average of 13 years in the US and an average of 6 years in Mexico since returning. Most migrants had returned to escape the limitations of living in the US without immigration authorization (n = 27) or as a result of their own or their family members' deportations (n = 13; n = 8). Four respondents described their return as "voluntary" but two of these respondents also reported constraints they faced living in the US without citizenship. In order to protect the identities of the persons interviewed, all names have been replaced with pseudonyms.

Uprooted, Paralyzed and Lost in Transition

Participants in this study by and large recalled growing up in the US fondly. They discussed their childhood toys, middle school field trips, graduation, and their first jobs. They had developed strong relationships with their US-based relatives, classmates, teachers, and coworkers. Some had started families of their own. In short, they had built lives in the US, and few had considered ever returning to Mexico. As they aged into adulthood, however, many realized they could not develop to their full potential without authorized immigration status, and others became entangled in the wide net of immigration enforcement. Thus, both deported and compelled returnees were forced to reimagine their futures in Mexico.

Several of the young adults in this study were taken by their parents to the US as infants. And while others had spent more of their childhoods in Mexico, few had visited their birth country since moving to the US. Thus, respondents had limited memories of Mexico. Moreover, about a quarter of the returnees in this study were deported. While deportees' long-term educational and occupational trajectories did not significantly differ from the other migrants in our study, the months immediately following their returns were often more challenging. Given their abrupt and unplanned returns, people who were deported were unable to prepare mentally or materially for building a new life in Mexico.

Those who were detained prior to deportation lost weeks and months in detention. This time can never be recovered. Moreover, many experienced threats, abuse, and a total lack of autonomy while in detention, which made their adaption once in Mexico far more challenging. For example, Santiago was deported after he drove through a traffic checkpoint without a license in Los Angeles. At 22, he had not visited Mexico for over a decade. He describes the process of returning as jarring: "One day I just woke up and got deported and then [the] next [thing I know] I'm in Mexico, so it's really hard for your brain to actually process that. The peso, the food, the weather, it's really hard. From one day to another that you're in another country. It takes time." While in detention, Santiago could not plan his return to Mexico. He thus felt a sense of whiplash upon being thrust into another country and culture when he was deported.

While in detention, Santiago felt as though time was not his own. As others have meticulously detailed (Canning 2019a; Khosravi 2009, 2018), individuals in detention lose autonomy over their time, their activities, and their daily routines. For Santiago, the scars of the abuse as well as the manipulation of his time continued to haunt him. He recalled that the guards at the detention center would question him about the whereabouts of his parents, "in the morning or at night, or at dawn or two or three in the morning." He continued, "They would do it randomly, just to see if they would catch me off guard." The lack of autonomy over his time scarred him emotionally. Not only could he not plan or prepare for his move back to Mexico; he also lacked the ability to plan his daily movements down to his own sleep and wake patterns. For Santiago, and others who endured months in detention prior to deportation, the trauma of detention and stolen time followed them to Mexico.

Like Santiago, Boris was completely unprepared to begin his new life in Mexico when he was deported from Arizona after several minor driving infractions. He explained:

> I never thought of coming to Mexico before I got deported. I don't know. I went in panic. I didn't know where to go. I didn't even know where I was from. I had to call my mom. I stayed over a week in Nogales in the

bus station [where I was deported to] because to be honest, I didn't know where to go. I didn't know where to run.

Boris lost a week of time while he remained in a bus station paralyzed with uncertainty. His entire life as he had known it in the US collapsed when he was deported, and he found himself immobilized from the trauma upon arrival in Mexico. After he spoke with his mother who connected him with his grandfather in San Miguel de Allende, he began to move again, but his journey to reunite with his extended family was not a smooth one.

In his first failed attempt to navigate the bus system in Mexico, Boris passed through San Miguel de Allende without realizing it, and ended up in Leon. Lost, he returned to Nogales, again passing by San Miguel on the way, before eventually making it to his grandparents' house in San Miguel several days later. Once in San Miguel, Boris continued to get lost in the city and would have to call his relatives to give him directions or take taxis to get back to his grandparents' house. Thus, even after arriving to his destination following his deportation, Boris continued to feel uprooted and lost for months after his return.

Nearly all of the deported and compelled returnees described similar struggles as they lost both time and money trying to get their bearings in their new communities of residence. They explained that it took them months, and sometimes years, to learn their new neighborhoods and establish a sense of safety and belonging. However, even as the shock of starting a new life started to recede, obstacles to structural incorporation remained.

Struggling to Overcome Language Barriers and Access Education

The initial challenges that young migrants faced upon arrival in Mexico were exacerbated by language barriers. Nearly everyone we interviewed reported struggling to learn Spanish, and this lack of Spanish fluency obstructed their educational development and career prospects. Returning to Mexico at 14, after living approximately a decade in the

Atlanta, Priscila recounted that she only knew "the basics" of Spanish and had trouble expressing her thoughts. Priscila returned unexpectedly with her family after her brother was deported. Unsurprisingly, she described this time of her life as challenging and explained "there were times when I didn't even want to go back to school because I just didn't understand what they were doing." Though she was on an advanced math track in the US, in Mexico she was one of the lowest-performing students because she could not understand the lessons taught in Spanish. She felt as though her academic development moved backward instead of forward as she embarked on her studies in Mexico.

When Priscila moved from the US to Mexico, she experienced an interruption in her education that stalled and arguably stunted her intellectual growth as she adjusted to her new school and language. Instead of continuing her schooling in the US, where she was on a college preparatory trajectory, she returned to Mexico to complete high school. Though she enrolled in college after high school, financially it made more sense for her to work, and she dropped out of college. She explained, "I was in college for about 5 months, but then I got a really good job offer because of the whole English [thing] so it was like, I could either … go to school or work." Her fluent English facilitated Priscila's move into a relatively well-paid position in a call center, but this job security came at the cost of her educational attainment. Although it is not certain whether she would have been able to enroll in college in the US without immigration authorization, her migration history impacted her educational attainment in Mexico for different reasons. And while her position at the call center was well-paid compared to her peers who did not speak English, she was limited in her opportunities for growth without a college degree. Furthermore, her pay in Mexico was far less than what it would have been if she were working in a similar position and with the same company in the US (Anderson 2015).

Similar to Priscila, other young migrants who moved back to Mexico after traversing the US school system also experienced backslides. Mario, who returned to Mexico because he could not afford to finish college in the US, describes how he struggled to complete academic work and find a good job in Mexico due to his challenges with Spanish:

Obviously, my English is better as far as writing and reading, because most of my education was in the US...When I got here from the US, it wasn't good. Like my writing level was a 5th grader. 4th grader. It wasn't at the level that I was supposed to be [at] to live in Mexico City, to work in Mexico City.

Beyond needing to communicate in Spanish to navigate their new communities and build relationships, these language skills were necessary to navigate schooling in Mexico. Furthermore, fluency in Spanish continued to be consequential to securing desirable jobs in which they used both English and Spanish on a daily basis.

Indeed, while migrants often credited their ability to secure jobs to their English skills, fluency in both languages was necessary for their adaption and mobility in Mexico. Thus, learning English in the US, and improving their Spanish after returning to Mexico proved to be a valuable investment of these returnees' time. That said, lacking fluency in Spanish also impeded some return migrants' plans, particularly their ability to continue their education uninterrupted. In this sense, their compelled or forced returns also robbed them of the ability to advance due lengthy, and sometimes indefinite, interruptions in their educational trajectories.

Of course, many of the individuals we interviewed were also unable to realize their educational aspirations in the US due to the inability to secure financial aid or as a result of fears surrounding their lack of post-college opportunities without immigration authorization in the US. Returning to Mexico, however, did not facilitate easy transitions into the educational system in their country of birth. To continue their educations in Mexico, they needed to have their transcripts from the United States validated and translated. This process often took several months in which returnees were not able to move forward with their goals.

Though a small number of migrants (n = 7) were able to resume their educations in Mexico with minimal delays, most who continued their educations waited at least a few months for their transcripts to be validated. Moreover, not all migrants were successful in having their education recognized. Though Miguel nearly completed high school in Michigan, many of his US elective classes, such as physical education and cooking, did not transfer. He was required to repeat two years of schooling, but he explained that it took three years since he "barely knew any Spanish" upon returning to Mexico.

Other returnees were unaware that they could transfer educational credentials across countries and thus spent years redoing their schooling. Brought to the United States when he was one and half years old, Abraham enjoyed school in Texas and was proud to be part of a high school program called Genesys, which provided academic counseling and a generous scholarship upon completion. He explained that neither his mother or sister attended high school, and he wanted to make his mother proud by finishing high school for her. However, Abraham's plans to complete high school were derailed when he and his mother returned to Mexico to attend to a family emergency when Abraham was a high school sophomore. Not aware that he could transfer his education credentials from the US, he spent his first two years in Mexico going to school with adults to demonstrate completion of his elementary and middle school education. Though he was eligible to start high school in Mexico, he explained, "by that time, I was already 17. And I was like 'Well, I'm already working. I'm already making money. I don't need school. So, it's fine [that I don't complete] school. Besides, I'm making fair money anyways.' Until I realized I wasn't. You know?".

After five years in Mexico, Abraham achieved economic advancement despite having not completed high school. Indeed, he was able to shift from labor-intensive work in the clothing industry to call center employment where he utilized his bilingual skills. He also completed Hola <code/>, a software engineering program helping return migrants gain valuable coding skills. He hoped to leverage these skills to secure a higher-paying job in the technology industry like other Hola <code/> students had before him.

Though Abraham experienced impressive mobility since returning to Mexico, he also lost a considerable amount of time along with highly significant adolescent experiences such as attending school and socializing with his peers. Not only was he unable to seamlessly resume his high school education, he also spent an additional two years redoing his elementary and middle school education. In total, he lost three years to only be able to demonstrate in Mexico a lower education level than the one he achieved in the United States. In this sense, the forward momentum he had achieved in the US not only stalled, but also reversed upon his return to Mexico.

In addition to facing bureaucratic obstacles to education, some migrants were unable to immediately resume their educations because they lacked the Spanish proficiency required to succeed in school. For example, Rafael and Belinda, who had both grown up in the US from very young ages, felt it necessary to postpone their schooling a year so that when they resumed they could keep up with their Mexican peers. Though this time improving their Spanish can be considered time invested given how crucial Spanish is for return migrants' incorporation and mobility, if Rafael and Belinda were able to stay in the United States, they could have accomplished their educational goals more quickly. Nonetheless, mastering Spanish helped them succeed in school and improved their employment prospects.

In contrast, Miguel and Abraham faced barriers beyond their control to completing their educations. Time waiting for transcripts to be validated, spent on replacing US coursework that did not transfer, or redoing years of schooling resulted in precious time lost. Instead of contributing to returnees' advancement, time waiting for administrative processes or repeating years of education was effectively time stolen.

Combined, Miguel, Abraham, Rafael and Belinda lost a total of eight years making up school, waiting for educational credentials to transfer, or working on improving their Spanish prior to enrolling in school. Though their circumstances varied, nearly all of the returnees who continued their educations in Mexico waited at least a few months to have their US transcripts or diplomas verified. In addition to needing their official US transcripts, they also needed to have registrars' signatures notarized and receive Apostilles from the state governments in which they were notarized. Once the documents were presented in Mexico, they needed to be translated by Mexican school officials who then evaluated whether the students' coursework would transfer.

A seamless transfer into the school system would ease the adjustment period for Mexican nationals, yet many Mexican-born individuals who grew up in the US encountered layers of obstacles that impeded and sometimes blocked their entrance into school in Mexico in spite of their citizenship. The Apostille system is confusing and tedious, and many respondents were asked to demonstrate their elementary and middle school diplomas even though they had graduated from high school. Several returnees spent months and sometimes years, replacing coursework that did not transfer. Given the complexity of transferring their education credentials, it is not surprising that some returnees abandoned their efforts to validate their US educations and either redid their schooling or set aside their educational aspirations entirely.

Traversing Bumpy Roads Toward Upward Mobility

Just as many returnees and deportees were unprepared to navigate schooling in Mexico, most also returned without clear plans for employment. Upon arrival in Mexico, they found themselves struggling to envision new lives for themselves in a country that felt foreign to them. For example, Miguel had planned on working full-time for his parents' clothing company in the US after graduating from high school. However, his family could not renew their visas and they were forced to return to Mexico. Though he eventually graduated high school in Mexico, he faced significant delays repeating coursework that did not transfer. His difficulties continued after high school as he began to seek work. He explained:

> Finding a job also [was difficult] because it's like "What have you done so far?" "I was in the States!" It's like "Yeah, but, like, professionally?" It's like "Well, not really [anything] because I had another kind of thought for my life." Another path that I was going to. And then it's like you get moved. Everything gets moved around. And it's like you're standing in a place you don't know. So that also makes it difficult.

After returning to his country of birth, Miguel felt as though the ground shifted beneath his feet at every important milestone.

Like Miguel, many young return migrants and deportees lacked work histories from both their birth and host countries. They also lacked preparation and long-term planning for life and work in Mexico. Thus, their adaptions after return depended more heavily on their ability to transfer language skills and cultural knowledge.

Indeed, nearly all interviewees discussed how their English skills and knowledge of American culture made them desirable candidates for particular jobs. In tourist regions, returnees found employment in hotels, restaurants, and other service positions predominantly catering to American visitors. In Mexico City and Guadalajara, returnees worked in call centers or more advanced administrative and sales positions serving English-speaking clients. Thus, while having work histories in Mexico or the United States surely helps return migrants secure employment, nearly all of the young returnees and deportees in this study benefited more directly from skills learned outside of the employment context.

Some found work easily, but others discussed struggling to find employment because they lacked connections to potential employers. This was the case for Boris. After Boris was deported, he returned to San Miguel and applied for a job at a hotel in the historic tourist center of the city. Lacking recommendations, however, he was not offered the position, and he settled for work at a car wash. From there, he leveraged prior knowledge about pool cleaning to get a job at a different, less central, hotel. He then proceeded to find a better position at a nicer hotel, before finally obtaining a job at a restaurant closer to his house. He explained that he secured his last two positions through recommendations from friends who worked at each establishment. He credits his comparatively high wages to both the work history he built in Mexico and the connections he gradually made over several years:

> I think that to get inside of a good job here in San Miguel, you gotta get recommended. You can't go inside…say a store, a restaurant, a hotel, motel, and show 'em your currículum [resume]…and expect to get a good job. You gotta have somebody inside there bring you in. Because otherwise they won't hire you. That's how it is in [the restaurant I work in now], to be honest.

As indicated by Boris, while returnees may possess qualities desired by employers such as being fluent in English and being able to relate to

American clients, these skills are often insufficient to get hired. Building a work history in Mexico and having connections are important to finding employment, with the latter cited more frequently by returnees. For example, Abraham found out about Hola <code/>, a coding program for returnees and deportees, through a friend. Similarly, Belinda learned from a previous colleague of a position available at the telecommunications corporation where he worked, which was more secure and paid better than her previous call center job. Because most of the young migrants in this study arrived in Mexico with limited work histories, they thus relied to a greater extent on transferable skills and social ties to find employment. Though migrants ultimately benefited from the social networks they formed, forging these connections took time.

Young returnees were grateful that their networks eventually helped them find employment, but several also emphasized how in the months immediately following return, they were isolated and lacked knowledge of the Mexican labor market. In particular, many return migrants were initially unaware of how they could take advantage of their bilingual and bicultural skills. For example, Ezequiel was deported to Mexico for a minor driving infraction shortly after completing high school. As he never planned to move, he did not have savings he could rely upon when he arrived in Mexico. Though his mother provided him a small amount of money to get established, it was not enough. He explained:

> [My mom] thought that I had money saved up when I got deported and I didn't. So, she sent me some money… [and] I had to make just that one thousand pesos last for a whole month. So at that point in time, I just I had to go out and shine shoes…until one of my cousins asked what I was doing for work and I told him that I was shining shoes. I mean the first day [I made] 20 pesos. I had no idea about call centers. And he told me "You're wasting your time. You need to work in a call center." I didn't have a clue about call centers.

Ezequiel was fortunate to have access to family housing when he arrived in Mexico. Thus, while he did not save for his return and was making very meager money shining shoes following his deportation, he was able to get by. It was not until he learned of call center employment through his cousin, however, that he was able to secure a living wage.

Like previous research has found (Anderson 2015; Golash-Boza 2015), several returnees expressed frustration about the monotonous, impersonal, and emotionally demanding nature of call center work, but others mentioned enjoying their jobs. They connected to other returnees and made better salaries than their non-migrant friends and relatives. Though call centers provided earnings and community to many migrants after compelled return or deportation, migrants' limited opportunities outside this line of work also suggests a powerful lack of autonomy in their occupational trajectories. Not one of the migrants we interviewed mentioned hoping to work in a call center or had even heard about call centers prior to returning to Mexico. Similarly, none had long-term ambitions of remaining in call center work. Though the communities they formed were meaningful to their lives, the work, by and large, was not. Just as many put their lives on hold while they waited to validate their educational credentials or redo their schooling, many put their occupational aspirations on hold to make money in a call center while figuring out how they might find a more fulfilling job in the future.

Telecommunications jobs, moreover, were only available in cosmopolitan cities, and were thus only accessible to those who lived close to urban areas. Though nearly all returnees initially moved into a relative's house upon returning to Mexico, many of their families lived in remote parts of the country that provided few opportunities for them to take advantage of the skills they gained in the United States. For example, Yolanda, who returned from Arizona after her father was arrested for driving under the influence of alcohol, initially returned to her family's ranch. Mario, who left Arizona after struggling to renew his student visa, first moved to his parents' small beach town. Finally, Emiliano, who was deported from Chicago after various legal issues involving reckless driving, moved to his grandparents' town in the heavily forested terrain of Campeche. Having limited opportunities for employment and advancement, all three of them moved to Guadalajara or Mexico City where they could garner higher wages. Others, however, lacked the means to move out of their extended families' homes and thus endured hours-long commutes each day to cities where they could find better paying work.

In summary, returnees struggled to find employment for four reasons. First, having arrived in the US from Mexico as children and adolescents, returnees often lacked work histories in both countries. Second, even though returnees held valuable language skills and cultural capital that were transferable across borders, their lack of connections to potential employers hindered their access to positions where they could apply these skills. Third, returnees' limited knowledge of the Mexican labor market resulted in many migrants working in less profitable occupations in the months following return. Finally, some returnees were unable to apply the bilingual and bicultural skills they gained in the US in their families' hometowns where they initially moved after they returned.

Compared to their educational journeys, it is less clear how much time and money migrants lost due to the barriers they faced finding employment in Mexico. Returnees and deportees were mostly in their late teens or twenties upon return. Given their ages, it is unsurprising that few had extensive or high-level work experience in either the United States or Mexico prior to return. Thus, it is plausible that they would have spent comparable amounts of time in the US searching for jobs. It is also likely that returnees would have had limited connections to potential employers in the US. Many specifically stated that they left the US because their immigration status limited their employment prospects. That said, gaining connections to employers and references in Mexico took time. In this sense, returnees may have spent more time unemployed in Mexico than they would have in the US. Moreover, several returnees who had worked in the US prior to moving to Mexico noted how much easier it was for them to make money in the US working in restaurants or in construction than it was for them to make money given Mexico's weaker economy. Finally, time wasted unemployed or underemployed, even when relatively short, resulted in earnings unrealized during a period when resources were scarce and the costs of rebuilding one's life high. The economic costs of those early months after return were of course entangled with even larger emotional costs for individuals who faced layers of obstacles impeding their incorporation in Mexico.

Conclusion

The trauma of compelled or forced return weighed heavily on young returnees and deportees who struggled to advance in Mexico without the anchors of their institutional attachments and social ties in the US. Returnees and deportees lost valuable time and money as they waited to acclimate to their surroundings, improve their Spanish, transfer and validate educational credentials, and find employment. Although most of the returnees felt as though they were "starting from scratch" when they first arrived in Mexico, they ultimately found that they were able to build on the capital they gained in the US to adapt and gradually advance their educations and careers in Mexico.

Despite gradually adapting to life in Mexico, all of the participants in this study experienced considerable losses of time and autonomy as they struggled to establish themselves in their birth country. In some cases, losses in education or earning potential had not been recovered by the time that we interviewed these migrants, years after their removal or return to Mexico. As De Genova (2018) and Peutz (2006) emphasize, deportation, and we would argue compelled return, do not occupy a single moment in these migrants' trajectories. Instead, forced and compelled migration to Mexico inflicts enduring harms on migrants and their families. After years of residence in Mexico, the majority of returnees we interviewed had abandoned their desires to return to the US permanently. They emphasized how they were unwilling to return to the circumstances of living as undocumented and liminally legal migrants. They spoke at length about the lack of freedom and opportunity they felt living under a harsh climate of immigration enforcement in the US, and directly compared their freedom in Mexico to their recollections of fear and frustration in the US. Some hoped to return permanently to the US, but they emphasized that they only would do so with a visa. Thus, many noted that their mobility remained constrained, and they were not free to even visit the country where they spent their formative years and began to establish their lives.

Though many young people who had been returned or deported began developing strong connections to Mexico after years of residence, they emphasized that they did not fit seamlessly in either the US or

Mexico. They suffered stifling legal and institutional obstacles in the US, and confronted substantial social, bureaucratic, and institutional barriers to incorporation in Mexico. For some, the trauma of being forced out of the US remained fresh even after years of living in Mexico. Santiago, who was deported from Los Angeles at 22, explained that he had not adopted Mexico as his home after living there for three years. He grieved the losses that he felt, saying, "My family. My friends. My life. I feel like, [Mexico] is my country, this is where I was born. But I wasn't raised here. I didn't create anything here, so basically, I'm like an outcast here. I'm just living day to day. And over there I have my life." While he had experienced labor market incorporation and developed social networks in Mexico, he maintained that his emotional life, his sense of membership, and his roots remained firmly planted in the US. Separated from his family, Santiago felt unable to plan or envision his long-term prospects in Mexico. Instead, he condensed his lived experience of time to the present moment and only experienced his "day to day" existence.

While all migrants lost time and money as they adapted to their new lives in Mexico, individuals who endured lengthy detentions while awaiting deportation lost the most time and suffered extensive trauma. Though a thorough examination of detention is beyond the scope of this chapter, deported persons in this sample endured irrecoverable losses of time, social connections, and autonomy while in detention. They experienced lengthy periods of isolation, as well as threats of violence, rape, and family-member deportation. The time and support structures necessary to recover from this type of trauma were simply not available to the vast majority of people who had been deported.

Returnees and deportees who were separated from their families also lost support networks crucial to wellbeing, particularly during times of stress. While losses suffered from being away from educational institutions and stalls in occupational trajectories can be measured or approximated, it is impossible to quantify the costs of the time separated from family members, particularly children. And while most compelled and deported returnees slowly gained their footing in Mexico, they continued to face restrictions over their freedom of movement, their autonomy and ultimately their time.

References

Anderson, Jill. 2015. "Tagged as a Criminal": Narratives of Deportation and Return Migration in a Mexico City Call Center. *Latino Studies* 13 (1): 8–27.

Bhatt, Wasudha and Bryan R. Roberts. 2012. "Forbidden Return": Return Migration in the Age of Restriction. *Journal of Immigrant & Refugee Studies* 10 (2): 162–183.

Brotherton, David C. and Luis Barrios. 2011. *Banished to the Homeland: Dominican Deportees and their Stories of Exile*. New York: Colombia University Press.

Canning, Victoria. 2019a. Keeping up with the Kladdkaka: Kindness and Coercion in Swedish Immigration Detention. *European Journal of Criminology*. https://journals.sagepub.com/doi/abs/10.1177/1477370818820627.

Canning, Victoria. 2019b. Reimagining Refugee Rights: Addressing Asylum Harms in Britain, Denmark and Sweden. *Migration and Mobilities Bristol*. https://www.statewatch.org/news/2019/mar/uk-dk-se-reimagining-refugee-rights-asylum-harms-3-19.pdf.

Cassarino, Jean-Pierre. 2004. Theorising Return Migration: A Revisited Conceptual Approach to Return Migrants. *International Journal on Multicultural Studies* 6 (2): 253–279.

Cassarino, Jean-Pierre. 2008. Return Migrants to the Maghreb Countries: Reintegrations and Development Challenges. Rober Schuman Centre for Advanced Studies, European University Institute, Florence. https://cadmus.eui.eu/handle/1814/9050.

Coutin, Susan B. 2016. *Exiled Home: Salvadoran Transnational Youth in the Aftermath of Violence*. Durham, N.C.: Duke University Press.

De Genova, Nicholas. 2010. The Deportation Regime: Sovereignty, Space, and the Freedom of Movement. In *The Deportation Regime: Sovereignty, Space, and the Freedom of Movement*, eds. Nicholas De Genova and Nathalie M. Peutz, 33–65. Durham: Duke University Press.

De Genova, Nicholas. 2018. Deportation: The Last Word? In *After Deportation: Ethnographic Perspectives*, ed. Shahram Khosravi, 253–266. Palgrave Macmillan. https://www.palgrave.com/gp/book/9783319572666.

Dingeman, Katie. 2018. Segmented Re/Integration: Divergent Post-Deportation Trajectories in El Salvador. *Social Problems* 65 (1): 116–134.

Dumon, W. 1986. Problems Faced by Migrations and Their Family Members, Particularly Second Generation Migrants, in Returning to and Reintegrating into Their Countries of Origin. *International Migration* 24 (1): 113–128.

Dustmann, Christian. 2003. Return Migration, Wage Differentials, and the Optimal Migration Duration. *European Economic Review* 47 (2): 353–369.

Gmelch, George. 1980. Return Migration. *Annual Review of Anthropology* 9:135–159.

Golash-Boza, Tanya M. 2015. *Deported: Immigrant Policing, Disposable Labor, and Global Capitalism.* New York: New York University Press.

Gonzales Roberto G and Leo R. Chavez. 2012. Awakening to a nightmare. *Current Anthropology* 53 (3): 255–281.

Hagan, Jacqueline Maria, Rubén Hernández-León, and Jean-Luc Demonsant. 2015. *Skills of the "Unskilled": Work and Mobility among Mexican Migrants.* Oakland, California: University of California Press.

Hagan, Jacqueline, Joshua Wassink, and Brianna Castro. 2019. A Longitudinal Analysis of Resource Mobilisation among Forced and Voluntary Return Migrants in Mexico. *Journal of Ethnic and Migration Studies* 45 (1): 170–189.

Hagan, Jacqueline Maria, and Joshua Thomas Wassink. 2020. Return Migration Around the World: An Integrated Agenda for Future Research. *Annual Review of Sociology* 46 (1). https://doi.org/10.1146/annurev-soc-120319-015855.

Hazán, Miryam. 2014. Understanding Return Migration to Mexico: Towards a Comprehensive Policy for the Reintegration of Returning Migrants. Working Paper 193. San Diego, CA: Center for Comparative Immigration Studies. https://ccis.ucsd.edu/_files/wp193.pdf.

Hernández-León, Rubén, Víctor Zúñiga, and Sarah M. Lakhani. 2020. An Imperfect Realignment: The Movement of Children of Immigrants and Their Families from the United States to Mexico. *Ethnic and Racial Studies* 43 (1): 80–98. https://doi.org/10.1080/01419870.2019.1667508.

Kanstroom, Dan. 2012. *Aftermath: Deportation Law and the New American Diaspora.* Oxford: Oxford University Press.

Khosravi, Shahram. 2009. Sweden: Detention and Deportation of Asylum Seekers. *Race & Class* 50 (4): 38–56. https://doi.org/10.1177/0306396809102996.

Khosravi, Shahram, ed. 2018. *After Deportation: Ethnographic Perspectives.* Global Ethics. Palgrave Macmillan. https://www.palgrave.com/gp/book/9783319572666.

King, Russell. 1986. *Return Migration and Regional Economic Problems.* London: Croom Helm Ltd.

Kuschminder, Katie. 2017. *Reintegration Strategies: Conceptualizing How Return Migrants Reintegrate.* Palgrave Macmillan.

Márquez, Adolfo Albo, Ordaz Díaz, Juan Luis, and Li Ng, Juan José. 2012. Inserción Laboral y Características de Los Migrantes Mexicanos de Retorno 2005–2011. Comparación Urbana-Rural. In *El Estado de La Migracion: México Ante Los Recientes Desafíos de La Migración Internacional*, eds. Telésforo Ramírez García, and Manuel Ángel Castillo, 237–269. México, D.F.: Consejo Nacional de Población. https://www.researchgate.net/public ation/269633676_Insercion_laboral_y_caracteristicas_de_los_migrantes_ mexicanos_de_retorno_2005-2011_Comparacion_urbana-rural.

Masferrer, Claudia, and Bryan Roberts. "Going Back Home? Changing Demography and Geography of Mexican Return Migration." *Population Research & Policy Review* 31, no. 4 (August 2012): 465–496. https://doi. org/10.1007/s11113-012-9243-8.

Menjívar, Cecilia and Leisy J. Abrego. 2012. Legal Violence: Immigration Law and the Lives of Central American Immigrants. *American Journal of Sociology* 117 (5): 1380–1421.

Pemberton, Simon. 2016. *Harmful Societies: Understanding Social Harm.* Bristol: Policy Press.

Peutz, Nathalie. 2006. Embarking on an Anthropology of Removal. *Current Anthropology* 47 (2): 217–241. https://doi.org/10.1086/498949.

Silver, Alexis M. 2018. Displaced at "Home": 1.5-Generation Immigrants Navigating Membership after Returning to Mexico. *Ethnicities* 18 (2): 208–224.

Waldinger, Roger D. 2015. *The Cross-Border Connection: Immigrants, Emigrants, and Their Homelands.* Cambridge, Mass.: Harvard Univ. Press.

8

The Mexico City Runaround: Temporal Barriers to Rebuilding Life After Deportation

Ruth Gomberg-Muñoz

Introduction

Left to fend for themselves, deportees in Mexico City have done just that: establishing community organizations to help fellow deportees navigate the bureaucratic maze of reinscription in Mexican society. As "Deportees United in Struggle," they work to provide clear and accurate information regarding Mexican identity documents and social programs, they help deportees secure necessary documentation and access public services, and they advance policy recommendations to streamline Mexican government programs ostensibly designed to help deportees like them. As they work to reduce deportees' wasted time, they draw on their life experiences as undocumented migrants, deportees, and citizens in their homelands to assert belonging and rebuild their lives.

R. Gomberg-Muñoz (✉)
Department of Anthropology, Loyola University Chicago, Chicago, IL, USA
e-mail: rgombergmunoz@luc.edu

Twenty to Life

When Ana Laura López was deported to Mexico in December of 2016, her only thought was to get back to the United States as quickly as possible. She had lived in Chicago for nearly twenty years and deportation separated her from her house, job, partner, and two young children. In hopes of preventing such a separation, Ana Laura had decided to pursue an application for a U.S. immigrant visa but was required to file the application at a U.S. consulate in Mexico. As she waited on the jet bridge at Chicago's O'Hare airport to board a plane bound for Mexico City, two U.S. Border Patrol agents took her into custody. The agents brought her to an office and informed Ana Laura that she either had to sign a "voluntary departure" or they would place her indefinitely in immigrant detention. Ana Laura signed, and the agents escorted her back to the very same flight to Mexico she had been attempting to board in the first place.

Stunned, Ana Laura landed in Mexico City determined to return to her family. She called immigrant-rights advocates in Chicago, spoke with lawyers, and even asked her U.S. employer to help. But the Border Patrol agents had barred Ana Laura from returning to the United States for 20 years, and there was nothing that anyone could do to change that. After months of futile attempts to fight her deportation and the 20-year bar, Ana Laura began to build a life for herself in Mexico City.

While Ana Laura's spatial displacement as a result of deportation was apparent and jarring, her experience was also permeated with temporal concerns. Her life in Chicago, while prolonged and full, was ultimately temporary. The very durability of her Chicago residence made life in Mexico seem impossible at first; only time convinced her otherwise. In order to expedite her deportation, U.S. Border Patrol agents used the threat of indefinite time in detention to compel Ana Laura to sign away her rights. And her final punishment? A bar on U.S. re-entry that separates Ana Laura from her partner and children for at least 20 years.

Prolonged delays, processing inefficiencies, and indefinite detention stays have been interpreted by migration scholars as important components of migrant governance and policing in the contemporary period (Andersson 2014; Gomberg-Muñoz 2016; Khosravi 2018b). Here, I show that the temporal disruptions caused by deportation do not end with expulsion. Instead, Ana Laura and Mexican deportees like her find themselves hindered in their ability to build post-deportation lives in their country of citizenship. The barriers they face are related to the amount of time they spent in the United States: deportees whose absence from Mexico was relatively brief may be able to return to homes, jobs, and families with relative ease. But most, including Ana Laura, have spent a decade or more in the United States and need to attain Mexican identity documents, apply for housing and jobs, transfer educational and training credentials, file for custody and/or dual citizenship for U.S.-born children, and otherwise reincorporate themselves into Mexican society. When they attempt these processes, deportees encounter governmental inefficiency, lag time, apathy, and long delays, which combine to create the "Mexico City Runaround," a period during which deportees' time is systematically wasted and their efforts to rebuild their lives are indefinitely stalled.

An emergent scholarship of removal (Peutz 2006) has theorized deportation as a politics of exclusion that culminates in the expulsion of people from the national territory, resulting in their alienation, abjection, and even "political death" (e.g., De Genova and Peutz 2010; Foucault 1992 cited in Walters 2010; Kanstroom 2010, 2012; Khosravi 2018a; Nyers 2010; Walters 2010). Yet for most people, deportation is not a final endpoint; it also marks the beginning of protracted struggle to build meaningful post-deportation lives (see e.g., Boehm 2016; Coutin 2016; Hasselberg 2018; Khosravi 2018a; Rodkey 2018). While analyses of state practices of deportation have tended to focus on the nation-state from which people are expelled, deportees' interactions with state agents continue long after they are deported. Mexican deportees interface with both national and international agencies at various points during and after their deportation: in addition to their detention and processing by U.S. Immigration and Customs Enforcement (ICE) agents, they may also be visited by Mexican consular officials at U.S. centers of detention and deportation; they board planes contracted by ICE and the United Nations High Commissioner for Refugees that take them to Mexico City; and they are received by agents of the *Instituto Naciónal de Migración* (National Migration Institute or INM), a branch of Mexico's

Secretaría de Gobernación (Secretary of State). In the months following their return, they visit several additional Mexican agencies to apply for identity documents and government resources; those with immediate U.S. citizen family members will probably also have ongoing exchanges with U.S. Customs and Immigration Services (USCIS) and, in custody cases of U.S.-born children, the U.S. Department of Children and Family Services (DCFS) and Mexico's *Desarollo Integral de la Familia* (Integral Family Development, or DIF). All of these interactions prolong deportees' engagement with agents of both the state of their expulsion and that of their citizenship.

The Mexican state has promoted a public face as a welcoming bastion for returning migrants, institutionalized in governmental mantras such as *Bienvenido a Casa, Paisano*! (Welcome home, countryman!) and the *Somos Mexicanos* (We Are Mexicans) program. Yet when deportees interact with Mexican agencies, they encounter bureaucratic obstacles to applying for identity documents, accessing social programs, securing dual citizenship for U.S.-born children, and attaining documents and other resources housed in the United States. If bureaucratic indifference "is the rejection of common humanity" (Herzfeld 1993, 1) and lag time a tool of migrant governance (Andersson 2014), then bureaucratic inefficiency, opacity, and delay can be interpreted as a signal to deportees that their time, and their lives, remain devalued in their country of citizenship.

This chapter builds on Khosravi's (2018a) conceptualization of abandoned citizens (see also my 2016 discussion of alienated citizenship) to explore temporal dimensions of post-deportation life in Mexico City. I draw on more than 250 semi-structured interviews with recent deportees, deportee rights advocates, and state agents that have been collected as part of a collaborative project designed and undertaken by myself, Chicago-based immigrant-rights organizers Reyna Wences, Rosi Carrasco, and Martin Unzueta, and deportee rights organizers in Mexico City: Ana Laura López of *Deportados Unidos en la Lucha* (Deportees United in Struggle or DUL), Dolores Unzueta and Adriana Sandoval of *Yaoyaotlcihuatl Ameyal* (A Well of Warriors or Ameyal), and Maggie Loredo and Esmeralda Flores of *Otros Dreams en Acción* (Other Dreams in Action or ODA). While I wrote the bulk of this chapter, the data and analyses developed here were generated as part of a team effort in which my colleagues played central roles.

Our findings suggest that one of the most significant challenges that deportees face in Mexico is bureaucratic wasting of their time. Time wasting comes in many forms: when deportees seek to file an application for documents or services at a governmental office, they stand in long lines often to be told that what they seek is housed elsewhere. They traverse the city on long rides through Mexico City's transit system, only to find that they need documents from a different place in order to be processed. Often, deportees must produce documentation from offices and employers in the United States to prove eligibility for employment, education, health care, housing, dual citizenship for children, and government services. Some officers will accept documents issued in the United States, while others will not. This happens over and over again: one document is needed to attain another, and there is no clear procedure in place nor agreement among Mexican agencies about which documents are acceptable. The difficulties inherent in navigating Mexico's bureaucratic red tape long delay deportees' abilities to rebuild their lives in their state of return.

States of Return

While the relationship of deportation with sovereign power in nation-states of expulsion is well analyzed (see e.g., De Genova 2010; Walters 2010), the ways in which states of return also mobilize and manipulate mass deportation is less well understood. For example, in recent years, the Mexican government has capitalized on mass U.S. deportation practices to create nationalist narratives of Mexico as a benevolent state (in contrast to the United States) that reaches out to help returning Mexican citizens reintegrate into Mexican society. In response to mass deportations during the Obama administration, the Mexican government instituted a program, *Somos Mexicanos* [We are Mexicans], which is supposed to help Mexican deportees attain financial security through job placement or small entrepreneurial loans, transforming them into model neoliberal citizens. But this program is fraught with barriers to access, often requiring deportees to attain documents such as letters of recommendation from past employers that are housed in the United States (Gomberg-Muñoz 2020). In addition, Mexican government agents often refuse to recognize U.S.-issued documents, such as birth certificates of U.S.-born children and educational credentials, creating additional bureaucratic barriers to resources such as dual citizenship and enrollment in Mexican schools for deportees and their children (Gomberg-Muñoz 2020; Medina and Menjivar 2015). More broadly, Mexico's narratives of benevolence obscure its own racialized politics of nationalism, criminalization of migrants and deportees, and complicity with the extension of U.S. dominion throughout Mexico via economic and foreign policies (De Genova 2010; Vogt 2013).

For "sending" states, the emigration of large numbers of workers has relieved some of the pressures of surplus labor and bolstered national economies through remittances (Coutin 2007; Hernandez and Coutin 2006; Wiltberger 2014). Even as sending states' complicity with neoliberal policies has helped to propel emigration, sending states have sought to court their "transborder citizenry" through policies such as dual citizenship and voting from abroad, as well as programs such as Mexico's 3-for-1 program, which matches migrants' remittance investments in infrastructure with state money, encouraging the sending of remittances through government channels (e.g., Coutin 2007; Glick-Schilller and Fouron 1998; Mahler 1998; Smith and Guarnizo 1998; Wiltberger 2014). Mass deportation not only involves the "return" of large numbers of migrants, but it also diminishes remittance flows; both of these processes are likely to weaken national and regional economies in the short term. Thus, for deportees, their state of citizenship has failed them twice: first in creating the circumstances that propelled their emigration in the first place, and second, in failing to provide meaningful assistance to them upon their return. This double failure is not lost on deportee rights organizers—it undergirds their critiques of neoliberal policies in Mexico. And as sending states increasingly become states of return, the question arises whether state negligence toward people who have been deported is best understood as a bureaucratic failure or as a logical response to their diminished value as failed remitters in their nations of citizenship.

For deporting states, the capacity to exclude broadly, and to bodily expel in particular, constitute and affirm state sovereignty as they imbue value to state-based citizenship (Bosniak 2006; De Genova and Peutz 2010; Peutz 2006). Thus, far from being superfluous or invisible to the state (Peutz 2006), deportees are highly symbolic instruments of nationalism whose expulsion validates claims to security and sovereignty in the nation-state of deportation, as well as narratives of national benevolence in the state of return. Immigrant policing and deportation practices also uphold and reinforce categorical inequities related to race, class, and gender, reproducing longstanding intranational and global inequalities (Golash-Boza and Hondagneu-Sotelo 2013; Gomberg-Muñoz 2015). As Andersson (2014) and Khosravi (2018b) argue, migrant policing practices control and usurp migrants' time through detention, delay, and, especially, expulsion. Deportation robs migrants of time they have invested in work, family, and community; it blocks their progression along the life course, returning them to "square one," and displacing their vision of the future (Khosravi 2018b).

While the scholarship on deportation has largely focused on the expelling nation-state, an emergent literature follows deportees to their nations of return. This research has found that deportees face a host of profound challenges to life in their nations of birth, including family separation (Drotbohm 2015; Glenn-Levin Rodriguez 2017; Hagan, Eschbach, and Rodriguez 2008; Hagan, Rodriguez, and Castro 2011), sociocultural disorientation and alienation (Boehm 2016; Coutin 2007, 2016; Golash-Boza 2015), stigmatization and criminalization (Boehm 2016; Brotherton and Barrios 2011; Coutin 2016; Golash-Boza 2015; Zilberg 2011), blocked access to social esteem (Coutin 2016), and underemployment and financial insecurity (Boehm 2016; Brotherton and Barrios 2011; Coutin 2016; Gerlach 2018); all of these ordeals are permeated with racial, gendered, and sexual inequalities (Drotbohm 2015; Gerlach 2018; Golash Boza 2015). Considering these challenges, it is not surprising that many deportees seek to re-migrate or, despairing, even take their own lives (Brotherton and Barrios 2011; Hagan, Eschbach, and Rodriguez 2008; Khosravi 2018a; Majidi 2018).

Yet deportees, like people everywhere, also prove resilient: many carve out social esteem and tenuous financial security by tapping into their cultural capital as long-term "global north" residents to find employment (Golash Boza 2015; Rodkey 2018) and create community with other return migrants (Andersson 2014; Hasselberg 2018). In Mexico City, for example, deportees like Ana Laura have formed community self-help organizations to assist new arrivals and push for changes in public policy that would reduce the time that deportees spend navigating governmental red tape in Mexico.

Deportees United in Struggle

With a population of nearly 9 million people, Mexico City is one of the largest cities in the world and the political and social capitol of Mexico. Deportees who arrive in the city find themselves adjacent to government offices, internet cafés, and emergent networks of civil organizations that offer support for return migrants, as well as private businesses that provide jobs and job training for the well-educated and English-speaking. Thus, far from being cut off from global processes, deportees in Mexico City remain highly connected to broader national and international networks. This concentration may offer some relative advantages for urban deportees over their rural counterparts, but navigating the urban landscape can be challenging and time-consuming, particularly for deportees who have spent many years in the United States and lack familiarity with Mexican society. The public transit system is efficient but sprawling and crowded, and it can take hours to traverse the city during rush hours. Streets in the city center are dense with people, buildings, and cars. Government offices are often packed, with long lines of people stretched onto the sidewalk waiting for hours to be attended. Many deportees arrive in this complex urban terrain uncertain where to go or how to begin rebuilding their lives. Their needs are varied and often urgent, and they include housing, employment, and health care.

Ana Laura co-founded Deportees United in Struggle, or DUL, in 2017 as a response to her own frustrating journey attempting to rebuild her life after deportation. When she arrived in Mexico City in 2016, Ana Laura described her first encounters with the runaround:

I didn't remember how to be in this city. I found the people hostile, unfriendly, I was used to Chicago. I was very depressed…. I looked for a place to rent. But the places would tell me, we need your INE [Instituto Nacional Electoral, or Voter ID card]. I said, but I have my passport, and they said, no we need pay stubs, we need references, we need this and that. I didn't have any of that.

It took Ana Laura more than a year to amass the documents that she would need to carve out a life in Mexico. This frustrating waste of her time prompted Ana Laura to begin organizing to help other deportees as they begin the process of establishing a bureaucratic identity in Mexico.

I met Ana Laura in the fall of 2017. I had spent that summer in Zapotlanejo, Jalisco, Mexico with a group of community organizers and students seeking to learn more about return migrants and their family members. Drawing on that experience, I worked with Loyola undergraduate Melissa Hernández to create Know-Your-Rights materials for people in the United States who want to prepare for possible return to Mexico. Among the information in those materials, we included descriptions of Mexican governmental agencies and programs that claim to provide support for deportees. But when I disseminated the materials among my contacts, a community organizer friend of mine reached out. "A lot of your information is not going to really help," he told me about the materials, "My sister Dolores works with deportees in Mexico City, and the Mexican government says it provides those resources, but in reality, they do very little to help deportees." I asked to be connected with Dolores, and the following month I traveled to Mexico City to meet with her community organization, Ameyal, as well as Ameyal's close collaborators, DUL and ODA.

Together, Dolores, Ana Laura, Chicago-based community organizers Reyna Wences, Martin Unzueta, and Rosi Carrasco, as well as members of ODA, and I designed a translocal (Mexico City/Chicago) research project aimed at understanding and facilitating the efforts of deportees and their family members as they rebuild their lives after deportation. As part of this project, we have so far conducted semi-structured interviews with more than 300 recent deportees in Mexico City that focus on understanding current U.S. immigrant policing practices and identifying the urgent needs of recent arrivals in Mexico after many years of residence in the United States.

Our interviews largely affirm existing studies of deportation (e.g., Slack 2019, Boehm 2016, see also Golash-Boza and Hondagneu-Sotelo 2013) in finding that the overwhelming majority of deportees are men (90%), lived in the United States for more than ten years (76%), and are separated from U.S. family members as a result of their deportation (75%). We also find that the overwhelming majority had been unable to make preparations prior to their deportation (85%) and arrived in Mexico to an uncertain future. In fact, 63% of the people in our sample report that they do not have permanent housing in Mexico, and 40% do not have a job. Fifty percent of recent deportees reported that they have not received any government support since their arrival, and no one who we interviewed has received benefits from the *Somos Mexicanos* program. High rates of precarious housing, unemployment, and family separation among deportees in Mexico have a variety of causes, and they are compounded by opaque, arbitrary, and dehumanizing bureaucratic practices in Mexican government agencies, which I explore in more depth next.

The Mexico City Runaround

As Ana Laura gradually accepted that she would not be able to return to Chicago and would need to build a life for herself in Mexico, she assessed her resources. She reached out to what remaining family members and friends she had in the city, and she researched employment opportunities and assistance. Her first stop was SEDEREC, the *Secretaría de Desarrollo Rural y Equidad para las Comunidades* [Secretary of Rural Development and Equity for Communities], an assistance program run by Mexico City's municipal government that has since been discontinued. SEDEREC had a job assistance program for deportees, but Ana Laura soon learned that she did not have the right documents to prove her eligibility. She recounted:

I started to look for a job, I went to SEDEREC, and they asked for my papers from ICE. They said, no we need your *certificación de repatriación* [certificate of repatriation]. I hadn't heard of any of that. They said, [this document you have] is not going to help us. It's in English. I showed them where it said removal, where it said penalty. They said no, this is not going to help us. You have to prove you arrived within a year of [today's] date. I showed them my *matricula consular* [Mexican consulate ID, in order to prove she had been in the United States], but they said no, that's not valid because it was issued more than a year ago. I showed them my passport, which luckily I had applied for before I left, so it was within the year, so they accepted that.

Even as Mexican bureaucracies delay deportees' ability to access programs and resources, they demand proof of deportees' recent arrival: only deportees who can prove they have been in Mexico for less than a year qualify for job assistance. And proving her eligibility for the program was only the first hurdle that Ana Laura had to clear. With mounting frustration, she found herself being shunted from place to place in an attempt to meet the program's bureaucratic criteria. She continued:

I had to leave [the office] and return. I didn't have the documents, I didn't have the residency documents, proof of housing. I had to look for my dad who was the only person I knew who lived in the city, and I found him and he loaned it to me, but had a million questions, what do you need it for? Are you going to get me in trouble? Oh no, no. [A]fter all that, it took two months to get my documents. I had to get a CURP [*Clave Única de Registro de Población*, Unique Population Registry Code] first, I had to investigate, what is that? How do I get one?

[A]nd you don't know. You go and get in a long line and then you get to the front and they tell you, you don't have your copies, you need to have copies. So you go get copies and then you return and have to get in the back of the line again. And I was lucky, I had my phone, I had some money. But for other people....

So then they sent me to the Employment Secretary for unemployment [insurance]. That wasn't hard, the only problem is that you have to prove that you've been looking for work. They give you a bank card [on which unemployment funds are supposed to be deposited]. But the problem is that there is never any money [on the card]. They tell you that the money is not released.

I applied in October or November for unemployment insurance [and] they said, you'll get it at the end of the year, in January. And then in January, they tell you March. "Don't worry, you'll get the total amount," but they only give you two months [worth]. By the time you get the money, you've spent it on transportation getting there and back so many times to see if the money has been released.

Ana Laura soon found that she was not alone. From educational institutions, to public hospitals, to agencies that issue identity documents, deportees describe running an endless obstacle course to get the documents they need to fill out applications for jobs, housing, schooling, and health care. As they are shunted from one office to another, forced to wait in long lines, and spend hours taking trains and busses across the city, deportees spend hours, days, weeks, and months amassing documents to meet bureaucratic criteria. After all the time they invest to qualify for programs, the resources they do qualify for, such as unemployment insurance, are inexplicably delayed.

Even programs designed specifically for deportees impose criteria that return migrants have trouble satisfying. In 2016, we visited the Office of Social Programs in Zapotlanejo, Jalisco, Mexico to ask about one 2015 government program that offered deportees modest cash assistance to invest in opening their own business. The municipal officer explained that their office was only able to identify three residents who met the documentary requirements of the program, even though nearly ten thousand people were deported to the state of Jalisco that year. Other would-be applicants, including those who were compelled to return to Mexico but not formally deported, those who left the United States in an attempt to adjust their legal status and were subsequently barred, or those who merely declined to attain or keep their deportation documents, were ineligible for the program. In another example, in late 2016, my friend Luis was deported from the United States after nearly twenty years in Chicago. Late one night as Luis watched television, he saw an ad for the *Somos Mexicanos* program. But when Luis called the number on the screen, the operator told him that he would need school transcripts and evidence of work experience to get support. "I worked in a car wash in Chicago," Luis told me, "how am I supposed to get that?".

For some people, the wait for government services proves too long. During the summer of 2019, organizers with ODA described a disturbing trend of people with grave illnesses being deported to Mexico with no plan for their follow up care. Once in Mexico, deportees who need urgent medical care face an impenetrable maze of documenting eligibility for treatment before they will be treated at public hospitals or clinics. Recently, ODA had worked with a deportee in Mexico City who died of renal disease after his deportation from the United States. The man's prolonged incarceration in a Tacoma, Washington detention center without adequate medical care worsened his illness, but the final blow was delivered by Mexican authorities who accused him of possessing fraudulent documents and denied his health insurance application. Shortly after, the man died "a completely preventable" death (La Resistencia 2019).

Not only do deportees contend with arbitrary requirements that create long delays to their own incorporation in Mexican society, their children also experience temporal interruptions to their citizenship, education, and health care. For example, U.S.-citizen children of Mexican nationals are eligible for dual citizenship. Yet when parents in Mexico attempt to access Mexican citizenship for their U.S.-born children, they face a requirement that few anticipate: they must produce their children's long-form U.S. birth certificates with an "*apostilla*," or apostille, affixed within the past year. An apostille is an official acknowledgment of the authenticity of government documents and their accompanying signatures and seals, and it allows the authority of documents issued in one nation to be recognized in another. Only birth certificates with the apostille are accepted by Mexican government authorities, who can then issue dual citizenship. But the apostilles are only affixed by specified authorities in the U.S. states where the birth certificates were issued—usually in the Secretary of State office. And because the parents are often unable to return to the United States to get their children's birth certificate "apostillada," U.S.-born children in Mexico can go for long periods of time without Mexican identity documents. During this time, they may be unable to enroll in school and ineligible for social services such as health insurance.

Without Mexican citizenship, U.S. citizen children in Mexico are left "without an identity," in the words of one parent, or "illegal in Mexico," in the words of another. One certified translator described a case in which she had translated the U.S. birth certificate of a young man into Spanish so his parents could apply for his dual citizenship. But the birth certificate lacked the apostille, and he was unable to get Mexican citizenship and enroll in Mexico's health care program. Subsequently, when the boy became gravely ill, he was refused treatment at the public hospital. Eventually, his parents took him to an urgent care clinic that would see him without insurance, and it turned out that the boy was suffering from childhood leukemia.

Because they are typically unable to travel themselves, deported parents resort to less secure, and often expensive and prolonged, ways of attaining the apostille. There are "professionals" who leverage their ability to travel internationally to courier documents such as birth certificates to the United States, and they will, for a fee, take the documents to get an apostille affixed. Parents could also mail the birth certificate to trusted family members or friends in the United States and ask them get the apostille, or they could mail the document directly to the Secretary of State's office—a process that can take months and result in lost documents. Understandably, many parents are reluctant to entrust the only proof of their child's citizenship to this process, and they are often unable to afford the fees to have the document professionally couriered. Instead, parents whose U.S.-born children are eligible for Mexican citizenship but lack the requisite documents often feel compelled to buy them fraudulent Mexican birth certificates so they can enroll the children in school and government programs. But this de facto citizenship switch leaves the children without a strong claim to their U.S. citizenship, jeopardizing potential benefits of dual citizenship down the road.

These examples demonstrate that the ability of deportees to retain possession of U.S.-issued documents, such as birth certificates, consular passports, and deportation orders is critical to their ability to receive wired money, find jobs, open accounts, access government services, and in general, reincorporate into Mexican society. Yet 2013 research by Daniel E. Martinez and Jeremy Slack found that U.S. authorities routinely seize and fail to return the possessions of deportees, including money, cell phones, and identity documents. The longer that detainees are in U.S. custody, the more likely it becomes that their documents and possessions become "lost." And one official with Mexico's *Programa Paisano* told us that U.S. Customs and Border Protection officers have begun deporting Mexican citizens through border ports of entry where the INM does not have offices, in violation of international agreement. This practice leaves deportees unable to attain their Evidence of Repatriation, delaying their registration for Mexican identity documents and government services upon their return even longer. U.S. policing practices such as these, compounded by unforgiving Mexican bureaucratic requirements, continue stealing deportees' time long after their removal from the United States.

Time Marches On

Five months after his deportation from the United States, a young man I will call Mateo went to an event for return migrants organized by the Secretariat of Labor and Social Welfare in Mexico City. He describes the event as packed with deportees just like him. He began talking with one young man about their shared frustrations, then another. He met Ana Laura, and they proposed forming a group of people who had been deported. The group began meeting twice a week to strategize about developing solutions to their common problems. They started going to the airport to provide moral support and assistance to deportees as they arrived. And to raise money for their burgeoning collective, they began selling candies and then created a print shop where they make T-shirts and bags under the *Deportados* [Deportees] Brand. They also built a shelter on the second floor of the print shop so that deportees with nowhere else to go have a safe space to sleep. Slowly, they began to build new lives in the city and time once again began moving forward. Ana Laura explained, "I am deported, but my life will go on. I will associate it with activism, with struggle, with business. I am starting over."

As deportees and deportee rights advocates, DUL members affirm their belonging in Mexico. Indeed, the tag line for the Deportados Brand is "100% Mexicano." This line is not merely an assertion of identity or citizenship, but a claim to belonging for people who routinely experience mistreatment and exclusion from the state of their citizenship. If living for many years as undocumented immigrants in the United States taught them that a lack of citizenship status leaves their time vulnerable to theft, their experiences of abandonment in Mexico have taught them that as citizens, their time is not valued, either. Indeed, much of the work of DUL and other deportee-led organizations in Mexico City and across the country is oriented toward demanding that the Mexican government provide resources in a more transparent, efficient, and timely manner.

In 2018, the U.S.-based airplanes carrying deportees destined for Mexico City were rerouted to Central America to more expeditiously deport Guatemalan, Honduran, and El Salvadoran migrants. Meanwhile, Mexico has increasingly become itself a nation of deportation in which migrants' time is stolen through kidnapping, confinement, detention, and expulsion. As organizations such as DUL work collaboratively with migrants in transit and their advocates, common experiences of displacement, immobilization, and temporal disruption become ever more apparent. In response, Ana Laura, Mateo, and their colleagues draw on and cultivate a global sensibility informed by their experiences of expulsion from one state and abandonment in another to challenge the theft of their families, their jobs, their time, and their lives.

References

Andersson, Jill. 2014. "Tagged as a Criminal": Narratives of deportation and return migration in a Mexico City call center. *Latino Studies* 13 (1): 8–27.
Andersson, Ruben. 2011. Time and the Migrant Other: European Border Controls and the Temporal Economics of Illegality. *American Anthropologist* 116 (4): 795–809.
———2014. *Ilegality Inc.: Clandestine Migration and the Business of Bordering Europe*. Berkeley: University of California Press.

Boehm, Deborah. 2016. *Returned: Going and Coming in an Age of Deportation.* Berkeley: University of California Press.
Bosniak, Linda. 2006. *The Citizen and the Alien: Dilemmas of Contemporary Membership.* Princeton: Princeton University Press.
Brotherton, David and Luis Barrios. 2011. *Banished to the Homeland: Dominican Deportees and Their Stories of Exile.* New York: Columbia University Press.
Coutin, Susan Bibler. 2016. *Exiled Home: Salvadoran Transnational Youth in the Aftermath of Violence.* Durham: Duke University Press.
———2007. *Nation of Emigrants: Shifting Boundaries of Citizenship in El Salvador and the United States.* New York: Cornell University Press.
De Genova, Nicholas. 2010. The Deportation Regime: Sovereignty, Space, and the Freedom of Movement. In *The Deportation Regime: Sovereignty, Space, and the Freedom of Movement*, edited by De Genova and Peutz, 33–68. Durham: Duke University Press.
———2005. *Working the Boundaries: Race, Space, and "Illegality" in Mexican Chicago.* Durham: Duke University Press.
———2004. The Legal Production of Mexican/Migrant "Illegality." *Latino Studies* 2: 160–185.
Drotbohm, Heike. 2015. The Reversal of Migratory Family Lives: A Cape Verdean Perspective on Gender and Sociality pre- and post-deportation. *Journal of Ethnic and Migration Studies* 41 (4): 653–670.
Gerlach, Alice. 2018. Helping Women Prepare for Removal: The Case of Jamaica. *In Life After Deportation: Ethnographic Perspectives*, edited by Shahram Khosravi, 63–80. Palgrave Macmillan.
Glenn-Levin Rodriguez, Naomi. 2017. *Fragile Families: Foster Care, Immigration, and Citizenship.* Philadelphia: University of Pennsylvania Press.
Glick Schiller, Nina, and Georges Fouron. 1998. Transnational Lives and National Identities: The Identity Politics of Haitian Immigrants. In *Transnationalism From Below*, edited by Michael Peter Smith and Luis Eduardo Guarnizo. New Brunswick: Transaction Publishers.
Golash-Boza, Tanya Maria. 2015. *Deported: Immigrant Policing, Disposable Labor, and Global Capitalism.* New York: New York University Press.
Golash-Boza, Tanya and Pierrette Hondagneu-Sotelo. 2013. Latino immigrant men and the deportation crisis: A gendered racial removal program. *Latino Studies* (11): 271–292.
Gomberg-Muñoz, Ruth. 2020. Knowing Your Rights in Trump's America: Paper Trails of Migrant Community Empowerment. In *Paper Trails:*

Migrants, Documents, and Legal Insecurity, edited by Sarah Horton and Josiah Heyman. Durham: Duke University Press.

———2016. The Juárez Wives Club: Gendered Citizenship and US Immigration Law. *American Ethnologist* 43 (2): 339–352.

Gomberg-Muñoz, Ruth. 2015. The Punishment/El Castigo: Undocumented Latinos and US Immigration Processing. *Journal of Ethnic and Migration Studies* 41 (14): 2235–2252.

Gomberg-Muñoz, Ruth and Melissa Hernández n.d. Preparing for Return. Materials prepared for distribution to community organizations helping people with pending or possible deportation cases prepare for return to Mexico.

Hagan, Jacqueline, Karl Eschbach, and Nestor Rodriguez. 2008. "U.S. deportation policy, family separation, and circular migration." *International Migration Review* 42 (1): 64–88.

Hagan, Jacqueline Maria, Nestor Rodriguez, and Brianna Castro. 2011. "Social effects of mass deportations by the United States government, 2000–10." *Ethnic and Racial Studies* 34 (8): 1374–1391.

Hasselberg, Ines. 2018. Fieldnotes from Cape Verde: On Deported Youth, Research Methods, and Social Change. In *Life After Deportation: Ethnographic Perspectives*, edited by Shahram Khosravi, 15–36. Palgrave Macmillan.

Hernandez, Ester, and Susan Bibler Coutin. 2006. Remitting Subjects: Migrants, Money and States. *Economy and Society* 35 (2): 185–208.

Herzfeld, Michael. 1993. *The Social Production of Indifference: Exploring the Symbolic Roots of Western Bureaucracy*. Chicago: University of Chicago Press.

Kanstroom, Daniel. 2010. *Deportation Nation: Outsiders in American History*. Cambridge: Harvard University Press.

———2012. *Aftermath: Deportation Law and the New American Diaspora*. New York: Oxford University Press.

Khosravi, Shahram. 2018a. Introduction. In *Life After Deportation: Ethnographic Perspectives*, edited by Shahram Khosravi, 1–14. Palgrave Macmillan.

———2018b. Stolen Time. *Radical Philosophy* RP 2.03 (December 2018).

La Resistencia. 2019. "Deportado a su Muerte: Hombre Deportado desde Tacoma con necesidades de atención médica muere en México." Press Release, June 27, 2019. Tacoma, Washington.

Lecadet, Clara. 2018. Post-Deportation Movements: Forms and Conditions of the Struggle Amongst Self-Organising Expelled Migrants in Mali and Togo. In *Life After Deportation: Ethnographic Perspectives*, edited by Shahram Khosravi, 187–204. Palgrave Macmillan.

Mahler, Sarah J. 1998. Theoretical and Empirical Contributions Toward a Research Agenda for Transnationalism. In *Transnationalism From Below*, edited by Michael Peter Smith and Luis Eduardo Guarnizo. New Brunswick: Transaction Publishers.

Majidi, Nassim. 2018. Deportees Lost at "Home": Post-deportation Outcomes in Afghanistan. In *Life After Deportation: Ethnographic Perspectives*, edited by Shahram Khosravi, 127–148. Palgrave Macmillan.

Martinez, Daniel E. and Jeremy Slack. "Bordering on Criminal: The Routine Abuse of Migrants in the Removal System. Part II: Possessions Taken and Not Returned." Immigration Policy Center, 2013.

Medina, Dulce and Cecilia Menjívar. 2015. The context of return migration: challenges of mixed-status families in Mexico's schools, *Ethnic and Racial Studies*, 38 (12): 2123–2139. https://doi.org/10.1080/01419870.2015.1036091.

Nyers, Peter. 2010. Abject Cosmopolitanism: The Politics of Protection in the Anti-Deportation Movement. In *The Deportation Regime: Sovereignty, Space, and the Freedom of Movement*, edited by De Genova and Peutz, 413–442. Durham: Duke University Press.

Peutz, Nathalie. 2006, April. Embarking on an Anthropology of Removal. *Current Anthropology* 47 (2): 217–241.

Peutz, Nathalie and Nicholas De Genova. 2010. Introduction. In *The Deportation Regime: Sovereignty, Space, and the Freedom of Movement*, edited by De Genova and Peutz, 1–32. Durham: Duke University Press.

Rodkey, Evin. 2018. Making it as a Deportee: Transnational Survival in the Dominican Republic. In *Life After Deportation: Ethnographic Perspectives*, edited by Shahram Khosravi, 169–186. Palgrave Macmillan.

Slack, Jeremy. 2019. *Deported to Death: How Drug Violence Is Changing Migration on the US–Mexico Border*. Berkeley: University of California Press.

Smith, Michael Peter and Luis Eduardo Guarnizo, eds. 1998. *Transnationalism From Below*. New Brunswick: Transaction Publishers.

US Department of Homeland Security. 2016. Tables 39, 40, 41 https://www.dhs.gov/immigration-statistics/yearbook/2016/table39.

Vogt, Wendy. 2013. Crossing Mexico: Structural violence and the commodification of undocumented Central American migrants. *American Ethnologist* 40 (4): 764–780.

Walters, William. 2010. Deportation, Expulsion, and the International Police of Aliens. In *The Deportation Regime: Sovereignty, Space, and the Freedom of Movement*, edited by De Genova and Peutz, 69–100. Durham: Duke University Press.

Wiltberger, Joseph. 2014. Beyond Remittances: Contesting El Salvador's Developmentalist Migration Politics. *The Journal of Latin American and Caribbean Anthropology* 19 (1): 41–62.

Zilberg, Elana. 2011. *Space of Detention: The Making of a Transnational Gang Crisis Between Los Angeles and San Salvador*. Durham: Duke University Press

9

State Violence in India: From Border Killings to the National Register of Citizens and the Citizenship Amendment Act

Monish Bhatia

Border Killing and the Violent Stopping of Time

> On either side of this strange line
> That separates yours from mine
> For whose existence we rely
> Entirely on our inward eye
> This border by whose callous side
> Our inert wheel lies stultified
>
> This border that cuts like a knife
> Through the waters of our life
> Slicing fluid rivers with
> The absurdity of a new myth

M. Bhatia (✉)
Birkbeck, University of London, London, England, UK
e-mail: m.bhatia@bbk.ac.uk

© The Author(s), under exclusive license to Springer Nature Switzerland AG 2021
M. Bhatia and V. Canning (eds.), *Stealing Time*,
https://doi.org/10.1007/978-3-030-69897-3_9

> That denies centuries
> Of friendships and families
> This border that now decrees
> One shared past with two histories
> This border that now decides
> The sky between us as two skies
> This border born of blood spilt free
> Makes *you* my friend, my enemy. ('This Border', Bashabi Fraser, 2008: 593–594)

On a cold morning of 7 January 2011 at approximately 6.00 am and just after the call for dawn prayer (*Fajr Azaan)*, Felani Khatun, a fifteen-year-old child attempted crossing the Indo-Bangladesh border through Anatapur post in Cooch Behar District—also referred to as International Border no. 947. Felani was born in the state of Assam in India to parents who were undocumented, and she was eldest of the six children. Her father, Mohammad Nurul Islam, moved to India at a young age to escape severe poverty and harsh conditions in Bangladesh. For most of his life, Nurul Islam worked as a labourer and his wife (Felani's mother) was a street betel leaf (*paan*) vendor. Whereas, Felani lived and worked in the capital, New Delhi, as a domestic maid. The father and daughter were heading to Bangladesh, as Felani's marriage was arranged and due to take place on the 8th of January 2011. Nurul Islam paid some 3000 rupees to the local brokers who facilitated their border crossing. Following the brokers instructions, he climbed the short 2.5-metre fence with the help of a ladder and successfully moved on to the other side. Felani followed him, but somehow her dress (*shalwar kameez*) got entangled in the barbed wire of the fence and she was stuck midway. Her stricken cries caught the attention of the Border Security Force (BSF)—a paramilitary unit tasked with patrolling the boundary. The BSF officer (*jawan*) of 181 Battalion opened fire without a warning. The bullet pierced through the upper right side of Felani's chest. Nurul Islam quickly jumped off on the Bangladeshi side and scratched several parts of his body. He started screaming in distress for Felani. However, when BSF aimed their guns at him, he had no choice but to move away. Nurul Islam then lost consciousness. Eyewitnesses stated that Felani was alive for around an hour, and she was left hanging upside down on the Indian side of the fence. After four hours or so, her lifeless body was moved down and BSF slung her hands and feet to a bamboo pole and took the body away.

The next day and 30 hours since the killing, the body of the deceased teenager was handed over to the Border Guard Bangladesh (BGB). The first post-mortem was conducted by the Indian authorities, and it was alleged that the body was returned by the BSF without the wedding jewellery that Felani was wearing at the time of crossing—for which her parents made numerous sacrifices and saved up the money over many numbers of months. The body was then taken to the police station close to the Bangladesh border for inquest and other formalities. This was followed by a second post-mortem, which concluded that death was homicidal in nature. From here on, her grieving parents embarked on a time dragging, painful journey of seeking justice and accountability. The picture of Felani's body hanging on the fence was published in some of the Bangladeshi and Indian news outlets, and subsequently the 181 Battalion *jawan* was charged under the Indian Penal Code Section 304, i.e., culpable homicide not amounting to murder (in other words, having no knowledge that the act in all probability would cause death or 'unintentional killing').

In August 2011, Felani's parents appeared before the Security Force Court (SFC) to give evidence in the trial of BSF officer, but they were not allowed to attend or observe. The SFCs are closed bodies and the proceedings and verdict are not made public. In 2013, the officer was acquitted by the court. The parents went through yet another process of complaints, urging the Indian authorities to take action against the officer. Nurul Islam was once again invited to give evidence but he was not allowed to attend or observe the revision trial. The officer was once again cleared of all the charges. Needless to say, the SFC trials appear to be partisan in nature as security forces prosecute their own *jawan*. After Felani's death, the family could not live in India and had to move to a village in Bangladesh, close to the border (where Nurul Islam originated from). Felani received a respectful burial in the backyard of her parents' home, where her memories and past will remain un-erased. The family relentlessly pursued justice, and through a strategic intervention and cooperation of lawyers and activists on both sides of the border, a petition was filed before the Supreme Court of India in 2015 requesting for an independent investigation and open trial. After five long years (and over nine years since the killing) it was announced that further hearings will take place in 2020.[1] Nevertheless, the family were pushed into poverty and not allowed to live/work in India any longer (which in itself was a lifetime punishment) and were finding it difficult to make the ends meet.

When compared to documented migrants the capitalist class, wealthy and financially secure, and global travellers—the undocumented global poor have vastly different relationship to the temporalities of journey (and this also includes time experiences in the host country, of lacking citizenship/legal status, discrimination and injustice—explored in the latter half of this chapter). They are affected by the violences of patrolled border fences, watch towers, and various other surveillance and control measures, all of which are designed to restrict their mobilities. Clandestine migrants take dangerous risks to cross borders, and for some these risks end in death. While reflecting on bodies washed up on the beaches of Lampedusa (Italy) and Lesbos (Greece), Donnan et al. (2016) argue that militarisation of the Mediterranean and lack of safe passage have resulted in migrants responding with desperate new strategies, and boarding overcrowded, under fuelled and fragile boats. Many drown and die during the crossing, and so their time is stopped altogether. Not only do these people have their futures stolen, but for many the absence of documents and identifying kin also acts to erase their past and their identities are vacated (Iliadou, this volume). With regard to the deaths at the Indo-Bangladesh border, the time has not simply stopped due to the latent (but deliberate) violence of borders, but rather *violently stopped and stolen* due to overt, state sanctioned killings.

Felani was one of 1185 people killed by the BSF between 2000 and 2019 and whose *time was violently stopped* and future stolen at the border (Odhikar, 2020). A further 1118 people were injured and 1401 kidnapped by the organisation during this period (Odhikar, 2020). In 2019 alone, 41 people were killed by shooting or torture and 40 injured (Odhikar, 2020). These figures only include Bangladeshi nationals, and

---

[1] Facts about this case can be found here: http://odhikar.org/teenage-girl-felani-killed-by-the-bsf-firing-at-anantapur-border-under-kurigram-district/.

no information is available on Indian nationals subjected to the same fate (or perhaps it is not clear as to how many of those killed were Indian nationals). The governments on either side do not release the statistics on the number of people killed or injured and reasons behind the decision to shoot. The true scale of killings is unknown. Also, it is uncertain as to what happens to the bodies of those who have no identifying kin. The laws governing borders and foreigners stipulate that people caught crossing/entering 'illegally' should be passed on to the civil/criminal justice authorities and penalised for transgressions—with (unfair) punishments ranging from (hefty) fines to (lengthy) imprisonment.[2] The shootings are not only violently disproportionate to the so-called 'crime' committed, but it is also in serious violation of human rights protocols. While responding to the various allegations of extra-judicial killings, the former Director-General of the BSF, Raman Srivastava stated: 'We have made it clear that we have an objection to the word "killing," as it suggests that we are intentionally killing people. We fire at criminals who violate the border norms … The deaths have occurred in Indian territory and mostly during night, so how can they be innocent?' (Human Rights Watch, 2010: 16). The only 'crime' of Felani and others in similar situations, besides atempting at crossing the boundary line clandestinely, was their presumed 'illegality', their inherent 'riskiness' and 'criminal' nature, and most crucially their apparent lack of belonging to *Hindu-sthan* (land of Hindus—also see Pandey, 1993). When such official attitudes are combined in the absence of effective accountability mechanisms, it often means that violence goes unnoticed and unpunished, becomes a routine part of bordering, and sends a message that border crossers can be killed with impunity. Despite the sheer number of deaths, kidnappings and injuries, the issue has not yet received a sufficient and sustained level of attention, scrutiny and outrage. As argued by Mahmud (2020), there is a lack of interest in these killings by the foreign governments—for instance, a single killing by US law enforcement makes headlines, whereas, killings of large numbers by Indian forces is ignored. The Indian officials maintain a *shoot to kill policy* at the Indo-Bangladesh borders (Oztig, 2013).

---

[2]For instance: https://www.loc.gov/law/help/illegal-entry/chart.php#_ftn60.

An Illogical Partition and the Erosion of Cultural Spatiality

Before going further, it is important to draw attention to the partition, which was at the time seen as the only remedy to Hindu-Muslim 'communalism' and a 'departing gift' from the British (Talbot & Singh, 2009). In 1947, Cyril Radcliffe, a barrister from England, was appointed by the boundary commission to carry out the task of border demarcation. It is argued that, within the British Indian civil administration, jobs with the highest level of responsibility were often passed on to amateurs lacking the technical knowledge and understanding (Chatterji, 1999). Despite having no background in Indian administration, nor having any experience or expertise of adjudicating border disputes, Radcliffe was tasked with carrying out a boundary vivisection.

The partition ended up dividing people belonging to the same ethnic/tribal, linguistic and geographical groups. It was in no way a single act and neither was it tidily concluded in 1947. On the contrary, the process had only just begun and still appears to be unfinished. According to Jalal (2013), partition is a moment that has neither beginning nor end—it is somewhat boundless in time—and 'continues to influence how the peoples and states of postcolonial South Asia envisage their past, present and future' (2013: 4). Similarly, Ghosh (2017: 7–9) observes, 'sometimes those assigned to run the pencil do so, without realising the impact that their line is going to have on humankind …[the surgical scars] will remain as long as India, Pakistan and Bangladesh exist as separate countries. The scars, considered together, are called the Radcliffe Line'. While these are indisputable facts and they highlight the violent impact of colonialism and the manner in which borders were hastily drawn; nevertheless, it is also crucial to acknowledge the role of politicians and intellectuals from within the Indian subcontinent in partition. As Chatterji (1999, 2002) argues, the nationalist version of partition only holds the British policy of divide and rule (and Muslim League leader Muhammed Jinnah's collusion with it) as responsible for the events of 1947. However, partition is not something that was simply done to India and she was not a passive object of the surgeon's knife—and agency and culpability of nationalist leaders and elites must be equally recognised

(Chatterji, 1999). For instance, in the neo Orientalist belief in the naturalness of Hindu-Muslim divide Muslim majority province of Bengal, the *bhadralok* (which translates to respectable people—Hindu intelligentsia, mostly belonging to high caste and middle-upper class, who were landlords and moneylenders to an overwhelmingly large Muslim peasantry) leadership pioneered an All India Nationalist Movement, which became increasingly anti-Muslim in the fifteen years leading up to the partition (Chatterji, 1999, 2002).

A similar analysis is presented by Nair (2011), who (amongst other aspects) de-emphasises the role of Jinnah and his Muslim separatist two-nation-theory as responsible for partition. Nair instead turns the attention to the powerful Hindu elites and Hindu politics four decades leading up to the partition in Punjab and their role and complicity. Whereas, Jalal's (1994) research suggests that Jinnah never wanted a separate Muslim state and his political objective from 1940 was to strengthen Muslim minority voice in the future Hindu dominated Indian state. These divergent views are necessary as they rupture the 'official nationalist historiography' (Nair, 2011: 261), and need to be fully considered so as to understand and contextualise the present. This is engulfed in rampant Hindu nationalism, Hindu grandiosity combined with toxic discourses of collective victimhood, anti-Muslim hate, anti-immigration and xenophobic politics, and changing temporal conditions, exclusions and restrictions placed on Bangladeshi migrants and Muslim people, and those living in the borderlands. The border/ing destroys communities and their social life, causes serious ruptures in people's ways of being, denies rights and resources to minorities. All of this is a form of cultural harm (see Tombs, 2019).

Structural Erosion of Fluidity and the Infliction of Cultural Harm

The Indo-Bangladesh border is approximately 4095 km long and runs across five states, making it the world's fifth-longest border (Datta, 2018). The border passes through hilly terrains, flat land, rivers and forests, and densely populated areas occupied by farmers and landless peasants (Das, 2008). In many parts it is difficult to clearly distinguish boundaries due to constant rivulets and unclear markers and in monsoon it is almost invincible. The farmers, villagers and landless peasants on both sides have struggled to make ends meet due to poor irrigation, environmental crisis, and rapid population growth in the region, coupled with limited employment opportunities. The marginalisation and disenfranchisement in borderland drive this group to attach a normal informality to the border (see Samaddar, 1999). Informal activities or as officials have increasingly termed it 'smuggling' (mostly involving people, animals, pharmaceuticals and food products) has become an important source of livelihood for many poor border inhabitants (Das, 2008). In many cases, farmers, villagers and peasants can be shot, tortured, killed or injured by the BSF for cattle 'smuggling' or casually crossing the boundary line or accidentally crossing/coming close to it while looking after the livestock and/or farming (Human Rights Watch, 2010).

This border is somewhat paradoxical: it is a line that divides two nations, but it is also a place where people live. It can be argued that borders are attached to the bodies of their inhabitants, and these inhabitants are increasingly treated as 'wrong bodies' and subjected to border control measures. The people living in the borderlands are neither arriving nor departing, but their relationship to temporality is similar (if not identical) to so-called clandestine border crossers—as coming close to the contested line changes their status in that moment. It is then that they are subjected to state sanctioned killing and their time is violently stopped. Further, authorities create time friction—for instance, the officials on both sides of the border enforce informal curfews in the immediate surrounding villages, so as to 'prevent' people from getting shot, and BSF patrol goes further few kilometres inside the Indian territory and restricts the movement of residents (Human Rights Watch, 2010). Such actions have resulted in people's social world being truncated and livelihoods further threatened. Many *jawan's* are deployed to the Indo-Bangladesh border duty after tense tours around the Indo-Pakistan border in Kashmir and tend to display aggressive behaviour towards the villagers, and police does not register any complaints of harassment and abuse made against the BSF (Human Rights Watch, 2010; also see Bose et al., 1990; Mathur, 2016). The border inhabitants living in/below the poverty line and in-between spaces of belonging and non-belonging often find multiple layers of debilitating control exerted over their time-space through an array of exclusionary, restrictive and aggressive practices, poverty and economic marginalisation. For them, time consistently slows, space shrinks and mobility constricted.

In her book *Border: Journey to the Edge of Europe* (2017), Kapka Kassabova highlights the cultural erosion of historic mobilities between the Middle East and Eastern Europe through the constructions of borders—a similar erosion has arguably occured through the creation of the Indo-Bangladesh border. People on both sides of the border have shared histories, languages, culture, and economic and (most importantly) kinship ties, and individuals cross the borders to meet family members, friends and relatives, and attend festivities and events (Mehta, 2018). However, there are also other push-pull factors that drives the migration of Bangladeshi's to India, such as, demographic pressures, climate disasters, persecution, economic conditions and better employment opportunities. Bangladesh's economic growth is rising, however, 28 and 13.4% of the total youth labour force with secondary and tertiary education remained unemployed during the year 2016–2017 and the share of unemployed youth in total unemployment was 79.6% (Centre for Policy Dialogue website).[3] It is argued by Bangladesh's economists that the country is currently experiencing a 'jobless growth'. For many years people (most not possessing passports and permits, as they cannot afford one) have casually crossed the porous border during the day to work as manual labour, others cross to work and stay temporarily, and some choose to settle and build lives outside of the official channels. The youth unemployment is also said to be a contributing factor for informal activities around the border areas (Centre for Policy Dialogue website) and cattle 'smuggling' is regarded as one of the most lucrative of all trades.

The slaughtering and sale of cows, and consumption of beef and related products is forbidden in India and banned in certain states. Therefore, containing the cross-border 'smuggling' has been the focus of the Bharatiya Janata Party (BJP) government ever since they came

---

[3] See: https://cpd.org.bd/time-to-address-youth-unemployment-dr-fahmida-khatun/.

back into power in 2014. The Hindu upper caste politics dictates the politics of border controls. On the other hand, it is legal to slaughter and consume beef products in Bangladesh, and demand exceeds supply due to limited land and growing demand. There is no definite estimate of cattle trade, however, unofficial figures suggest that it is in the region of 1.8 million to 2 million animals per year (Suresh & Karmakar, 2017). The trade itself is somewhat legal or rather informal, as oppose to outright illegal. Once the animals are in Bangladesh, the trade is taxable and recorded. The restrictions and controls implemented by the Indian state have led to corrupted practices at the border and clashes over bribe money that BSF demands from border inhabitants, 'smugglers' and migrants (Das, 2008).

Besides cow protection, one of the other reasons that is deployed to maintain violent militarised borders is to prevent organised crime and cross-border trafficking of women and children. Within the official discourses it is often raised that many Bangladeshi women and girls are sold into brothels in Mumbai, Delhi or Kolkata, and others end up in domestic servitude—and they need to be protected. Some scholars have argued that escalation of borders disproportionately impact women and children and have violent consequences for them. For instance, Pickering and Cochrane (2013) analysed border-related deaths in EU, US and Australia and revealed that women disproportionately die at the frontiers. Whereas, South Asian scholars have raised concerns with dominant narratives of trafficking and organised crime in border controls, wherein women's cross-border mobility is primarily addressed through the framework of victimisation, and conservative Hindu morality that sexualizes their safety and ignores the agency (Ghosh, 2015). Once inside the country, any gendered and sexual violence often goes unreported and unaddressed because of undocumented status and fear of repercussion, and poverty (Rai, 2011), and on getting caught women can be imprisoned and deported (Mehta, 2018). Further, Rai (2011) argues that BSF themselves are leading customers of sex workers around the border regions, and some of the women are victims of trafficking.

The state has also deployed the rhetoric of 'infiltrators' and 'terrorism' to justify the shootings and violence. According to Jones (2009), border crossers are frequently merged with violent criminals in the narratives of border protection, and all people from Bangladesh become suspects within India (292–293). This issue has increasingly taken a centre stage due to BJP's muscular securitisation agenda that castes doubt over the motives of 'illegal' border crossers. Inspired by the racist settler-colonial Israeli state practices and borders in the West Bank, the BJP government has started implementing an enhanced surveillance system called BOLD-QIT (Border Electronically Dominated QRT Interception Technique) under CIBMS (Comprehensive Integrated Border Management System)[4]—so as to block the 'violent' and 'backward' people from entering the civilised and forward *Hindu-sthan*.

Hindu nationalists have consistently claimed that an influx of 'illegals' is altering India's demography. According to one official document, the number of 'illegal' Bangladeshi nationals in India is estimated to be between 15 and 18 million, with 350,000 or more people entering into country each year (Law Commision of India, 2000: 7). The document does not explain the methodology or how the government arrived at this staggering figure (which was at the time approximately 15% of Bangladesh's overall population). This figure was further inflated to 20 million in 2003, and it has been consistently used by BJP as a point of reference to highlight the scale of Muslim 'problem' and to justify harsh measures. Recently, in his 2019 public speech, the BJP Minister of Home Affairs,[5] constructed Bangladeshi nationals as 'threats' and compared them with vermin stating: 'Infiltrators are like termites … Bharatiya Janata Party government will pick up infiltrators one by one and throw them into the Bay of Bengal' (Ghoshal, 2019). The speech was given at the time when a large number of Bangladeshi nationals and Rohingya people were drowning while crossing the Bay. According to the UNHCR South East Asia Report (2016), approximately 12 of every 1000 people who embarked on mixed maritime movement from the Bay of Bengal did not survive the boat journey. The anti-Muslim and unwelcomed foreigner theme has continued in public speeches given by various BJP politicians. Some human rights organisations have called out the

---

[4]For instance, see: https://economictimes.indiatimes.com/news/defence/electronic-surveillance-of-indo-bangla-border-to-begin-tuesday/articleshow/68254084.cms.
[5]The Home Ministry is headed by the Union Minister of Home Affairs. The Ministry is (amongst other things) responsible for border management and security.

use of dehumanising language and compared it to Nazi Germany and argued that it is paving the way for mass atrocities against Muslims and minorities (also see Avaaz Report, 2019).

On one hand, there is a proliferation and militarisation of external borders and state sanctioned brutality and violence against border crossers and those living in the borderlands. On the other hand, the divisive rhetoric, policies and practices have triggered an implosion of borders—causing further chaos, confusion and misery, and atmosphere of panic and fear of becoming permanently excluded. Increasingly, there is a permanent state of liminality and insecurity created for the undocumented (Muslim) people in India—where they cannot foresee their future and the erratic nature of present renders it completely unpredictable. Most importantly, the contemporary Indian citizenship regime is designed to steal their most precious resource—*time*—explored further in the next section.

Orientalism and Hindu Nationalism: Border Implosions, Temporalities and Harm

To make sense of the current citizenship/bordering regimes and its impact on people, it is important to go back in time so as to understand the emergence of divisions within the Indian society and how the Muslim 'foreigner' was constructed and vilified. Orientalists attempted at tracing the roots of Aryan or Western civilisation in ancient Hindu scriptures. They glorified India's ancient past and constructed a narrative that Aryan civilisation declined due to the Muslim rule and that Hindus prospered and flourished before the Muslim invasions in the eleventh and twelfth centuries (Van der Veer, 1994). This in turn laid a foundation for Hindu nationalist interpretation of Indian history, which was heavily influenced by Orientalist historiography. Both Van der Veer (1994) and Bhatt's (2001) work have covered the enormous influence of Orientalism on India, however, such an influence was not a one-way imposition that was passively accepted—instead ideas were absorbed through an intense scholarly exchange between Orientalists and Indian (Hindu) intellectuals. Van der veer also goes on to develop a critique of Edward Said's work and the notion that Orientalism created a reality in which Indians had to live—according to him, such idea was too simplistic, erroneous and it ignored the complexities and deep intertwining of Western and Indian discourses.

After the 1857–1858 civil rebellion in Northern India, the East India Company[6] was abolished, and direct and violent rule of India by the British government began. Much of the nineteenth century saw a large-scale state project undertaken by a group of British officers so as to classify around 300 million Indian people and enable the rule by records. The data included information about caste and religion. This census also resulted in identity formation, as people started imagining their relation to one another on a much larger scale (Van der Veer, 1994). There was an establishment of Muslim minority and Hindu majority as social and political categories, and this was entirely the result of census classifications. The divisions between the groups existed in pre-colonial period too, however, counting of the communities and having leaders to represent each community was a colonial creation, and it resulted in the emergence of religious nationalism (Van der Veer, 1994). Within the narratives of colonial Orientalism, the division and differences between Hindus and Muslims formed a powerful legitimising force for British rule as an 'enlightened race', and these divisions also blocked any future alliance between the groups that would weaken the rule (Van der Veer, 1994).

Orientalist belief in the naturalness of Hindu-Muslim divide has continued into the present time. The Hindu nationalists view Islam as a foreign element despite its long presence in the country, and Muslims are considered as 'outsiders' or foreign 'enemy' who weakening India from the inside. The nationalists have also dramatised the Muslim fertility rates, linking religion to sexuality and contemporary politics of fear—Anand (2011: 1) terms this nationalist obsession with 'predatory' Muslim sexuality as 'porno-nationalism'. More recently, right-wing parties have referred to the apparent growing Muslim population as threat to India and obstructing the development of nation and called

---

[6]For more information on East India Company and its operation, see: Robins, N. (2002). Loot: In search of the East India Company, the World's First Transnational Corporation. *Environment and Urbanization, 14*(1), 79–88.

for compulsory sterilisation. It can be argued that Hindu nationalists are constantly attempting to take the nation back to a point in (Orientalist constructed) history, with an hope to achieve a glorious future that does not exist. They see the country constantly besieged by the outsiders—first Muslims, then British and Muslims again; thereby, alternating messages of Hindu victimhood on the one hand, and Hindu grandeur on the other (see Tripathi et al., 2019). The nationalists ascribe to the modern idea of nation state and they accept capitalism, science and technology with open arms: what they do not ascribe to is secular state and they see secular thought as Westernised, one that is rotting India and colonising it all over again (Van der Veer, 1994).

In 2019, the right-wing Hindu nationalist Bharatiya Janata Party (BJP) made history by achieving a second consecutive landslide victory, giving prime minister Narendra Modi a powerful mandate to pursue ethnocentric policies. Historically speaking, BJPs success relies on two leading Hindu nationalist movements—Vishva Hindu Parishad (VHP; translates to Universal Hindu Council) and Rashtriya Swayamsevak Sangh (RSS; translates to National Volunteer Organisation). The VHP is an organisation of religious leaders and later is a militant youth organisation. It is widely known that Modi himself was a former full-time fieldworker of the RSS, however, he distanced himself from the organisation to broader his electoral appeal. The BJP's alliance with these organisations has resulted in the use of religious discourse in the political arena. The BJP espouses the *Hindutva* ideology and seeks to define Indian culture solely in terms of Hindu values and equates religious and national identity, and Muslims are outside of this equation and therefore outside of the nation (Pal et al., 2016). The Hindutva project heavily relies on the discourses of territory and the construct of *Hindu-rashtra* (Hindu nation), and this has been increasingly accompanied by vitriolic violence that is carefully planned and targeted against the Muslim 'other'.

Many of the BJP leaders have direct links to either VHP or RSS. According to Casolari (2000) organisation's founding fathers expressed open admiration for European fascist movements. Today, neither of these organisations are simply extreme right, at the periphery, and far removed from the mainstream of the Indian society—on the contrary many in the high-level bureaucracies are linked to them (also explained in Van der Veer). Since coming back into power in 2014, BJP executed two key actions—updating the National Register of Citizens (NRC from here on) in Assam and promised to extend this NRC on an all India level, and also updating the Citizenship Act (CAA)—both directly relevant to the core aims of this collection.

The National Register of Citizens and the Citizenship Amendment Act: Time Theft and Disenfranchisement

The NRC contains names, addresses and photographs of all the 'legal' citizens who are residing in the state of Assam. It was first compiled in 1951 and was based on the census exercise undertaken the same year. The decision to maintain a register for the state was due to the Immigration (Expulsion from Assam) Act, 1950. In the initial years following the partition, there was a large movement of people into Assam from East Pakistan (now Bangladesh) and NRC emerged as a tool to pushback those who had entered the country without official authorisation. Nevertheless, to fully understand the opposition to so-called 'illegal' immigration in this and subsequent periods, one has to look into the past.

In the late nineteenth century, the British decided to extend the railway line to remote corners of the North East and brought in labour migrants into Assam to work on the construction (Ahmed, 2006). The parts of Assam and Bengal eventually became connected, and the peasant population from East Bengal (which was East Pakistan post-partition) started moving into the sparsely populated and fertile lands of Assam. This was in part also due to peasants wanting to escape exploitative landlords (*zamindars*, who were largely *Bhadralok*) in East Bengal (Ahmed, 2006). These wage labourers were important to the imperial agrarian policy and colonial economy, and British consciously encouraged people to leave their mother state and settle in Assam (Ahmed, 2006). The beginning of twentieth century saw a large-scale migration from East Bengal due to the British government's policy of establishing jute industries. Travel was heavily subsidised for peasants and the British also published news adverts giving details of large wastelands in Assam waiting to be occupied, thereby, enticing people to move (Ahmed, 2006). The British had facilitated movement and a nexus between temporality and spatiality through unscrupulous and deceptive means and through violence and oppression, only to end such now necessary freedoms later.

In 1931, C. S. Mullen (British census superintendent) recorded the influx and stated that 'vast horde of land-hungry immigrants, mostly Muslims' are likely to destroy Assamese culture and civilisation' (quoted in Baruah, 1999: 57). Mullen's statement stoked fear amongst indigenous Assamese and fuelled the anti-immigration sentiments. In nineteenth century and near half of twentieth century the migration was inter-state (and 'legal') as India was undivided at that point, and people from East Bengal were citizens of India (Ahmed, 2006). After the 1947 partition, time and again some movement of people from East Pakistan into Assam (and vice versa) occurred due to riots and disturbances and/or natural disasters. The year 1971 witnessed a large number of people fleeing from the Bangladesh Liberation War. There was a growing discontent amongst Assamese that the ethnic character of the state was under threat—resulting in the Assam Agitation 1979–1985 (Hardgrave, 2019). The RSS became increasingly active in regional politics and circulated the Orientalist narrative of Assam being overrun by Muslims (Hardgrave, 2019). The harmful actions of the British, followed by nationalists, resulted in the rupturing of the forward movement in time for Muslim people, and they were removed from the domains of belonging and exposed to unmediated violence and suffering. Thousands of Bengali Muslim peasantry in rural Assam were killed in what came to be known as the Nellie massacre. Eventually and to end the Agitation, the Assam Accord was signed in 1985, dividing the undocumented entrants into pre-1971 (to be granted full citizenship, including the right to vote) and post-1971 (detected, removed from the electoral register and expelled). In line with the secular constitution of India, the Accord did not include any provision for preferential treatment for Bengali Hindus and/or exclusion of Bengali Muslims, despite RSS's divisive politics (Hardgrave, 2019). This secular view was widely supported by the people of Assam. However, RSS and BJP remained active in the region.

After around forty years since the Accord and 70 years since the first NRC exercise, the update of the register was initiated by the BJP government in 2015. The NRC includes names of people who are able to prove their Indian citizenship through the submission of personal/family legacy documents that have pre-1971 validity. The update was happening against the backdrop of rampant anti-Muslim and anti-immigration discourses and surge in hate-crimes and lynching's of Muslim people in various parts of the country. Increasingly, the pejorative 'outsider' narrative and subsequent actions have resulted in the attempts to delegitimize Muslim citizenship in India, and it has pushed the group into an existentially immobile state. Hage's (2015) notion of stuckedness accurately describes this condition of immobility—where people are stuck in the existential confinement that moves beyond physical spaces. Here they are left waiting to be accepted as citizens, waiting to be treated as equals, waiting to belong.

The undertaking of NRC update was an enormous bureaucratic exercise in which some 32 million people searched for identity documents spanning over six-decade timeframe and tried to connect pieces of family history. The relationship between time and citizenship became a key factor here. Individuals (and families) who were seemingly secure were now stuck in precarious situation until they've proved their connection to the Indian soil through gathering and furnishing of legacy documents. Of course, being included in the register translates to being recognised as the citizen of *Hindu-sthan,* and consequences of getting excluded and its marginalising effects are at the centre of public debates and concerns. One of the most problematic aspect of NRC (and the Citizenship Amendment Act—explained later) in the twenty-first century is that it moves away from the principle of *ius solis,* i.e. citizenship by birth, which was also enshrined in the secular constitution of independent India (also see Chatterji, 2012 on histories of citizenship between 1946–1970). The nationalist government has actively pursued *ius sanguinis,* i.e. citizenship by blood or descent.

The update exercise in itself was time wasting, discriminatory and caused immense stress and anxiety amongst underprivileged and marginalised groups. The process required communication reaching not just to those living in the urban areas, but also remote tribal communities, farmers and peasants in rural Assam (which has very low literacy rates and live in or below poverty line). Certain media outlets, non-governmental organisations and activists frequently reported the inconsistencies and dehumanising effects of the exercise, and the sheer pressure on these groups who had to gather historic documents. The North East of India is severely affected by monsoon and heavy rainfall, and consequent landslides, flooding, and river erosions. Each year, hundreds and thousands of villages in Assam are submerged by the Brahmaputra River, and some have been erased altogether—therefore, maintaining and gathering legacy documents is not only difficult, but also impossible for some. Furthermore, according to research conducted by Field et al. (2019), the main source of information about NRC and form filling came from media platforms or word of mouth. A small number of officials were also appointed to assist villagers having limited bureaucratic and digital literacy. The study highlighted several issues, first being the ever-changing rules around document eligibility and deadlines from the Supreme Court, which exacerbated the chaos and uncertainty. Second, bureaucrats themselves were not always updated, which created gaps in knowledge and people turning to informal networks, leading to misinformation and errors. Third, some people were given different information on different days, making the entire process even more complicated and resulting in multiple wasted journeys. Field et al. argue that, as per the Electoral Commission of India, the polling stations need to be within 2 km reach of voter residence, so as to ensure equal access; however, for NRC, people (especially those in rural Assam) had to travel dozens and several hundreds of kilometres to submit the application and verify their claims. Women in particular were severely affected by poor communication and lack of infrastructure around NRC. Besides this, patriarchal norms meant that women did not have entitlements to land or lineage, making it difficult to prove the legacy (Singh, 2019). The initial three drafts were published in December 2017, July 2018, and June 2019, and the final list was released in August 2019. A total of 19,06,659 (approximately 2 million) did not make it on the register. While the consequences of exclusion are yet to come, the process in itself caused harms to the communities, amplified vulnerabilities and pushed people into time wasting bureaucratic limbo on a large-scale. The NRC update is labelled as one of the biggest exercises in disenfranchisement in the twenty-first century, and it is likely to destroy the international efforts of ending statelessness by 2024 (Avaaz, 2019).

Exclusion, Incarceration and Detained Temporalities

People excluded from NRC in Assam are allowed to appeal the decision at the Foreigners Tribunal, which is set-up to exclusively make decisions on the citizenship cases. These bodies are quasi-judicial and operate in a highly discriminatory manner and is geared to reject (Avaaz, 2019). Those who are not satisfied by the Tribunals decision can pursue the matter in the Supreme Court, and once all the legal options are exhausted, people are classified as 'foreigner'. On the other hand, the Bangladesh government has consistently denied that its citizens are living in India 'illegally' and does not recognise Bengali Muslims in Assam as nationals of their country and refuse to accept their deportations (Gowen, 2018). Individuals whose names did not make it in the NRC are at risk of detention and considered as deportables (until proven otherwise). This, according to De Genova (2019), can make everyday life riddled with precarity, multiple conditionalities and inequality, as detainability renders ones way of life and life plans tentative and tenuous. The very condition exemplifies time theft by the state, as pasts are rendered irrelevant, present stranded and future obscured. Several news reports have documented the increasing numbers of individuals excluded from NRC being held in one of the six detention centres in Assam. Nevertheless, to increase capacity and detain growing numbers of stateless (deportable) people, a mass enclosure camp is being constructed and it is spread over 6.15 acres of land (roughly the size of seven football pitches), containing 15 buildings, and surrounded by 20 feet walls and watchtowers (Choudhury, 2019).[7]

Some of those who were excluded from NRC experienced time in which change was happening suddenly and rapidly—or as Griffiths

---

[7]Throughout India, there are 10 centres operational (6 being in Assam), 3 under construction (including mass detention camp mentioned above) and 3 for which land has been obtained.

(2014) calls it frenzied time—and they were quickly moved to one of the detention sites. Furthermore, the NRC in itself was filled with grave errors and omissions. News reports have confirmed that many of those with valid documents did not make it on the list (Gowen, 2018) and were subjected to forced illegalisation. For instance, Saleha Begum, a 40-year-old Muslim woman and Assam resident explained: 'My parents were born here. We have all the documents. Still, my family's names are not on the list. I'm scared. I don't know if the police will put us into a detention centre or deport us to Bangladesh' (quoted in Gowen, 2018).

Saleha likewise highlights the bureaucratic violence and the dark abyss in which people are thrown, where they have to wait in agony, into the unknown future. In another case, Joynal Abedin, a 50-year-old Muslim man, daily wage labourer and an Indian citizen made it on the NRC and was yet held in detention for 14.5 months, he recalled:

> Despite sending all the papers and documents that I had in my possession, I was called to the police station … From there I was sent to the office of superintendent of police … It was here that my handprints were taken and I underwent a medical check-up. From there I was sent to the detention camp … Neither was a notice sent not was I informed about anything. My name has been included in the NRC as are my children's names. I was just trying to get my name enrolled in the voter list and the authorities suspected that I was a foreigner.
> (quoted in Das, 2018)

There have also been numerous deaths in the detention centres (and according to the Indian state, deaths were due to 'natural causes'). Outside of detention, number of suicidal deaths have occurred, and all been linked to NRC including suicides occurring after individuals finding out their names not being included on the register and/or due to fear of marginalisation and banishment (and existential immobility) arising from being branded as 'foreigner' (New Delhi Television, 2019). Despite the sheer scale of trauma and psychological harms caused by the exercise and mounting criticisms and concerns, the BJP Home Minister announced in November 2019 that government will be rolling out NRC on all India basis so as to identify and remove 'illegal immigrants' from the country and have set 2024 as the deadline. This news came at the time when the parliament also passed the controversial Citizenship Amendment Act, 2019 (CAA from here on). The amendment created a category of 'persecuted minorities' and included six religious communities (namely, Hindu, Sikh, Buddhist, Jain, Parsi and Christian) who migrated from the neighbouring Muslim countries of Bangladesh, Pakistan and Afghanistan. Only these listed groups are considered for amnesty. The CAA was strongly criticised by civil society organisations for excluding Rohingya and Muslim refugees (for instance, Baha'is, Hazaras/Shias and Ahmadiyyas who are labelled as incompatible with Sunni-Islam and face persecution in neighbouring countries) and it was branded as unconstitutional and discriminatory. The CAA is empty on its own. However, when combined with NRC—it could result in disenfranchisement and exclusion of certain religious groups on an unprecedented scale. The administration of the regime remains a cause of concern, as many poor and dispossessed groups are likely to find it difficult to furnish necessary documents to prove their status,[8] and it is likely to illegalize Indian citizens. Several civil society organisations have linked the CAA to Nuremberg Laws. The Indian government maintains that law is not discriminatory, and other groups can apply for naturalisation through existing provisions. The government also insists that deportations are not discriminatory either as 'illegal' foreigners will be processed accordingly under different legislations. Nevertheless, the inclusion and exclusion of religious groups and the motivation behind it has not yet been justified. The announcement of CAA (and All India NRC) triggered one of the most fierce but peaceful protests that will go down in country's history. Braving the near freezing weather, women of all ages, castes and religion (but overwhelmingly Muslim) gathered in Delhi's working class Shaheen Bagh neighbourhood to lead a resistance movement, fight for rights and stop the mass time theft of minorities—as explained by a protestor:

---

[8]According to the National Health Population Survey (2017), approximately 36% of children under the age of five do not have birth certificates, and these numbers are said to be even higher for the older generations. Also, there are other reasons for lacking documents, including, floods and natural events, nomadic lifestyles, home births, poor record keeping and so on.

Ask (Prime Minister) Modi why we are protesting (?) Why did we have to see a day like this? That I will have to sit in protest? I am against CAA. He wants us to furnish documents to prove citizenship? There are so many people in this country who have no papers. Many lose their papers to natural calamities like floods and rain. Where will they get their documents from? I dare Modi to name 7 generations of his family [on the Indian soil]. I will name 9 ... I want to tell the future generations that we fought for their rights

Asma Khatun, 90-year-old protester; quoted in NDTV, 2020. Asma Khatun, 90-year-old protester; quoted in Upadhyay, 2020.

Conclusion

Borders are often accompanied by the strong desire to order. It is an exercise of power that requires the construction of the 'other' as someone that exists outside of the borders, and both visible and imaginary demarcation lines differentiate this other from oneself or 'us' from 'them'. The Indo-Bangladesh borders are the toxic legacy of colonialism and Hindu nationalism. Instead of uniting people who belonged to same ethnic, linguistic and tribal communities—they ended up dividing along the religious lines. While the demarcation line was drawn over 70 years ago, the harm continues to be felt. The desire to keep the Muslim other out has led to the brutal *shoot to kill policy* at border—one that *violently stops time* and steals future of poor undocumented border crossers, and also those living in the borderlands.

At the same time, the nationalist government has triggered exacerbations in bordering through the anti-Muslim, xenophobic and anti-immigrant discourses, and through an array of hostile policies and bureaucratic practices that illegalise and disenfranchise people and steal their time—such as, the National Register of Citizens and the Citizenship Amendment Act. Those excluded from the domains of citizenship are stuck in the waiting, with an erratic present and uncertain future. Furthermore, people who could not make it on the citizens register due to lack of legacy documents or errors in the process are increasingly subjected to detention and suffering. Some individuals who were excluded ended their lives due to fear of banishment, and their time was stopped as an indirect consequence of bordering policies/practices. Currently, India is constructing more sites of confinement to accommodate those who cannot provide legacy documents and/or unable to challenge the decision to exclude them from the NRC. To end this chapter, I would like to emphasise that, while the state is exerting violent and oppressive powers over undocumented people's time, there are also emerging resistance movements to combat such actions and protect minority rights. These movements need cooperation and support of activists at transnational levels to collectively challenge authoritarianism and violent borders.

References

Ahmed, S. (2006). Identity issue, foreigner's deportation movement and erstwhile East Bengal (present Bangladesh) origin people of Assam. In *Proceedings of the Indian History Congress* (Vol. 67, pp. 624–639). Indian History Congress.

Anand, D. (2011). *Hindu nationalism in India and the politics of fear*. Palgrave.

Avaaz. (2019). *Megaphone for hate: Disinformation and hate speech on Facebook during Assam's citizenship count*. https://avaazpress.s3.amazonaws.com/FINAL-Facebook%20in%20Assam_Megaphone%20for%20hate%20-%20Compressed%20(1).pdf. Accessed on 20 April 2020.

Baruah, S. (1999). *India against itself: Assam and the politics of nationality*. Pennsylvania Press.

Bhatt, C. (2001). *Hindu nationalism: Origins, ideologies and modern myths*. Routledge.

Bose, T., Mohan, D., Navlakha, G., & Banerjee, S. (1990). India's 'Kashmir War'. *Economic and Political Weekly, 25*(13), 650–662.

Casolari, M. (2000). Hindutva's foreign tie-up in the 1930s: Archival evidence. *Economic and Political Weekly*, 218–228.

Chatterji, J. (1999). The fashioning of a frontier: The Radcliffe line and Bengal's border landscape, 1947–1952. *Modern Asian Studies, 33*(1), 185–242.

Chatterji, J. (2002). *Bengal divided: Hindu communalism and partition, 1932–1947*. Cambridge University Press.

Chatterji, J. (2012). South Asian histories of citizenship, 1946–1970. *The Historical Journal, 55*(4), 1049–1071.

Choudhury, R. (2019). *India's 1st illegal immigrant detention camp size of 7 football fields.* https://www.ndtv.com/india-news/assam-detention-centre-inside-indias-1st-detention-centre-for-illegal-immigrants-after-nrc-school-ho-2099626. Accessed on 15 April 2020.

Das, P. (2008). India–Bangladesh border management: A review of government's response. *Strategic Analysis, 32*(3), 367–388.

Das, G. (2018). *Labourer freed from goalpara detention camp.* https://www.telegraphindia.com/north-east/labourer-joynal-abedin-freed-from-goalpara-detention-camp-after-over-a-year/cid/1680457. Accessed on 18 April 2020.

Datta, A. (2018). Barbed wire border fencing: Exclusion and displacement at the Indo-Bangladesh borderland. *India Quarterly, 74*(1), 42–60.

De Genova, N. (2019). Detention, deportation, and waiting: Toward a theory of migrant detainability. *Gender a výzkum/Gender and Research, 20*(1), 92–104. https://doi.org/10.13060/25706578.2019.20.1.464.

Donnan, H., Hurd, M., & Leutloff-Grandits, C. (2016). *Migrating borders and moving times: Temporality and the crossing of borders in Europe.* Manchester University Press.

Field, J., Tiwari, D., Hemadri, R., Singh, P., & Rastogi, T. (2019). *Bureaucratic failings in the National Register of Citizens process have worsened life for the vulnerable in Assam.* http://www.daji.org.in/images/NRC-Brief-final.pdf. Accessed on 14 April 2020.

Fraser, B. (2008). *Bengal partition stories: An unclosed chapter.* Anthem Press.

Ghosh, S. (2015). Anti-trafficking and its discontents: Women's migrations and work in an Indian borderland. *Gender, Place & Culture, 22*(9), 1220–1235.

Ghosh, B. (2017). *Gazing at neighbours: Travels along the Line that partitioned India.* Tranquebar Press.

Ghoshal, D. (2019). *Amit Shah vows to throw illegal immigrants into Bay of Bengal.* https://www.reuters.com/article/india-election-speech/amit-shah-vows-to-throw-illegal-immigrants-into-bay-of-bengal-idUSKCN1RO1YD. Accessed on 3 April 2020.

Gowen, A. (2018). *India's crackdown on illegal immigration could leave 4 million people stateless.* https://www.washingtonpost.com/world/asia_pacific/indias-muslim-migrants-fear-deportation-after-4-million-are-left-off-citizens-list/2018/07/30/0d5c28fc-bbd7-4934-821c-17e9520c0d60_story.html. Accessed on 18 April 2020.

Griffiths, M. B. (2014). Out of time: The temporal uncertainties of refused asylum seekers and immigration detainees. *Journal of Ethnic and Migration Studies*, *40*(12), 1991–2009.

Hage, G. (2015). *Alter-politics: Critical anthropology and the radical imagination*. Melbourne University Publishing.

Hardgrave, R. L. (2019). *India under pressure: Prospects for political stability*. Routledge.

Human Rights Watch Report. (2010). *Trigger happy: Excessive use of force by Indian troops at the Bangladesh border*. https://www.hrw.org/sites/default/files/reports/bangladesh1210Web.pdf. Accessed on 14 January 2020.

International Institute for Population Sciences (IIPS) and ICF. (2017). *National Family Health Survey (NFHS-4), 2015–16: India*. Mumbai: IIPS.

Jalal, A. (1994). *The sole spokesman: Jinnah, the Muslim League and the demand for Pakistan*. Cambridge University Press.

Jalal, A. (2013). *The pity of partition: Manto's life, times, and work across the India-Pakistan divide* (Vol. 3). Princeton University Press.

Jones, R. (2009) Geopolitical boundary narratives, the global war on terror and boundary fencing in India. *Transactions of the British Institute of Geographers*, *34*(3), 290–304.

Kassabova, K. (2017). *Border: A journey to the edge of Europe*. Graywolf Press.

Law Commission of India. (2000). *The foreigners (Amendment) bill*. http://lawcommissionofindia.nic.in/reports/175thReport.pdf. Accessed on 12 March 2020.

Mahmud, F. (2020). *Death toll rising in the India-Bangladesh border*. https://asiatimes.com/2020/01/death-toll-rising-on-the-india-bangladesh-border/. Accessed on 19 January 2020.

Mathur, S. (2016). *The human toll of the Kashmir conflict: Grief and courage in a South Asian borderland*. Palgrave.

Mehta, R. (2018). *Women, mobility and incarceration: Love and recasting of self across the Bangladesh-India border*. Routledge.

Nair, N. (2011). *Changing homelands*. Harvard University Press.

New Delhi Television. (2019). Congress leader Shashi Tharoor criticises centre over Assam citizenship list. https://www.ndtv.com/india-news/congress-leader-shashi-tharoor-criticises-centre-over-assam-citizenship-list-2072225. Accessed on 18 April 2020.

Odhikar Report. (2020). *Human rights violation by Indian Border Security Force (BSF) against Bangladeshi citizens 2000–2019*. http://odhikar.org/wp-content/uploads/2020/02/Statistics_Border_2000-2019.pdf. Accessed on 13 March 2020.

Oztig, L. (2013). *Why do border guards shoot? An explanation of shoot to kill policies which target illegal border crossers*. PhD. Dissertation.

Pal, J., Chandra, P., & Vydiswaran, V. V. (2016). Twitter and the rebranding of Narendra Modi. *Economic & Political Weekly, 51*(8), 52–60.

Pandey, G. (1993). *Hindus and others: The question of identity in India Today*. Viking.

Pickering, S., & Cochrane, B. (2013). Irregular border-crossing deaths and gender: Where, how and why women die crossing borders. *Theoretical Criminology, 17*(1), 27–48.

Rai, U. (2011). *The Indo-Bangladesh border: No-woman's land*. https://www.thehindu.com/features/magazine/the-indobangladesh-bordernowomans-land/article2018578.ece. Accessed on 20 March 2020.

Samaddar, R. (1999). *The marginal nation: Transborder migration from Bangladesh to West Bengal*. Sage.

Singh, A. (2019). *Women 'worst victims' of NRC: Gendered and discriminatory nature of the register revealed*. https://www.thecitizen.in/index.php/en/NewsDetail/index/7/17924/Women-Worst-Victims-Of-NRC-Gendered-and-Discriminatory-Nature-Of-The-Register-Revealed. Accessed on 16 April 2020.

Suresh, A., & Karmakar, R. (2017). *Cows make up tiny share of cattle smuggled into Bangladesh*. https://www.hindustantimes.com/india-news/cows-make-up-tiny-share-of-cattle-smuggled-to-bangladesh/story-bxmI2eGBKaxqBMmFxCqMuL.html. Accessed on 20 March 2020.

Talbot, I., & Singh, G. (2009). *The partition of India*. Cambridge University Press.

Tombs, S. (2019). Grenfell: The unfolding dimensions of social harm. *Justice, Power and Resistance, 3*(1), 61–88.

Tripathi, R. C., Kumar, R., & Tripathi, V. N. (2019). When the advantaged feel victimised: The case of hindus in India. *Psychology and Developing Societies, 31*(1), 31–55.

UNHCR Report. 2016. *Mixed movements in South-East Asia*. https://reporting.unhcr.org/sites/default/files/UNHCR%20-%20Mixed%20Movements%20in%20South-East%20Asia%20-%202016%20-%20April%202017_0.pdf. Accessed on 11 April 2020.

Upadhyay, S. (2020). *CAA protests: In biting cold, 'Dadis' of Delhi's Shaheen Bagh protest citizenship law*. https://www.ndtv.com/india-news/caa-protests-shaheen-bagh-protest-in-winter-dadis-of-shaheen-bagh-delhi-protest-citizenship-act-2157818. Accessed on 19 April 2020.

Van der Veer, P. (1994). *Religious nationalism: Hindus and Muslims in India*. University of California Press.

10

"Violence Continuum": Border Crossings, Deaths and Time in the Island of Lesvos

Evgenia Iliadou

Introduction

The International Organisation of Migration (IOM) estimates that in 2015 alone more than 5,400 border crossers[1] have died or are rendered missing globally (Brian and Laczko, 2016). Over the course of the last two decades "more than 60,000 migrants have embarked on fatal journeys around the world, never to return to their loved ones" (ibid., p. iii). The numbers of lives lost are a minimum estimate, given that deaths

---

[1] I use the term border crossers instead of the legal and bureaucratic terms "refugees", "asylum seekers" and "irregular migrants". The border regime generates border controls, visas and passports, "legal" or "illegal" mobilities, bureaucratic and legal classifications of people. Therefore, I politically engage with grassroots movements, which condemn the violent border regime and its fatal consequences by emphasising that the actual problem is the borders and not the people who cross them.

E. Iliadou (✉)
Department of Politics, University of Surrey, Bletchley, England, UK
e-mail: e.iliadou@surrey.ac.uk

are not always recorded by the national authorities, and many bodies are never identified or recovered (Singleton et al., 2017). Although represented as random, unforeseen, unpreventable events and "tragic" accidents, border-related deaths are the outcome of political decisions and the fatal policies surrounding the EU border regime (Canning, 2017; Iliadou, 2019). For the EU border regime, which has been enforced since the 1985 Schengen Agreement and proliferated in the aftermath of the so-called 2015 refugee crisis, some lives -mainly of the poorest- rendered "unliveable" (Butler, 2004) and, therefore, can easily become sacrificial on the altar of Fortress Europe.

Between October 2016 and June 2017, I carried out ethnographic research on the Greek Island of Lesvos, which since 2015 is in the epicenter of the refugee crisis. My research explored the EU responses toward the refugee crisis and the continuum of social harm and violence upon border crossers' lives. The research focused on the lived experiences of everyday violence and social harm border crossers experience while they traverse the multiple land and sea border pathways and while they stuck and wait in border zones, like Lesvos. Throughout my research, I conducted 60 in-depth interviews with border crossers, activists, NGO staff, the authorities and FRONTEX. In this chapter I focus on the continuum of politics of closed borders, and explore the human consequences of the thanatopolitical border regime upon the lives which are apprehended "unlivable." I particularly explore the continuum of border deaths, which occur off the coasts of Lesvos—while people cross the Aegean Sea—as well as inside the refugee camps on Lesvos.

This chapter is about (temporal) violence and state and policy facilitated stealing of time. In the existing academic literature time—temporality—is examined as a fundamental feature of the border and migration governance, and a border technique (Tazzioli, 2016). As the EU border regime and border controls proliferate and strengthen, temporal border controls multiply. For instance, in the light of the 2015 refugee crisis, the deployment of a "live governance" (Walters, 2016)—a real time, technological surveillance, governing, intelligence reporting, risk assessments, speedy and instant interventions—has increased upon people who are *en route* to Europe. According to social scientist Martina Tazzioli, "the temporality of control and temporal borders are functional to slow down and disrupt migrants' autonomous temporalities and geographies of movement (…)" (2018, p. 15). In the existing literature, temporal border controls are examined as stealing or usurping people's time (Andersson, 2014; Khosravi, 2018). The EU border regime—by raising barriers and walls, and by deploying enhanced border patrols and marine operations—makes more dangerous the border pathways to Europe, by increasing the risk of death. Parallel, the temporal borders delay and/or prevent border crossers from reaching Europe through the enforcement of various forms of stasis and stuckedness in transit zones. As a result, a border crossing itself can last for months, years or "even a lifetime," as Mohammad, an activist border crosser from Afghanistan told me. In this chapter I explore time and stuckedness as a form of institutional and structural violence which is inflicted upon the living, the dead and whole communities (Iliadou, 2019). The chapter examines how harms unfold and are cumulative. Harms exist historically and unfold over time, escalate, and thus their effects intensify, deteriorate and become greater over time. These harms are experienced as if, they interact, combine, and intersect by producing more and/or new types of harm.

The first section of this chapter begins with a self-reflexive vignette from a fatal shipwreck which took place in 2012 on Lesvos. This vignette is a border narrative and derives from more than a decade of activism, professional experience, first-hand lived experiences and witnessing of institutional and structural violence, border harms, deaths, dehumanization of border crossers as well as everyday resistance. It shows that there were early "warning signs" (Scheper-Hughes, 2004, p. 224) present, which indicated that the 2015 refugee crisis and border deaths was about to happen. The vignette also indicates the harm and violence continuum and, therefore, the historical development and continuum of the "crisis," the border regime and deterrence policies which have significantly escalated in 2015 onwards.

The second section explores the thanatopolitical border regime, characterised by deterrent policies and practices which have been enforced at, within and beyond the borders. These lethal policies have greatly escalated in the light of the 2015 refugee crisis by inflicting border deaths. The third focuses on the continuum of deliberate "deterring-killing"

(De León, 2015) policies and practices, actions and inactions—by state officials and border agents—of exposure and abandonment of border crossers to death or to a high risk of death. Here, I introduce a new type of harm which I call thanatopolitical harms, hereafter "thanatoharms."

The final section explores the ways under which violence continues in death. Violence continues to be inflicted upon the lifeless bodies which are washed ashore, the unidentified and missing persons, the shipwreck survivors, the families, and whole communities, who are stuck in a temporal limbo lasting for years and even a lifetime. The chapter closes with an argument on the fundamental right to life and dignity in death, and the moral, political and legal responsibility of preventing, documenting, counting and accounting for border deaths.

Frozen Death

One cold morning of December 2012 on Lesvos I woke up from the sudden ring of the phone. The sad voice on the other side of the line of one of the members of the local activist network I was involved with was urging me to wake up and go to help. "The sea has washed ashore dead bodies!" the voice said and suddenly burst into tears. A fatal shipwreck had taken place in the early hours off the coasts of Lesvos. Border crossers' dead bodies were found by local people, frozen on the coasts' pebbles near Mytilene, the center of Lesvos Island's capital. Dead bodies, shoes, clothes and various objects were scattered here and there reminding of a battlefield in a time of peace. These were the discarded bodies and belongings of those who were not allowed to belong (Davies and Isakjee, 2015, p. 93). A member of the rescue crew told me that day, that from the position which the dead bodies were found on the shore one could tell that some of the border crossers reached Lesvos alive but eventually froze to death. The frozen death found them on the threshold of Europe. In the next few days the sea washed up more corpses. The number of fatalities of the shipwreck was finalized; twenty-eight dead and one survivor. The mass media, and particularly the local news, reproduced over and over again the macabre details and photos of the tragic end of life of people who died while fleeing violence, conflicts and persecution. The one and only survivor, a boy from Afghanistan, was photographed and interviewed by journalists. He was also interrogated multiple times by the police and eventually he was abandoned to silently suffer and mourn of his family, who he had witnessed drowning in that same shipwreck.

Although Lesvos has been an important entry point for border crossers since the early 1990s, there were neither adequate facilities within the morgue to store the bodies nor social services and staff to manage the bureaucratic aspect of death. There was not even enough space within the town's cemetery for people to carry out the funeral arrangements and rites. All the bureaucratic procedures were performed by activists, like me, and the death rituals were carried out by border crossers who were living for many years in Lesvos and had, therefore, become experts by experience. The twenty-eight bodies were stored for several days within the hospital's fridges since there was no space available within the morgue. The burials delayed to take place due to the authorities' indifference and inaction. The authorities mainly wanted to get rid of the corpses, along with their annoying relatives, by relocating the burden of responsibility to activists and volunteers. As a result, the macabre smell of human flesh in the state of sepsis overwhelmed the hospital, disturbed and disgusted people hospitalised and working there. In the light of people's complaints about the smell, a representative of the local authorities finally suggested to me: "We should bury the dead in the dump so as local Christians will not be offended."

I remember that the funeral took place after an agonizing struggle and discomfort for all people involved. When the burial eventually took place, it was inappropriately performed. Without knowing the religious and cultural beliefs, municipality workers buried the dead bodies in the wrong direction, violating religious and cultural doctrines and inflicting cultural harm upon border crossers' relatives and their community. As a result, the workers had to exhume the dead bodies and bury them again. Even the process of repatriation of the corpses to the EU or the countries of origin was mentally harmful and exhausting. I remember that the relatives of some of the dead, who traveled from Sweden to Lesvos in order to complete the identification and repatriation procedures confronted misinformation, chaotic bureaucracy and enduring waiting. After weeks they also faced the cruelty of the prosecutor, who literally threw the documentation needed for the repatriation back in their faces by shouting at them, "Well, here you are! Take your bloody corpses."

That cold December of 2012 I witnessed what was then the most deadly shipwreck in the recent history of Lesvos. It is not that shipwrecks and border deaths did not occur before but the particular event was until then the one with most fatalities, which caused a collateral shock to Lesvos' people. Suddenly, the unauthorized border crossings—a phenomenon which has been unfolding on Lesvos over the last two decades- came out from its invisibility via the recovered dead corpses, shocked and sensitized even for a while the indifferent public opinion. This fatal event was the hallmark of what was about to come and framed as the "refugee crisis," since it inaugurated the increased arrivals of border crossers through Lesvos and Greece to Northern Europe.

Although I had buried the traumatic experience of the dreadful event of December 2012 deep in my subconscious, the macabre spectre of death—which was haunting Lesvos and which I confronted later throughout the research process—evoked the memory of trauma. The spectre of death was creeping all over Lesvos. This fact was vividly portrayed in the numerous disposed life jackets, plastic or wooden boats—the "refugee waste" (Gillespie, 2018)—which was scattered all around the coasts. The cruel irony was that the "refugee waste" had a formal place to be buried—in a municipal dump known as the life jackets' graveyard—but "refugees" themselves did not. Due to the lack of facilities and space, border crossers were buried in an allotment illegally operating as a graveyard. In a sense, this illegal site capitalized the cynic epilogue for the "illegal" lives which even in death were not allowed to belong, although their waste somehow was.

The Thanatopolitical Border Regime

The governing of undesirable human mobility through violevnce and death in the name of "humanitarian security" and "prevention through deterrence" has been a common feature of contemporary border politics

(Doty, 2011). According to the logic which underpins deterrent policies, the more border crossers suffer or die *en route*, by being exposed to abandonment, violence and extreme environmental conditions, the more the ones who anticipate coming to Europe will be deterred from taking the journey in the first place (Squire, 2017). Traces of death through corpses—in whole, in parts or decomposed—which are washed ashore or found in anonymous tombs and mass graves along the multiple land and sea border pathways, are preemptive and deterrent "messages" being left for the ones who have not reached Europe yet. According to the feminist anthropologist Rita Segato (2014), "corpses are being used as messages where the body is actually transmitting something the perpetrators want to say, show or enact" (in Délano et al., 2016, p. 528). Geographic landscape plays a significant role in the "fight" against the "illegal" migration. Since the 1990s, the Aegean and Mediterranean Sea has become, in Jason De León words, a tool of "boundary enforcement and a strategic slayer of border crossers" (2015, p. 67). It has also become an enormous graveyard wherein the politics of death has found its ultimate materialization.

In the aftermath of the 2015 refugee crisis, deaths and washed up bodies or remains have become a banality. Local people of Lesvos might not eat fish from fear that fish have fed on human flesh from bodies never recovered from the sea. Ali,[2] a Syrian man asked me, "Do you know how many Syrian people have been fed on by fish?" Fishermen are horrified every time they fish off Lesvos' coasts, since frequently human remains are caught within their nets. "We are just throwing them back to the sea," a fisherman told me. Anna, a long-term resident and activist noted, "I have a very intense feeling that while I swim I will come across a corpse since in most of the beaches that we used to swim corpses were found." The banality of death is one of the most pernicious and insidious features in the governance of the undesirable human mobility.

Governing migration through death and violence has become the Janus-face of deterrence, whereas policies of "killing" are masked as policies of "deterring." The "deterring-killing" (De León, 2015, p. 67) policies and enforcements which routinely expose border crossers' lives to

---

[2] All names are pseudonyms.

physical harms and death indicate "the lethal or thanatopolitical dimension of biopolitical governance" (Vaughan-Williams, 2015, p. 47). The intersection between biopolitical (Foucault, 2003) and thanatopolitical enforcements is very important in the understanding of the contemporary border practices which allow or create the conditions, spaces and "juridical voids" (Doty, 2011, p. 600) of ultimate dehumanization, abandonment and death. Those enforcements shed light on the circumstances and processes under which border deaths are naturalized by being presented as random, unpredictable events and tragic accidents, even though they are outcomes of political decisions and, therefore, can be better understood as an "integral operation of power" (Squire, 2017, p. 517). The biopolitical border management of undesirable human mobility through processes of militarisation, securitisation and humanitarian interventions—wherein border crossers' bodies, vulnerabilities and basic needs are intensively managed and regulated—systematically reduce border crossers into "security risky lives" or "lives to be saved" (Vaughan-Williams, 2015). Therefore, they generate segregations and hierarchies between "livable" and "unlivable lives" which are "worthy" or "unworthy" to be rescued, protected, and, thus, live. As Didier Fassin argues, "biopolitics presupposes not only risking others but also selecting those who have priority for being saved" (2012, p. 226). The politics of death as a mode of governance is founded on the existence of such "hierarchies of humanity" (ibid.).

In order for border crossers' sacrifices to be legitimated and justified in the name of humanitarianism and security, their humanity must be denied or devalued as hierarchical inferior and risky. Through various silent and quiet, interlinked and parallel processes of criminalisation, illegalisation, commodification, animalisation and devaluation (Bosworth and Guild, 2008; Vaughan-Williams, 2015), border crossers are stripped from their humanity and are reduced into liminal and disposable creatures—into "bare lives" (Agamben, 1998). According to Agamben, a bare life represents a liminal figure that is depoliticised by being stripped from any social and legal rights and whose life is deemed by the sovereign as unworthy to enjoy rights and the protection of the law; therefore her/his death is of little consequence (Agamben, 1998). "Bare lives" are considered exceptions to the norm, and are consigned, excluded and abandoned to "zones of exception" (Agamben, 2005), wherein the law is suspended and "creates a juridical void which permits abuses and killings without punishment" (Doty, 2011, p. 602). Therefore, when a life is devalued as no longer a life,[3] and humans are reduced and apprehended as "no longer humans" (Prem Kumar and Grundy-Warr, 2004, p. 36), their slaughter within border zones does not count as murder and their deaths "are deemed of little consequence" (Doty, 2011, p. 600).

Borders and border zones are auspicious places of dehumanisation, since they generate "thresholds"—liminal spaces and zones of ultimate abandonment and exception (Agamben, 2005)—which are characterised by lawlessness and impunity, legally and geographically (Prem Kumar and Grundy-Warr, 2004). According to De León, "Border zones become spaces of exception-physical and political locations where an individual's rights and protections under law can be stripped away upon entrance" (2015, p. 27). In such thresholds the legal status of people is ambiguous, while the geographic isolation and remoteness make them hidden from view wherein not only "violence passes over into law" (Agamben, 1998, p. 25), but also naturalised and as such "death becomes a norm" (Squire, 2017). In this sense, nature and the geographic space plays a pivotal role in the implementation of the violent deterrent policies by providing, as Doty argues, "a moral alibi that enables the policy makers to deny responsibility for the deaths" (2011, p. 599).

---

[3] Borders might be "zones of exception", which can potentially reduce border crossers to bare lives, but they are also spaces of possibilities where anything can happen (Doty, 2011). Therefore, not all border crossers die or are necessarily reduced to bare lives, since many of them resist and survive border controls (see Yahya, this volume). Survival itself is a form of resistance. Despite the increased fortification and militarisation of borders, border crossers defy, disobey, and figuratively speaking mock borders by crossing them. According to the political geographer Reece Jones, "By refusing to abide by a wall, map, property line, border, identity document, or legal regime, mobile people upset the state's schemes of exclusion, control and violence. They do this simply by moving" (2016, p. 180). Regarding Lesvos, agency and resistance is more than evident through the continuous protests and demonstrations by border crossers and locals as well as acts of solidarity in respect to deaths and funerals, as I argue later in this chapter.

Thanatoharms

The thanatopolitical border regime is actualised and enforced through multi-layered, deliberate "deterring-killing" policies and practices, actions and inactions—by state officials and border agents—of exposure and abandonment of border crossers to death or an increased risk of death. According to Doty, "After the apparatus of security fabricate and organise a milieu- i.e., after physical barriers, increased numbers of border patrol agents, and high-tech surveillance are put in place- agents of security can just let things take their 'natural course'" (2011, p. 606). The "deterring-killing" policies and practices are outcomes of a continuum of political decisions, acts of omission and commission which ultimately kill or endanger the very lives they claim to protect. I introduce the concept of "thanatoharms" from the Greek word "thanatos" which means death and the concept of harm which is routed in the "social harm approach" (Hillyard and Tombs, 2007). I define as "thanatoharms" all physical harms which are related to and are an outcome of the thanatopolitical violence enforced at, within and beyond borders.

On an institutional level, thanatoharms are outcomes of political decisions which enforce deterrent policies—instead of safe passages—in the name of protection and security. Through political decisions, search and rescue operations in the Mediterranean and Aegean Sea are systematically prohibited. Similarly, everyday acts of solidarity by citizens, who transit unauthorized border crossers, are prosecuted—a condition which is predominantly referred to as criminalisation of solidarity (Tazzioli, 2018). On a local level, thanatoharms are produced through the actions (acts of commission) and inactions (acts of omission) of border agents and state officials who in practice make the deterring-killing policies possible. Such actions include push-back operations, intimidation, torture and other forms of physical abuse, and such inactions include left-to-die practices and abandonment of border crossers in distress to the forces of nature (Weber and Pickering, 2011). Inactions also include the abandonment of border crossers into refugee camps and detention centers in conditions which tantamount to inhuman and degrading treatment, and where either death is inflicted or the risk of death is high. Both actions and inactions often intersect and collude and are actualised twofold: (i) when border crossers are *en route* and cross the land (Evros River) and sea (Aegean Sea) borders; (ii) after the border is crossed inside sites, like the Moria camp.[4]

A push-back occurs when border guards arbitrarily coerce border crossers back, across the land or sea border, denying them the right to seek international protection. Push-backs are common, deliberate and mundane deterrent practices which are enforced at the land and sea border pathways. Since the 1990's, the Mediterranean Sea (InfoMigrants, 2018b), the Sonoran desert between Mexico and the US (Squire, 2015), and the land and sea Greek-Turkish borders (Human Rights Watch, 2008) have become the violent geographic spaces where push-backs, violent and/or fatal (in)actions unfold silently and quietly. The aforementioned geographic spaces are deadly sites in which border crossers experience extreme violence, abandonment, drowning and fatal injuries, starvation and dehydration and extreme environmental conditions. As De León argues, "Nature 'civilizes' the way the government deals with migrants; it does the dirty work" (2015, p. 68). Greece has repeatedly been accused of systematic illegal push-backs, human rights violations and state violence (Amnesty International, 2015). In the aftermath of the 2015 refugee crisis evidence of violent push-backs have become the norm in the Aegean Sea (InfoMigrants, 2018a). Push-backs often intersect with left-to-die and intimidating (in)actions, such as disabling of boats via damaging or removing the engines or their fuel, puncture holes on boats, tow or abandonment of boats to Turkish waters frequently under the threat of guns and physical abuse or torture. These actions and inactions intend to endanger and horrify, prevent and deter, but very often to kill (Human Rights Watch, 2018). Farhad, an informant from Afghanistan, characteristically noted,

> I tried to enter Greece by boat four times but I failed. I was arrested twice by the Greek coastguards and twice by the Turkish. We were pushed back. When the Greek coastguards arrested us they removed our boat's rows, they punctured holes on our boat and then they left us at the Turkish

---

[4]Moria camp is the biggest detention and reception facility on Lesvos, where currently more than 20,000 border crossers remain stranded for indefinite periods of time.

territorial waters. We were abandoned in the middle of the sea all night until fishermen found us in the early morning hours.

Similarly, in Evros, the north land border between Greece and Turkey, push-back operations with the excessive use of violence, beatings with hands, batons, gunshots, and mock executions have also been documented (Forensic Architecture, 2020).

In the aftermath of the 2015 refugee crisis border deaths, fatal injuries and accidents continue taking place even after the border is crossed. Therefore, although border crossers might reach Lesvos alive—due to the inactions of state officials—die or face an increased risk of death. Such inactions include the abandonment in life-threatening conditions within sites, like the Moria camp. Within these sites border crossers might die or face a high risk of death due to insufficient reception accommodation, or medical and psychological support services (Legal Centre Lesvos, 2020). On January 2017, when I was conducting my fieldwork, in the space of one week I documented the deaths of three border crossers, because of of fumes in their tents. The brutality of this abandonment is epitomised in what Alex, an informant from Afghanistan, told me after a man from Pakistan died in Moria hotspot. "Poor Pakistani man, he traveled from so far away in order to reach Europe, but only to die alone in his frozen tent. Moria should not be called a refugee camp. It should be called a graveyard."

The thanatopolitical border regime turned border crossings into lengthy spatial and fragmented terrains wherein border crossers move, stuck, wait, and again move (Vogt, 2013). The stealing of border crossers' time is achieved through these enforced delays and stuckedness, given that the perilous journeys can be attempted unsuccessfully multiple times and, thus, last for months, years and even a lifetime. People ultimately waste precious time, grow old waiting or die at or within the borders hoping to reach Northern Europe. Given that life is made up of moments and thus time, what the thanatopolitical border regime eventually jeopardizes is life itself by stealing, not just time, but the time of border crossers' life—their lifetime.

Violence After Death

After the event of death, the living—survivors, families and whole communities—must adhere to the rules of a dysfunctional and Kafkaesque bureaucratic complex which is underpinned by multiple, lengthy, inconsistent and parallel procedures and sub-procedures, which exacerbate the feeling of pain, and grief. As Ellie, an activist and long-term resident of Lesvos noted, "You have your mourning and at the same time you have one million bureaucratic things which are impossible to be done." There are different procedures implemented in case a dead body is recovered. A separate procedure combined with a criminal investigation takes place, in case human remains are recovered. A different procedure is applied in case a person registers as missing. Additionally, there are different procedures in case there are relatives and/or survivors who can identify the bodies and other procedures if the bodies are rendered unidentified. Despite the fact that for more than two decades deaths occur at the Greek-Turkish borders, there are no standardised procedures, policies and guidelines for the management of bodies after the fatal event. This lack has produced a policy vacuum produced a policy vacuum (Mediterranean Missing Project, 2016), which itself produces more harm upon survivors, the families of those who lost their lives and even whole communities, who are stuck in a temporal limbo (see Canning, this volume) without knowing what to do. Martha, a social worker supporting survivors of shipwrecks argued,

> Sometimes procedures are done and sometimes they are not, because there are not any standard procedures. There are no guidelines that one can apply. Thus, from the one Port Police to the other and even from clerk to clerk, there is a different and conflicting administering of the procedures. The one clerk says something and then the other clerk says the opposite. Many of them have never done this procedure before and, hence, they seek advice from their superiors, who have also never done this before.

Due to the lack of interpretation services, socio-psychological and legal support for families (who in many cases are themselves survivors of the same shipwreck as well as witnesses of the death of their loved ones) the identification and bureaucratic procedures can take considerable time. Also, the identification procedures are carried out by the authorities immediately after the event, without survivors' and families' grief to be considered or respected. Survivors of shipwrecks are often held within Moria hotspot in degrading and life-threatening conditions. As Ellie argues,

> The way the whole procedure is taking place is a huge form of violence. Imagine that survivors are often held inside Moria hotspot. It is an enormous violence because losing your loved ones is a very traumatic experience and even within a very good context one can be emotionally torn apart. Imagine now someone in this psychological condition living inside Moria hotspot.

Frequently, identification of the dead is not successful due to the lack of evidence, the decomposition of bodies or the remains, as well as the expensive and lengthy procedures in finding and bringing the relatives for identification. Also, procedures can become particularly lengthy and time-consuming due to systematic delays in the identification of the dead through the DNA samples which are sent via the Greek authorities to other countries. As the coroner argued,

> In countries like Syria, Afghanistan and Somalia where there is war and conflicts it is very hard to contact the embassies there, in order for the DNA samples to be sent and thus to receive an answer. For this reason the identification procedures can be delayed or being impossible to take place in the first place.

Due to the dysfunctional bureaucratised system, the policy vacuum and this overall lack of information, the quest of tracing the truth for the destiny of border crossers becomes agonizing, but mainly impossible for the relatives. Many activists emphasised the difficult collaboration with the authorities as an additional problem in the whole process. According to Ellie,

The relatives who will contact the authorities on their own will often be ignored and sent away. If the relatives are not able to identify the dead from the existing evidence [photos, clothes, other personal belongings] they will be ignored and sent away by the authorities. No one will explain to them that they must complete a "missing person's declaration", that they must give a DNA sample, that all the Greek authorities must be informed and some supplementary information must be given on the temporal period of death. The authorities will send relatives away without showing them enough evidence or they will do it in a rushed manner. They are indifferent.

The competent authority to carry out the initial bureaucracy of death in sea is the Hellenic Coast Guard. The Hellenic Coast Guard is responsible for various and conflicting tasks wherein policing of borders and humanitarian practices take place simultaneously (Mediterranean Missing Project, 2016). Foremost, the coastguard is, on the one hand, a repressive body whose mandate is the "surveillance and control of sea borders," "the prevention of illegal migration," and "the protection of the sea borders" (Hellenic Coast Guard, no date a). On the other hand, its mandate is to also conduct search and rescue operations of border crossers in distress, and to recover the corpses or their remains from the sea and coasts (Hellenic Coast Guard, no date b). However, the Coast Guard has been involved in various lethal push-back operations, left-to-die practices, attacks on boats and tortures (AlarmPhone, 2020). Therefore its tasks become even more conflicting, if not obscuring, since apart from the bureaucratic procedures, it must carry out criminal investigations in order to define the causes of border deaths and, simultaneously, detect the perpetrators (in cases of attacks, tortures, push-backs, left-to-die practices) and press charges.

Due to these Kafkaesque procedures, relatives are reaching the Greek islands, often by being (mis)informed or deceived by smugglers—who themselves take advantage of the system's gaps and inconsistencies and profiteer from relatives' pain (Kovras and Robins, 2017). The lack of consistency of post-mortem data, and a map and a record of the graves in the cemetery, prevent the relatives from tracing the grave, exhuming and repatriating the body. As an activist on Lesvos, I have witnessed myself families wasting precious time in wandering, from island to island

and from port police station to port police station, looking for their loved ones with photos, clothes, shoes, personal belongings, marks on the skins, and tattoos. The pain of this quest intensifies and deteriorates in cases where families manage to detect their relatives but when they do, it is too late. The body is already buried as "unknown." As Anna, an activist supporting shipwreck survivors notes, "the whole process inflicts a lot of suffering and discomfort. Sometimes the process is just absurd."

The performance of burials and rituals is another brutalising process. The cemetery used after 2015 for the dead is an allotment which is rented by the Lesvos' municipality and managed by activists and border crossers, who also are the religious leaders. Both attributes—"cemetery" and "religious leaders"—are not formal since the cemetery operates without legal license and is temporary, while the religious leaders are two border crossers volunteers who had become experts by experience in completing the funeral rites and rituals. According to Inam, one of the religious leaders,

> I started performing the religious rituals since March 2015, when I first came in Lesvos and after I heard about a fatal shipwreck. I went to the funeral for the first time as a visitor. The situation I encountered was that there was not any ritual from Islam applied, that the people who were burying the dead were just taking the dead bodies from the hospital and were throwing them inside a dip, and that was all.

The religious protocols and rituals include cleaning and caring for the body before it is buried, the position of the body within the grave, and the direction of the grave. According to the religious leaders, initially these rituals were taking place inappropriately, due to the limited refrigerator facilities available in the morgue, and the limited period during which the bodies could be stored in them. Tariq, the other religious leader and volunteer in the cemetery noted,

> When funerals were taking place inside the old cemetery, no one really knew what to do. We were praying for the dead, but we were not following the ritual protocol. According to the protocol we must clean the dead body and put her/him inside a clean white bed sheet before burying. Most of the time, we used the same bed sheet from the hospital,

which was dirty with blood, and then municipality's workers were placing the dead inside the grave, and they were just throwing soil above them.

As such, often the performance of a culturally appropriate burial and ritual procedures could not be guaranteed, and the dignity and memory of the dead could not be respected. Burial procedures and rituals are of social, cultural, political and emotional significance for the families and the whole communities. The inappropriateness of burial procedures inflicts cultural harms[5] to the whole community—that is, harms which: (i) are produced from the post-mortem corporeal mistreatment; (ii) signify the violation of cultural, religious, moral, sacred norms—associated with one's culture, customs and identity; (iii) humiliate, and shame the living and whole communities, and ultimately insult the memory of the dead. According to the anthropologist Robert Hertz funeral rituals are a way of strengthening the social bond (Hertz, 1960). Without a proper burial the rite of passage from the world of the living to the world of the dead cannot be fulfilled. Therefore, the soul remains in a liminal and temporal threshold between earth and afterlife—a condition which Hertz describes through the metaphor of the "unquiet dead"; a soul which can never rest and is condemned "forever impinging on the land of the living" (in Taussig, 1992, p. 48). The anthropologist Mary Douglas showed that the absence of death rituals signifies the disruption of social order—a danger, pollution and impurity which is transmitted upon by contaminating the living and the communities (Douglas, 2003). Inam, the religious leader noted how impurity and shame is transmitted, and cultural harms are inflicted to the living and whole communities through the metaphor of the "sin,"

> It is a sin for us and not for the dead. It is a sin for us who are alive, and we are here. It is a sin for all the Muslims who know about another Muslim's death and do not pray and do not perform the rituals. All the living, who are aware of the death, must take the responsibility. But the

---

[5]The definition of cultural harms I propose builds upon the work of the criminologist Lynne Copson (2018) and the anthropologist Jason De León and his concept "necroviolence" (2015, p. 69). Copson defines cultural harms as: (i) harms to a culture; (ii) harms by a culture; (iii) harms as misrecognition (p. 3). De León's concept refers to the violence inflicted by the post-mortem treatment of the dead.

dead person even if s/he is thrown to the sea, or eaten by animals, there is no sin on her/him. The responsibility and the sin are distributed to the living ones, to those who knew about the death and did not do a ritual. But if someone performs the ritual, the sin eclipses from all. This is an obligation which must be taken by one person. If one person takes this responsibility, then the sin diminishes for all. If no one takes the responsibility, then all Muslims carry the sin. And when we say the whole Muslims, we mean the Muslims from the whole world.

Temporal violence continuum is exemplified in the figure of the missing and unknown person, and the remains of what was previously apprehended as human. Human remains might never be recovered or identified and, therefore, a person is rendered missing or buried as unknown. Until their death is actually confirmed missing and unknown, persons are not yet dead for the families, which anticipate that their loved ones will reappear. Missing people cannot be grieved and buried, but they cannot also give relief to the living, who are awaiting news, and questing of the traces of their loved ones. This quest, and hence stuckedness and waiting can last for months, years and even a lifetime. Families and communities cannot perform the rituals and, thus, the last parting words are never told. The rite of passage from mourning to closure cannot be fulfilled and the healing process is temporally frozen. Grief becomes protracted and complicated, loss remains unclear, unresolved and "ambiguous" (Boss, 2010). According to the clinical psychologist Pauline Boss,

> [ambiguous loss] is akin to the trauma that causes post-traumatic stress disorder (PTSD) in that it is a painful experience far beyond normal human expectations. But unlike PTSD, it remains in the present; that is, the traumatizing experience (the ambiguity) often continues for years, a lifetime, or even across generations as with slavery or the Holocaust. Because there is no social or religious ritual to deal with such losses, people are stuck alone in a limbo of not knowing, with none of the usual supports for grieving and moving forward with their lives. (2010, p. 139)

As such, death itself does not signify the end, but rather the perpetuation of violence and harm upon the dead and the living. The violence and harm one had experienced before, in and beyond the moment of death is transmitted to the families and whole communities, and is perpetuated for an indefinite period of time.

Conclusion: Violence Continuum and the Right to Life

Since the 1990s, NGOs, scholars and activists have developed long lists in an attempt to document border-related deaths. Such lists are important ongoing timelines of fatal events which are otherwise normalised and rendered invisible. These attempts demonstrate the political demand of "bringing the dead back into society" (Délano and Nienass, 2016a) by making deaths knowable, visible and recordable. The documentation of border deaths makes a political and moral argument about the dignity and protection of the human rights of the dead, and is an active demand for accountability, culpability of those deaths and restoration of justice. The names, data and information which are encompassed within "the hopelessly incomplete lists of dead or disappeared migrants" (Délano and Nienass, 2016b, p. xxii) symbolise the human cost of the thanatopolitical border regime. Therefore such long lists can only be perceived as the long lists of thanatopolitics.

In this chapter, I argued that border deaths are not new, random, unforeseen, unpreventable events or "tragic accidents". They are instead the outcome of lethal political decisions which have been enforced since the 1985 Schengen Agreement and have greatly proliferated in the aftermath of the 2015 refugee crisis. The thanatopolitical border regime is enforced through multi-layered, deliberate "deterring-killing" policies and practices, actions (acts of commission) and inactions (acts of omission)—by state officials and border agents—which expose border crossers to death or an increased risk of death. Such policies and practices produce thanatoharms by violating the inherent right for life embodied in article 3 of the Universal Declaration of Human Rights and articles 2, 4 and 6 of the International Covenant on Civil and Political Rights. The right to life is the most fundamental human right which is applicable without any discrimination, at all times and in all circumstances. It is the basis of all other rights, since any attempt to safeguard other rights is impossible if the right to life is not protected. According to the European Court of Human Rights (ECHR, 2020) the right to life defines two general obligations for states: (i) the protection by law the right to life, and (ii) the prohibition of intentional deprivation of life.

However, the systematic and deliberate disregard of life through push-backs and left-to-die deterrent border practices by state officials violate the right to life itself. They are state crimes (Weber and Pickering, 2011). Push-backs are also arbitrary, according to the international law, since they breach art. 33(1) of the 1951 Geneva Convention on the protection against refoulement which indicates that,

> No Contracting State shall expel or return ("refouler") a refugee in any manner whatsoever to the frontiers of territories where his or her life or freedom would be threatened on account of his or her race, religion, nationality, membership of a particular social group or political opinion.

Moreover, the duty to rescue persons in distress at sea is a fundamental rule of the international law of the sea, maritime law and international humanitarian law (Papanicolopulu, 2016). The left-to-die practices by state officials, consist of infringement of duty and violate the 1974 International Convention for the Safety of Life at Sea (SOLAS), and the 1982 United Nations Convention on the Law of the Sea (UNCLOS).

Yet, although one might think that death would be the last act of a lethal political game which is played at border crossers' expense, that death itself would serve as a figurative border beyond which violence could not continue inflicting harm, my research indicates that violence also continues in death and even beyond the moment of death. Violence is inflicted upon the lifeless bodies which are washed ashore, the unidentified and missing persons, the shipwreck survivors, the families, and whole communities, who are stuck in a bureaucratic and temporal limbo lasting for years and even a lifetime. Violence continues temporally beyond death due to the post-mortem corporal treatment of the dead, the inappropriate performance of burials, religious doctrines and rituals and, as Alison Mountz argues, "those who survive and those who perish both experience lives devalued" (2015, p. 196). The performance of undignified and culturally inappropriate burial procedures and rituals—including the widespread practice of mass graves—have taken place on Lesvos since the 1990s. These mundane practices and policies insult the memory of the dead and inflict cultural harms to the living. Everyday violent acts of dehumanizing speeches by state officials, vandalisms of graves and memorials dedicated to dead border crossers (Keep Talking Greece, 2018), and the lack of memoralisation insult further the memory of the dead. According to Article 365 of the 4619/2019 Greek Penal Code, insulting the memory of the dead or missing person with "cruel or malicious defamation or libel" is a criminal offence liable to punishment with up to six months imprisonment. However, such offensive acts remain unpunished, by normalizing, legitimizing and perpetuating violence which is inflicted upon the dead, the living and whole communities.

The dignified treatment of all missing and dead persons and their families is an undeniable universal human right (Mytilini Declaration, 2018). This right signifies that "all human beings have the right not to lose their identities after death" (ibid.), and that all lives should be valued, grieved and mourned. As Inam, the religious leader, noted,

> What we say is that this human thing [burial] is the least that should exist when one dies, even if one is a Muslim, Christian, Jewish. This person must be buried with the specific way that this person believes in. This is the minimum of the rights that one has after death; that is to be buried with dignity.

Through a continuum of political decisions, policies and practices in the EU, national and local levels, states routinely violate the universal right to life and dignity in death. These violations are state crimes and, therefore, states are culpable for the production of border deaths and the infliction and perpetuation of harm upon the living, the dead and whole communities.

References

Agamben, G. (1998) *Homo Sacer. Sovereign Power and Bare Life*. California: Stanford University Press.

Agamben, G. (2005) *State of Exception*. The University of Chicago Press: Chicago and London.

AlarmPhone (2020) *Push Backs: The New Old Routine in the Aegean Sea, AlarmPhone*. Available at: https://alarmphone.org/en/2020/05/14/push-backs-the-new-old-routine-in-the-aegean-sea/?post_type_release_type=post (Accessed: 14 May 2020).

Amnesty International (2015) *Refugees Endangered and Dying Due to EU Reliance on Fences and Gatekeepers*. Available at: https://www.amnesty.org/en/latest/news/2015/11/refugees-endangered-and-dying-due-to-eu-reliance-on-fences-and-gatekeepers/ (Accessed: 19 March 2019).

Andersson, R. (2014). 'Time and the Migrant Other: European Border Controls and the Temporal Economics of Illegality', *American Anthropologist*, 116(4), pp. 795–809.

Boss, P. (2010) 'The Trauma and Complicated GRIEF of Ambiguous Loss', *Pastoral Psychology*, 59(2), pp. 137–145.

Bosworth, M. and Guild, M. (2008) 'Governing Through Migration Control: Security and Citizenship in Britain', *British Journal of Criminology*, 48(6), pp. 703–719.

Brian, T. and Laczko, F. (2016) *Fatal Journeys: Identification and Tracing of Dead and Missing Migrants*. Geneva, Switzerland.

Butler, J. (2004) *Precarious Life. The Powers of Mourning and Violence*. London and New York, NY: Verso.

Canning, V. (2017) *Gendered Harm and Structural Violence in the British Asylum System*. London: Routledge.

Copson, L. (2018) *Understanding 'Cultural Harm'—Are We Part of the Problem?*, *Social Harm in a Digitalized Global World: Technologies of Power and Normalized Practices of Contemporary Society*. Ljubljana.

Davies, T. and Isakjee, A. (2015) 'Geography, Migration and Abandonment in the Calais Refugee Camp', *Guest Editorial/Political Geography*, 49, pp. 93–95.

De León, J. (2015) *The Land of Open Graves: Living and Dying on the Migrant Trail*. Oakland, CA: University California Press.

Délano, A., Domínguez Galbraith, P. and Nienass, B. (2016) 'Bringing the Dead Back into Society: An Interview with Mercedes Doretti', *Social*

Research: An International Quarterly Article Social Research, 83(2), pp. 511–534. Available at: https://muse.jhu.edu/article/631171.

Délano, A. and Nienass, B. (2016a) 'Deaths, Visibility, and Responsibility: The Politics of Mourning at the US-Mexico Border', *Social Research: An International Quarterly*, 83(2), pp. 421–451.

Délano, A. and Nienass, B. (2016b) 'Introduction: Borders and the Politics of Mourning', *Social Research*, 83(2), pp. xxi–xxxiii. Available at: https://muse-jhu-edu.libezproxy.open.ac.uk/article/631160/pdf.

Doty, R. L. (2011) 'Bare Life: Border-Crossing Deaths and Spaces of Moral Alibi', *Environment and Planning D: Society and Space*, 29(4), pp. 599–612.

Douglas, M. (2003) *Purity and Danger*. 3rd edn. London and New York: Taylor & Francis e-Library.

ECHR (2020) *Guide on Article 2 of the European Convention on Human Rights, 30 April 2020, European Court of Human Rights*. Available at: https://www.echr.coe.int/Documents/Guide_Art_2_ENG.pdf (Accessed: 24 June 2020).

Fassin, D. (2012) *Humanitarian Reason. A Moral History of the Present*. Berkeley and Los Angeles: University California Press.

Forensic Architecture (2020) *The Killing Of Muhammad Gulzar*. Available at: https://forensic-architecture.org/investigation/the-killing-of-muhammad-gulzar (Accessed: 13 May 2020).

Foucault, M. (2003) *'Society Must Be Defended' Lectures at the College de France, 1975–1976*, translated by David Masey. first. Edited by M. Bertani and A. Fontana. New York, NY: Picador.

Gillespie, M. (2018) 'Refiguring Refugee Waste: Regimes of Reception and Solidarity Networks in Lesvos', in Dodsworth, F. and Walford, A. (eds) *A World Laid Waste? Responding to the Social, Cultural and Political Consequences of Globalisation*. 1st edn. London: Routledge, Taylor & Francis Group, pp. 147–170.

Hellenic Coast Guard (no date a) *Control of Sea Borders (in Greek)*, *Hellenic Coast Guard*. Available at: http://www.hcg.gr/node/151 (Accessed: 14 May 2020).

Hellenic Coast Guard (no date b) *Search and Rescue (in Greek)*. Available at: http://www.hcg.gr/node/149 (Accessed: 14 May 2020).

Herz, R. (1960) *Death and The Right Hand*. Glencoe, Il: The Free Press.

Hillyard, P. and Tombs, S. (2007) 'From "Crime" to Social Harm?', *Crime, Law and Social Change*, 48(1–2), pp. 9–25.

Human Rights Watch (2008) *Iraqis and Other Asylum Seekers and Migrants at the Greece/Turkey Entrance to the European Union*. Available at: https://www.hrw.org/report/2008/11/26/stuck-revolving-door/iraqis-and-other-asylum-seekers-and-migrants-greece/turkey (Accessed: 20 March 2019).

Human Rights Watch (2018) *Greece: Violent Pushbacks at Turkey Border*. Available at: https://www.hrw.org/news/2018/12/18/greece-violent-pushbacks-turkey-border (Accessed: 19 March 2019).

Iliadou, E. (2019) *Border Harms and Everyday Violence. The Lived Experiences of Border Crossers in Lesvos Island, Greece*. The Open University.

InfoMigrants (2018a) *Greece Accused of Migrant Pushbacks*. Available at: https://www.infomigrants.net/en/post/12927/greece-accused-of-migrant-pushbacks (Accessed: 18 March 2019).

InfoMigrants (2018b) *Pushbacks on Spain's Southern Border—InfoMigrants*. Available at: https://www.infomigrants.net/en/post/7866/pushbacks-on-spain-s-southern-border (Accessed: 18 March 2019).

Jones, R. (2016) *Violent Borders: Refugees and the Right to Move*. London and New York: Verso.

Keep Talking Greece (2018) *Memorial for Drowned Refugees Completely Destroyed on Lesvos UPD, Keep Talking Greece*. Available at: https://www.keeptalkinggreece.com/2018/09/03/memorial-for-drowned-refugees-completely-destroyed-on-lesvos/ (Accessed: 20 June 2020).

Khosravi, S. (2018) 'Stolen Time', *Radical Philosophy*, pp. 38–41.

Kovras, I. and Robins, S. (2017) 'Missing Migrants: Deaths at Sea and Unidentified Bodies in Lesbos', in *Migrating Borders and Moving Times. Temporality and the Crossing of Borders in Europe*. Manchester University Press, pp. 157–175.

Legal Centre Lesvos (2020) *CALL FOR ACCOUNTABILITY: Apparent Suicide in Moria Detention Centre followed failure by Greek State to provide obligated care*. Available at: http://legalcentrelesvos.org/2020/01/19/call-for-accountability-apparent-suicide-in-moria-detention-centre-followed-failure-by-greek-state-to-provide-obligated-care/ (Accessed: 16 May 2020).

Mediterranean Missing Project (2016) *Missing Migrants: Management of Dead Bodies in Lesbos/Greece Summary Report*. Available at http://www.mediterraneanmissing.eu/wp-content/uploads/2015/10/Mediterranean-Missing-Greek-short-report-260817.pdf (Accessed 21st June 2021).

Mountz, A. (2015) 'In/visibility and the Securitization of Migration', *Cultural Politics*, 11(2), pp. 184–200.

Mytilini Declaration (2018) *We the Undersigned Make this Declaration for the Dignified Treatment of all Missing and Deceased Persons and their Families as a Consequence of Migrant Journeys*. Mytilini. Available at: https://drive.google.com/file/d/1n9ZZ5LjI9KkEf7Lfzqv_yB1R9bAy0G8B/view (Accessed: 30 August 2019).

Papanicolopulu, I. (2016) 'The Duty to Rescue at Sea, in Peacetime and in War: A General Overview', *International Review of the Red Cross*, 98(2), pp. 491–514.

Prem Kumar, R. and Grundy-Warr, C. (2004) 'The Irregular Migrant as Homo Sacer: Migration and Detention in Australia, Malaysia, and Thailand', *International Migration*, 42(1), pp. 33–64.

Scheper-Hughes, N. (2004) 'Violence Foretold: Reflections on 9/11', in Scheper-Hughes, N. and Bourgois, P. (eds) *Violence in War and Peace. An Anthology*. Blackwell Publishing Ltd, pp. 224–226.

Segato, R. L. (2014) 'Las nuevas formas de la guerra y el cuerpo de las mujeres', *Revista Sociedade e Estado—Maio*, 29(2).

Singleton, A., Laczko, F. and Black, J. (2017) 'Measuring Unsafe Migration: The Challenge of Collecting Accurate Data on Migrant Fatalities', *Migration Policy and Practice*, VII(2), pp. 4–9.

Squire, V. (2015) *Post/Humanitarian Border Politics Between Mexico and the US: People, Places, Things. Mobility & politics*. Basingstoke: Palgrave Pivot.

Squire, V. (2017) 'Governing Migration through Death in Europe and the US: Identification, Burial and the Crisis of Modern Humanism', *European Journal of International Relations*, 23(233), pp. 513–532.

Taussig, M. (1992) *The Nervous System*. London and New York: Routledge.

Tazzioli, M. (2016) *Concentric Cages: The Hotspots of Lesvos After the EU-Turkey Agreement*, openDemocracy. Available at: https://www.opendemocracy.net/mediterranean-journeys-in-hope/martina-tazzioli/concentric-cages-hotspots-of-lesvos-after-eu-turkey (Accessed: 6 March 2018).

Tazzioli, M. (2018) 'The Temporal Borders of Asylum. Temporality of Control in the EU Border Regime', *Political Geography*. Elsevier Ltd, 64, pp. 13–22.

Vaughan-Williams, N. (2015) *Europe's Border Crisis: Biopolitical Security and Beyond*. Oxford: Oxford University Press.

Vogt, W. A. (2013) 'Crossing Mexico: Structural Violence and the Commodification of Undocumented Central American Migrants', *American Ethnologist*, 40(4), pp. 764–780.

Walters, W. (2016) 'Live Governance, Borders, and the Time—Space of the Situation: EUROSUR and the Genealogy of Bordering in Europe', *Comparative European Politics*, 15(5), pp. 794–817.

Weber, L. and Pickering, S. (2011) *Globalization and Borders: Death at the Global Frontier*. 1st edn. London: Palgrave Macmillan.

Epilogue

Bridget Anderson

I am writing while much of the world is under 'lockdown', confined to domestic spaces with movement, both within and across borders, still highly restricted. The COVID-19 global pandemic has brought disproportionate hardship to the most impoverished and marginalised populations, and this includes migrants and refugees caught at, between, or within borders. Movement it seems is bad for our health. Looking to the future there are already plans for harsher border regimes. For example, states including Italy, Germany, Chile, the UK and the USA have suggested 'immunity passports' as a way of exiting lockdown, exempting holders from mobility restrictions. Such an approach has been deemed impractical, unethical, discriminatory and incentivising infection but this does not mean it will not be adopted (Phelan 2020). Isolation and the prevention of movement and interaction can be, in circumstances such as we are facing today, an important *emergency* public health measure to contain infection. But there is disquiet at the introduction of methods of surveillance and population control that affect everyone and are not confined to 'migrants'. Researchers, activists and institutions concerned with migration and asylum have drawn attention to the parallels, overlaps and tensions between COVID movement restrictions and those experienced by non-citizens. But far less attention has been paid to COVID temporalities. Yet COVID-19 has disrupted the normal rhythms of life and the ways many people experience and feel time changed quite significantly in the first half of 2020. This has the potential to be a new tool for us to find connections between the state differentiated populations of 'migrants' and 'citizens'.

In 2020 many of the institutional, cultural and bureaucratic markers that lend order to our time, from school years to summer festivals, have melted away or been transformed into digital shadows of themselves. For many of those lucky enough to still be in a job, daily work routines have also been disrupted. Flexible working has become normalised as the domestic space, from which many people are now working, adjusts to demands from children, the sick and the elderly. These changes in our social and subjective experiences of time are bound up with a new experience of uncertainty. When will this end? What will life be like when we emerge from lockdown? Will there be post-pandemic life, and if so, what will it be like?

Trapped in the tunnel of an overly powerful present enduring rather than leading a life, what is being experienced under lockdown is, however pale, a reflection of the nightmare of the 'migrant temporalities' described in this volume. Attention to time is desperately needed in the study of and political response to migration as time is critical to the governance of people who move across borders. Indeed, time is a critical element in defining who counts as a 'migrant'. The United Nations data on global migration define a migrant as: 'A person who moves to a country other than that of his or her usual residence for a period of twelve months or more so that the country of destination effectively becomes his or her new country of usual residence'. Notably there is no mention of citizenship status. What matters is *time*: time away (*usual* residence) and length of time planned to stay (*twelve months or more*).

Non-citizens, such as migrant workers, family members and other visa holders are almost always subject to restrictions on their length of stay on a territory, their subjection to a range of temporal regimes formally captured in bureaucratic papers. The time limitedness of documents, their renewability, and the relation between legal length of stay and access to permanent residence/citizenship is critical to the governing of migration. Immigration and asylum systems produce a hierarchy of security through different temporal limitations and many states have seen a marked shift from immigration statuses leading to settlement, to immigration statuses which do not lead to any permanent settlement rights. For example, in the UK, of those who enter the UK as 'economic migrants' only those constructed as highly skilled will find themselves able to legally remain for more than four or five years. The person of 'exceptional talent' may be given permission to stay for a maximum of five years (five years and four months if they apply outside the UK), but if they bring their domestic worker with them, she will only be permitted a six-month, non-renewable stay. Even those with refugee status cannot access the security of settlement until they have completed the 'safe return review' after five years. This is a slow-burning state violence that is not a spectacular display of physical domination and brutality, but a source of psychological harm and suffering and a means of leveraging law to justify separation from loved ones and denial of access to a social safety net.

The word 'limbo' has been used to describe COVID-19 lockdowns, it is an unwelcome unintended consequence. However, it is inbuilt into immigration and asylum systems. Emergency time over-extended, becomes limbo, and so too does chapping life stage into visa sized chunks, when visas are renewable, but never lead to permanent residence. 'Limbo' is plagued with uncertainty, unlike 'purgatory' where the faithful suffer but know there is an idyllic ending to their misery. Limbo is deeply destabilising and can mean people losing a sense of a recursive engagement with an imagined future. Like all forms of violence then, this form of state violence produces subjectivities, often shaped by an experience of a (temporary) lack of agency. Importantly this is not restricted to those designated as 'migrants'. For many people in the world, migrant or not, this engagement has been denied. Craig Jeffrey uses the term 'timepass' to explore the lives of young educated men in India, forced to wait indefinitely to find a job, reflecting the sense of having little to do other than spend/waste me (Jeffrey 2010). Indeed, the escape from 'stuckness' can also be precisely why people become migrants—Reuben Andersson describes how the search for 'deliverance from a world of extended youth and lack of fulfilment in reeling home economies' can motivate migration, and in some cases this is only for people to find themselves strapped in the distinct temporalities of a camp (Andersson 2014: 805) The experiences of anxiety about uncertain futures, what will happen next and how will uncontrollable externalities shape future lives now confronting new populations. Much can be learned from work on the processes and effects of 'waiting' in relation to asylum where temporary statuses can become so extended that they would be better characterised as 'permanent temporariness'.

Time as connection is not only restricted to COVID experiences. Indeed perhaps one reason that research on migration has tended to overlook the temporalities of immigration controls is that in practice certain forms of state control over time is normalised for all residents on a territory. Consider social assistance claimants for example. Across Europe different requirements apply but they are imbricated with controls over time: requirements to report at a certain time and place, to devote sufficient time searching for work, to be prepared to travel for a certain time to take up a job offer and so on. Moreover, those citizens who are out of the country for a certain length of time may find that they are not eligible for certain forms of welfare support that otherwise they would be able to access. For the purposes of claiming welfare support, time can turn those with citizenship status into 'migrants'. Furthermore, citizens' rights as workers are also temporally shaped: A person starting a new job even in a well unionised, formal sector, does not acquire all employment rights straight away but must generally work for a certain period. For example, in the UK a worker must have worked for the same employer for 26 weeks before they are eligible to make a claim for maternity pay and for two years before they can claim unfair dismissal. The duration of the qualifying period is typically determined in regulations rather than in law and is thereby buffered from political dispute.

It can be difficult to 'see' time and recognise when it is being stolen. Even the most visible cases which are exposed through working time, when workers are not paid for the full length of the time that they work, tend to be described as 'wage theft' rather than 'time theft' and despite their importance to the governance of employment, qualifying periods are treated as a rather arcane subject. Time theft is even more difficult to identify when it is out of the work place and when it is future directed. Who gets to imagine and make futures, and what our time horizons are, are matters that are gendered, raced and classed, but they are also fundamentally shaped by citizenship and immigration status. This does not mean that the use of time to brutally govern is a natural consequence of mobilities, but rather that migrants expose how citizenship can protect some people in certain contexts from the most egregious controls over their times.

It is important not to flatten experiences. The horrors of the ontological uncertainty that can lead in extremis asylum seekers to take their own lives in an effort to exercise control over their futures is not equivalent to middle-class European anxieties about post-COVID futures. But we might analyse the 'migrant' as one of the subjects who experiences extreme vulnerability in the face of state temporal controls, and use the temporal lens to explore the possibility for imagining new political alliances that trouble the borders between citizens and non-citizens.

References

Andersson, R. (2014). *Illegality, Inc.: Clandestine Migration and the Business of Bordering Europe*. University of California Press.

Jeffrey, C. (2010). *Timepass: Youth, Class, and the Politics of Waiting in India*. Stanford University Press.

Phelan, A. L. (2020). COVID-19 Immunity Passports and Vaccination Certificates: Scientific, Equitable, and Legal Challenges. *The Lancet*, 395 (10237): 1595–1598.

United Nations. (1998). "Recommendations on Statistics of International Migration, Revision 1," *Statistical Papers*, Series M, No.58, Rev.1. Sales No. E.98.XVII.14.

Index

A

Africa 35, 51
Agency xviii, xxii, 5, 25, 33, 37, 40, 41, 43, 44, 58, 59, 88, 109, 131, 132, 153–155, 159, 160, 162, 176, 180, 205, 225
Anderson, Bridget 84, 223
Andersson, R. 41, 116, 152, 154, 157, 199, 226
Arcel, Libby Tata 117
Asylum xvi, xxi, xxii, 20, 27, 34, 36, 39–48, 50–55, 57–59, 68, 86, 88, 90, 96, 105–107, 109, 111–113, 115, 118–120, 122, 223, 225–227
Asylum seeking xvii, xix, xxi, 3, 13, 43, 48, 49, 51, 53, 56, 57, 59, 65, 73, 85, 86, 107–122
Australia xviii, 2, 34, 65–67, 70–75, 77, 78, 97, 180

Autonomy xv–xviii, xx, xxii, 14, 40, 41, 59, 91, 101, 106, 107, 109, 110, 113, 114, 122, 131, 134, 143, 145, 146

B

Bharatiya Janata Party (BJP) 179, 181, 184, 186, 190
Bhatia, Monish xv, xvi, xviii, xxiii, 117
Boochani, Behrouz xix, xxi, xxii, 66–69, 72, 73, 77, 80
Border harms 199
Bordering xvii, xxi, xxiii, xxiv, 39–43, 49, 50, 52, 54, 59, 78, 120, 175, 182, 193
Borders xvi–xviii, xx, xxi, xxiii, 3, 7, 25, 26, 29, 31–33, 35, 37, 38, 40–45, 50, 56, 58, 70, 72,

73, 77–79, 84, 85, 88, 95, 96, 98, 100, 101, 109, 112, 115, 116, 119, 121, 131, 144, 165, 172–182, 192, 193, 197–212, 215–217, 223, 224, 227
Bourdieu, Pierre xix, 31
Britain xviii, xix, xxii, 107, 109, 120, 122

Calais camps 57
Canning, Victoria xv, xvi, xviii, xxii, 53, 59, 87, 101, 107, 108, 110, 112, 117–119, 121, 128, 131, 134, 198

Danish Institute Against Torture 108
Death xviii, xxiii, 14, 46, 71, 76, 77, 79, 80, 102, 110, 163, 173–175, 190, 197, 199–206, 208, 209, 211, 213–217
Death at borders xviii, xx, xxiii, 50, 59, 110, 180, 198–200, 202, 204, 208, 211, 215, 217
Dehumanisation 199, 204, 205
Denmark xviii, xxi, xxii, 85, 86, 91–93, 96–99, 106–109, 111–113, 115, 119, 120, 122
Deportation xvi, xvii, xix–xxii, 19, 33, 34, 41, 53–55, 78, 83–102, 106, 109–111, 114, 119, 122, 128–130, 132–135, 142, 143, 145, 146, 152, 153, 155–160, 162–166, 191
Deportees 129–133, 140–142, 144–146, 153–166

Detention xvi, xvii, xix–xxiii, 4, 31, 34, 37, 41, 46, 53, 54, 57, 65–67, 69, 71–73, 75–79, 85–89, 92, 93, 96, 100, 105, 108–112, 118, 122, 128, 134, 146, 152, 153, 157, 163, 166, 189, 190, 192, 206, 207
Dignity 99, 213, 215, 217
Dignity in death xxiii, 200, 217
Durkheim, Emile xv

European Union (EU) xvi, xxiii, 19, 29, 31, 33, 35, 41, 180, 198, 199, 201, 217
Exclusion xv, xx, xxiii, 3, 43, 83, 94, 108, 114, 122, 132, 153, 166, 177, 186, 188, 191, 205

Feminism 66, 118, 203
Forced deportation 33, 118
Forced migration 78
France xviii, xxi, 1, 15, 16, 45, 89

Gender 5, 132, 157
Gendered violence 180
Germany xviii, xxi, 1, 11, 12, 34, 36, 55, 89, 90, 94, 97, 98, 182, 223
Greece xviii, xxiii, 15, 31–33, 35, 174, 202, 207, 208
Green, P. 117

H

Hindu 177, 180–184, 191, 192
Humanitarianism xix, xxiii, 204
Human rights 69, 79, 97, 99, 175, 181, 207, 215, 217

I

Immigrants 152, 157, 160, 166, 186
Immigration xvi, xvii, xxi, xxii, 65, 73, 78, 96, 108–110, 112, 122, 128, 129, 133, 136, 137, 144, 145, 185, 225–227
India xviii, xxiii, 172–174, 176, 179, 181–184, 186–189, 193, 225
Iran xviii, 2, 9–11, 16, 67, 78

J

Jordan xviii, xxi, 27–30

K

Khosravi, Shahram xvii, 4, 84, 87, 88, 96, 98, 100, 107, 110, 115, 131, 134, 152–154, 157, 199

L

Lesvos Island xxiii, 198–203, 207–209, 211, 212, 217
LGBTQ 110

M

Manus Island xviii, xxi, 65, 69, 70, 73, 74, 76, 78, 80, 105
Mead, G.H. xv

Mexico xviii, 11, 128–146, 152–156, 158–166, 207
Migrants xvi, xviii–xx, xxii, xxiii, 2–5, 9, 17, 18, 20, 26, 30, 32, 38, 40–48, 50–56, 58–60, 87, 97, 112, 115, 121, 128–133, 135–146, 152, 154, 156–159, 162, 165, 166, 174, 177, 180, 185, 197, 199, 207, 215, 223–227
Migration xvi–xx, 5–9, 17, 19, 20, 25–27, 29, 30, 35, 37, 40, 41, 49–52, 84, 89, 95, 96, 100, 101, 129, 136, 145, 152, 179, 185, 186, 198, 203, 223–226
Mobility xix, 25, 78, 84, 90, 93, 130, 131, 137–139, 145, 174, 179, 180, 197, 202–204, 223, 227
Murder 173, 205

N

National identity xvii, 184
Nationalism xxiii, 45, 156, 157, 177, 183, 192
Nationality 216
New Zealand 68

P

Persecution xvii, 2, 43, 116, 121, 122, 179, 191, 201
Prosecution 173, 206
Psychotraumatologist 108, 119, 120

R

Racism 36

Rape 116, 146
Rashtriya Swayamsevak Sangh (RSS) 184, 186
Refugee 3, 10, 16, 19, 26–29, 31–34, 36, 37, 41, 43, 45, 48, 50, 51, 56, 59, 67–80, 97, 107, 108, 110–112, 114–120, 191, 197–199, 202, 216, 223, 225
Refugee rights 110
Returnees 129, 131, 133, 135, 137–146

S

Schuster, Liza xvii, xx, 5, 6, 15, 17, 44
Sexual violence 108, 116, 117, 119, 180
Sigona, Nando xvii
Social harm 198, 206
Spatial controls 106
Spatiality 186
State crime 216, 217
State harm xviii
States xvi, xix–xxi, xxiii, 3, 4, 16, 17, 19, 20, 26, 41–43, 47, 48, 50–52, 55, 58, 59, 67, 83–87, 89, 90, 93–95, 100–102, 107, 109, 112, 116, 117, 119–122, 130, 131, 139, 153–157, 162, 163, 166, 172, 174, 176–180, 182–187, 189, 190, 193, 198, 200, 201, 205–208, 216, 217, 223–225, 227
Stealing time xvii, xx, 95
Stolen time xvii, 72, 76, 109, 114, 131, 132, 134

Stress xxi, 12, 40, 48–51, 54, 58, 59, 80, 84, 87, 120, 121, 146, 187, 214
Structural harm 108
Structural violence 199
Sweden xviii, xxi, xxii, 18, 85–89, 92, 93, 107–113, 118, 120–122, 201
Syria xviii, xxi, 27, 30, 33–35, 55, 210

T

Temporal harm xviii, 105, 107, 114, 116, 119, 120
Temporality xv–xviii, xx, xxi, xxiii, 25, 39–43, 45, 48, 49, 52, 53, 58, 72, 73, 106, 109, 116, 118, 174, 178, 182, 186, 198, 199, 224, 226
Thanatoharms 200, 206, 215
Thanatopolitical border regime 198, 199, 202, 206, 208, 215
Time xv–xxiv, 2–5, 12, 14–16, 18–20, 25, 27, 29, 31, 32, 34–37, 39–47, 49–59, 66–70, 72–74, 76–80, 83–89, 92–96, 98–102, 106, 107, 109–116, 118, 121, 122, 129, 131, 132, 134–139, 142, 144–146, 152–155, 157–159, 162, 163, 165, 166, 173, 174, 176, 178, 179, 181–183, 186, 187, 189–192, 198–200, 203, 207–212, 215, 224–227
Tofighian, Omid xxi, xxii, 67, 68, 72, 77–79

Torture xxi, 37, 69, 72, 77, 78, 108, 116–118, 120, 122, 174, 206, 207, 211
Trauma 34, 111, 112, 116–122, 129, 131, 134, 135, 145, 146, 190, 202, 214
Turkey xviii, 15, 19, 29–31, 33–35, 208
Turner, S. 44
Turner, V.W. xv, 25, 26

United Kingdom (UK) xxi, 39, 44, 45, 47, 48, 50, 51, 53, 56, 57, 108, 109, 112, 113, 223, 225, 226
USA xviii, xxii, 128, 223

Violence xviii, xxi–xxiii, 32, 36, 40, 50, 56, 59, 67, 69, 73, 74, 77–80, 84, 93, 105, 116, 117, 119, 121, 122, 146, 174, 175, 180, 182, 184, 186, 190, 198–200, 202, 203, 205–208, 210, 213, 214, 216, 217

Ward, T. 117
Weaponisation 66, 67, 72
Women xxi, xxii, 2–11, 13, 14, 17, 18, 20, 55, 66, 108–110, 112, 114, 116, 119, 132, 180, 188, 191

Xenophobia xxiii, 177, 192

GPSR Compliance

The European Union's (EU) General Product Safety Regulation (GPSR) is a set of rules that requires consumer products to be safe and our obligations to ensure this.

If you have any concerns about our products, you can contact us on

ProductSafety@springernature.com

In case Publisher is established outside the EU, the EU authorized representative is:

Springer Nature Customer Service Center GmbH
Europaplatz 3
69115 Heidelberg, Germany

www.ingramcontent.com/pod-product-compliance
Lightning Source LLC
LaVergne TN
LVHW021336080526
838202LV00004B/191